BEASTLY JOURNEYS

LIVERPOOL ENGLISH TEXTS AND STUDIES 63

BEASTLY JOURNEYS
Travel and Transformation
at the fin de siècle

TIM YOUNGS

LIVERPOOL UNIVERSITY PRESS

First published 2013 by
Liverpool University Press
4 Cambridge Street
Liverpool
L69 7ZU

Copyright © 2013 Tim Youngs

The right of Tim Youngs to be identified as the author of this book has been asserted by him in accordance with the Copyright, Designs and Patents Act 1988.

All rights reserved. No part of this book may be reproduced, stored in a retrieval system, or transmitted, in any form or by any means, electronic, mechanical, photocopying, recording, or otherwise, without the prior written permission of the publisher.

British Library Cataloguing-in-Publication data

A British Library CIP record is available

ISBN 978-1-84631-958-7 cased

Typeset by XL Publishing Services
Printed and bound in the United States of America

For

John and Pauline Lucas

Contents

Acknowledgements	ix
Introduction: The Unchaining of the Beast	1
1 City Creatures	39
2 The Bat and the Beetle	74
3 Morlocks, Martians, and Beast-People	107
4 'Beast and man so mixty': The Fairy Tales of George MacDonald	140
5 Oscar Wilde: 'an unclean beast'	165
Conclusion	197
Bibliography	211
Index	220

Acknowledgements

This book has had a long gestation. Early stages of it were supported through research leave funded by the Arts and Humanities Research Board and through my own university department's sabbatical programme. I am grateful to both bodies. The following people have also helped through, variously, their provision of ideas, information, encouragement, and the hosting of lectures, seminars, and conferences at which early drafts of some material were tried out: Chris Barker, Dinah Birch, Joseph Bristow, Antoinette Burton, Viv Chadder, Stephen Donovan, Justin D. Edwards, R. J. (Dick) Ellis, Charles Forsdick, Shirley Foster, Christopher Gair, Indira Ghose, Mike Green, Lynne Hapgood, Tracey Hill, Peter Hulme, Philip Leonard, John Lucas, Roger Luckhurst, Gesa Mackenthun, Richard Pearson, Lyssa Randolph, Ray Russell, Wim Tigges, Richard White, Martin Willis, and David Woods. My thanks go also to the inter-library loans team at Nottingham Trent University. I am especially grateful to Anthony Cond for encouraging submission of the book to Liverpool University Press and for his patience and good humour in seeing it through to publication. Any weaknesses, oddities, and errors are my own.

Portions of Chapter One and Chapter Three have their origins in three earlier essays, whose ideas they develop: 'Stevenson's Monkey-Business: *The Strange Case of Dr. Jekyll and Mr. Hyde*', in Peter Liebregts and Wim Tigges, eds, *Beauty and the Beast: Christina Rossetti, Walter Pater, R. L. Stevenson and their Contemporaries* (Amsterdam: Rodopi, 1996), pp.157–170; 'Wells's Fifth Dimension: *The Time Machine* at the Fin de Siècle', in Tracey Hill and Alan Marshall, eds, *Decadence and Danger: Writing, History and the Fin de Siècle* (Bath: Sulis Press, 1997), pp.64–74; and 'The Plasticity of Living Forms: Beasts and Narrative in *The Octopus* and *The Island of Doctor Moreau*', *Symbiosis: A Journal of Anglo-American Literary Relations* 1, 1 (April 1997), 86–103. I am grateful to Rodopi, Tracey Hill, and Christopher Gair respectively for allowing me to draw on this nascent material. For permission to quote from H. G. Wells's works I am grateful to A. P. Watt.

As ever, the greater and lasting acknowledgement is to Gurminder and Natty for being who they are.

Introduction
The Unchaining of the Beast

Vile bestiality

In 1936, Georg Lukács wrote of the 'degradation and crippling under capitalism [that] is far more tragic, its *bestiality viler*, more ferocious and terrible than that pictured even in the best of these novels'. He was referring to modern realism, which, in his view, had 'lost its capacity to depict the dynamics of life, and thus its representation of capitalist reality is inadequate, diluted and constrained'.[1] The present study grapples with this vile bestiality, but examines its earlier manifestation in British texts between 1885 and 1900 – the period that saw the development of realism and its sister movement, naturalism, and which is most commonly described in literary and cultural studies as an 'age of transition'.[2]

During these years, '[t]he Late Victorians themselves were intensely conscious of their transitory state'.[3] The literary historian Peter Keating outlines, for example, the transformation of education into a system of social mobility; cultural transformation; the transformation, 'even perhaps the death', of the Victorian family; and a 'revolutionary transformation in every aspect of communications'.[4] To these, we might add urbanisation, whose 'whetted fangs of change/Daily devour the old demesne'.[5] John Davidson's lines growl with the sense of class menace.

The changes that many experienced in late nineteenth-century Britain are symbolised by the obsessive display of figures of indeterminate or altered shape: beasts with human characteristics; humans who are, or who become, beastly; creatures of dubious or shifting classification. Some of these have been the subject of considerable critical attention, but rather than timeless mythical or psychological examples of metamorphosis – for which they are often taken – these physical alterations might be viewed more productively as reflections of changes to the social body.[6]

In 'one of the most important documents of the fin de siècle', Max Nordau considers the notion behind the latter term:

> It means a practical emancipation from traditional discipline, which theoretically is still in force. To the voluptuary this means unbridled lewdness, the unchaining of the beast in man; to the withered heart of the egoist, disdain of all consideration for his fellow-men, the trampling under foot of all barriers which enclose brutal greed of lucre and lust of pleasure ... And to all, it means the end of an established order, which for thousands of years has satisfied logic, fettered depravity, and in every art matured something of beauty.[7]

Nordau's condemnation of the fin de siècle connects avarice, animality, and disorder – a linkage that the present study explores.

If the following pages risk assuming the character of a safari, the metaphors of animality and movement that they track provide an important vantage point from which to survey the literary and social terrain of the 1880s and 1890s. When, for instance, a modern editor of Walter Besant's *All Sorts and Conditions of Men* (1882) summarises that novel as one 'about transformation: crossings of class boundaries, metamorphoses of estate',[8] she is describing a situation that also applies to its context. Besant himself turns to animal imagery to make his point, writing:

> There is one consolation always open, thank Heaven, for the meanest among us *poor worms of earth*. We are gifted with imaginations; we can make the impossible an actual fact, and can with the eye of the mind make the unreal stand before us in the flesh. Therefore when we are down-trodden, we may proceed ... to take revenge upon our enemy in imagination.[9]

The immediate referent here is the vengeance pictured by the grasping, cheating Mr Bunker upon the heiress, Angela Messenger, who, in visiting her property and its East End environs incognito as Miss Kennedy, has humiliated him. In a broader sense, however, the passage glances at something else that is happening: Besant uses his imagination to bust Bunker. The author's remarks quoted above suggest the transformative power of imaginative literature, with both negative and positive effects. While revenge is not always a motive, the metaphors employed by writers of the late nineteenth century attempt to give shape to a society in which so much had become uncertain. The threats to social definition result not only in imaginative projections of beastly confusion, but are reflected, too, in narratives of mixed generic identity.

Surprising transformations

'Many Victorians were fascinated by transformation and the limits of metamorphosis', Gillian Beer observes.[10] The late Victorians' fascination with this process and its boundaries was distinctive: it followed a long tradition of interest and curiosity, but was of its own order, driven by circumstances unique to the last fifteen years or so of the nineteenth century. Each age and culture has its own monsters and transformations, often modifying those of its ancestors or neighbours. The Renaissance's rediscovery of the classics, and their prominence in nineteenth-century élite education, tied modern European culture to the times of Ovid, who proclaimed at the beginning of his *Metamorphoses*: 'My intention is to tell of bodies changed/To different forms.'[11] In a study of shape-shifting, Marina Warner recognises both the continuities and changes between the centuries. She detects in Ovid the fact that 'metamorphosis often breaks out in moments of crisis'; that, more generally, tales of metamorphosis often occur 'in spaces (temporal, geographical, and mental) that [are] crossroads, cross-cultural zones, points of interchange on the intricate connective tissue of communications between cultures'; and that 'it is characteristic of metamorphic writing to appear in transitional places and at the confluences of traditions and civilizations'.[12]

It is at such a moment of 'clash and conflict between one intellectual hegemony and another' that the texts of the 1880s and 1890s examined here are situated. Wim Neetens has described how, in the 1880s, 'an already precarious and internally eroded ideological dominant found itself faced with the social unrest in which the working class and a number of progressive, middle-class intellectuals began to produce their own, decentralising and potentially counter-hegemonic discourses'. Through its increased literary and scientific interest in the working class, the British bourgeoisie attempted to reassert its dominance and hegemony. 'Under these ideological and cultural pressures, naturalism was foregrounded in English literature as the artistic practice which carried the literature of working-class life to an extreme of colonial self-confidence.'[13] One might also refer to the significance of 'racial' encounter at this time of increased immigration into London and of heightened anxiety towards the figure of the 'mulatto'. Metamorphoses may be connected across the centuries, but the nature of the crises and contacts differs from case to case and from place to place.[14] In Warner's words, 'context changes meanings'.[15]

Warner extends the idea of metamorphosis by claiming that through its communication of 'principles and ideas', it 'transformed their receivers and readers'.[16] It does this partly because

> [t]ransformations bring about a surprise ... The breaking of rules of natural law and verisimilitude creates the fictional world with its own laws ... Moreover, some kinds of metamorphosis play a crucial part in anagnorisis, or recognition, the reversal fundamental to narrative form, and so govern narrative satisfaction.[17]

Such a process can be seen to operate in the texts that form the subject of *Beastly Journeys*. Since the social and cultural changes that were happening at the time are reflected symbolically in the alteration of shape that humans and (other) animals undergo, the shock of physical disruption may, if we pursue Warner's argument, be said to force recognition of the new social juxtapositions. In fact, while this might have been the case for some contemporary readers, who cannot fail to have seen the economic basis of the literary transformations, the recognition that Warner describes seems largely to have been overlooked or misapprehended by subsequent readers. The further changes that these late nineteenth-century tales of transformation have undergone in film, stage, and prose adaptations have diluted their radical force. The social and economic anxieties of the original texts have generally vanished. Dracula, Mr Hyde, Dorian Gray, the Martians and the Morlocks are not what they once were. *Beastly Journeys* is, in part, a journey backwards to (re)discover their former identities and situations.

The last couple of decades of the nineteenth century seem to have housed an especially remarkable menagerie. Apes (white, as well as black),[18] wolves, bats, beetles, hyenas, alien beings, and countless others swing, prowl, fly, creep, crawl, and slither along. Many are still gawped at uneasily. These are the years of the Beast-People, the Ripper, the 'Elephant Man', and others. There were overtly political beasts, too: 'Some of the political implications of Nietzsche's views were taken up by Shaw and Wells; references to the *Ubermensch*, "Superman", or "blond beast" occur with some frequency from the mid-1890s; and there were real enthusiasts, like John Davidson.'[19]

They are remarkable both in their number and in their transmutation from or into other forms. One can say of them, as one critic has of metamorphosis generally and its literary representations in particular, that 'it is obvious ... metamorphosis has something to do with the search for identity, or in some cases its antithesis, the refusal to develop'.[20] The condition of the creatures rounded up in this book is symptomatic of the society that has spawned them. For an understanding of them, we must add to the six broad headings of metamorphosis that Irving Massey proposes – scientific, philosophical, anthropological (including lycanthropy and vampirism), religious, psychological, and aesthetic[21] – a seventh: economic. It is the economic and social changes of the late nineteenth century that drive the shape-shifting of these years and the science of Darwinism that frames it.

Three aspects to these beasts underlie the present study. First, many of these creatures are avatars of humans, their transformation from their original condition due to the deforming effects of capital. And yet, second, the socio-economic environment that has so shaped these ghastly apparitions has disappeared from most retellings and readings of the original narratives. Third, the motif of travel forms an important part of the texts, effecting the alteration itself or leading to the discovery of that transformation. Both the mode of travel and the discoveries that are made throw light on the preoccupations of the period.

Framing the changes: beastly journeys

This will be a book about the fin de siècle, but I shall try to resist easy generalisations about the character of those years. Max Nordau objected to the idea of classifying parts of a century as though it were a 'kind of living being, born like a beast or a man, passing through all the stages of existence ... to die with the expiration of the hundredth year, after being afflicted in its last decade with all the infirmities of mournful senility'.[22] One can make a case for any period being a 'time of' something to someone. In doing so, one will dangerously overlook the counter-examples and anomalies that do not fit the general pattern. As Simon Dentith, denying the possibility of speaking of 'a *Zeitgeist* for the nineteenth century, or any portion of it, such as the "Victorian Age"', states: 'every period of history is characterised by multiple and contradictory ways of thinking, seeing and feeling'.[23] And as a critic of 1890s decadence has pointed out, plenty of people lived through the decade untouched by the reference point we give it. On the other hand, as the same critic has remarked, '[t]he origins of the nineties myth lie within the period itself'.[24] Generalisations are finally inescapable, and perhaps all that one can do is to treat them with caution. To claim that the end of the century was a time of nervous introspection, marked by anxiety about the social changes associated with shifts in power and class relations, about gender tensions and international relations, and precipitated by the feeling that the end of a long era was approaching, is no doubt true, even if it tends rather too neatly to remove similar fears from other decades and there were some in society who felt no such insecurity. Sturgis may be right to claim that

> [p]eople in the nineties were very aware of the distinctness and significance of the decade: it marked the end of the century. Side by side with the enthusiasm for the 'new' was a consciousness of the 'end'.[25]

But that is not to say that anxieties about change did not exist at other times. Nevertheless, the worries at the end of the nineteenth century have to do with uncertainties about identity. They are generated by many factors, including class mobility and conflict, sexual confusion, international competition and threats, loss of confidence in the ability to control one's environment, and a fear of being overtaken by latent urges. All of these owe their force and character to the social and intellectual contexts in which they occur. In particular, much of the imagery and the impetus for its expression are provided by Darwinian and psychoanalytic metaphors, and this imagery, too, must be historicised. Of course, Darwin's 'daring and momentous conviction that species were mutable' supplied both reason and image for much of this concern,[26] as we shall see below, but – as with Freud's ideas later – it is doubtful that the impact of Darwin's writings would have been so great had they not spoken to other contemporary fears. In Adam Phillips's words:

> The new Darwinian or Freudian person – born and growing up in the newfound flourish and terror of a mercilessly expansive capitalism – had to be committed to instability. It was, unsurprisingly, economies of loss, in their secular versions, that preoccupied Darwin and Freud.[27]

Both Darwinism and psychoanalysis depend also on ideas and metaphors of travel (evolution, reversion, and interior). The language in which these are communicated reflects the intellectual and social structures – and subsequent responses to them – that characterise the age. Outward and inward change preoccupies Darwin, Freud, and their contemporaries. Motifs of travel and animality predominate. Focusing on the presence of these in popular texts of the late nineteenth century allows us to recover the context and force of elements whose significance has often been underplayed in readings that concentrate on their generic qualities (science fiction, gothic, horror, and so on). The shape-shifting that is discussed in this study invariably happens within, or itself constitutes, some kind of journey. Travel functions as a structural metaphor within the literature: for example, the time travel of H. G.

Wells's *The Time Machine* (1895), the space travel that brings the Martians to London in the same author's *The War of the Worlds* (1898), the journey to the island on which are practised the ghastly experiments in *The Island of Doctor Moreau* (1896), again by Wells, and the journeys that precipitate the 'reverse colonization' of Bram Stoker's *Dracula* (1897) and Richard Marsh's *The Beetle* (1897).[28] More obliquely, perhaps, Jekyll's experiments in Robert Louis Stevenson's *The Strange Case of Dr. Jekyll and Mr. Hyde* (1888) can be interpreted as a psychological voyage into his unconscious (a not uncommon reading) or a social exploration of class differences in which the most frightening aspect is not Jekyll's turning into Hyde, but rather the latter's standing to inherit Jekyll's fortune of a quarter of a million pounds;[29] while the urban exploration of General Booth's *In Darkest England* (1890) consciously reverses the journey undertaken by Stanley in his *In Darkest Africa* (1890),[30] though its author seems unaware that Stanley himself, when writing about Africa, was reflecting on Britain. In all of these texts and many more, bestiality is present as a signifier of travel, as subsequent chapters will show.

Travel is especially important as a motif in the mid- to late nineteenth century, in view of what Raymond Williams has called the 'crisis of the knowable community',[31] which occurred with the transition from a predominantly rural to a mainly urban society and led authors to explore the new conditions and relationships of existence through a development of the novel form. Williams praises Dickens for the skill and curiosity with which he charts relationships, frequently between people who seem at first to have no connection to one another.[32] This concern provided the impetus for many of the 'condition of England' novels from the mid-century onward. One thinks, for instance, of Elizabeth Gaskell's description of the Davenports' cellar contrasted with the opulence of the factory owner Carson's home in *Mary Barton* (1848). For the later novelists this preoccupation continues, but it is often presented as a need to establish links between the surface and subterranean, preserving in its verticality the idea of a hierarchy, even as the security of those on top was threatened by the return of the socially and psychologically repressed. But at the close of the century, when Darwinism had taken root (*The Origin of Species* first appeared in 1859) and psychoanalysis was in its infancy, the poles of civilisation and savagery acquired a personal, psychological basis in addition to the familiar aspect of social investigation. The theme of duality, which had been used forcefully to convey the sense of a divided society, became more self-centred as evolutionary and degeneration theories combined with growing attention paid to the unconscious with the result that the emphasis fell on a split personal subject.

Travel offers a means of discovering, exploring, and connecting such divides. Wells's *The Time Machine*, which readily lends itself to social and psychoanalytic criticism, uses time travel as a device through which the relationship of the underground dwellers to those above ground can be examined, with the Time Traveller continually modifying his understanding of what he sees. In its very title, George Gissing's *The Nether World* (1889) symbolises the image of the socially subterranean (as, of course, does the label: the 'underclass'). Hardy's *Jude the Obscure* (1895) – not a focus of this volume, but worth noting here – charts the tragic journey of one of many hidden from view. In the chapters that follow, we shall encounter social exploration, time travel, space travel, interior voyages, sexual adventures, journeys to and from colonies, subterranean burrowing, and forays into fairyland.

The line between fictional and non-fictional treatments of social journeys is not always easy to find. In his introduction to an anthology of some of the important works of social exploration from the second half of the nineteenth century, Peter Keating argues that they are 'more a frame of mind than a literary form', and that the role of social explorer is assumed by novelists and characters as much as by figures like Mayhew.[33] There does seem to be a shared use of metaphor, structure, and rhetoric, but these need to be examined in their own particular contexts, otherwise this gives the false impression that these all originate in social exploration and spread beyond it. Rather, the language and typologies of social exploration are influenced by expressions and developments in other arenas. Indeed, without elaborating on it, Keating himself points to one of these: external travel, especially in the imperial sphere. In the literature of social exploration, Keating notes the 'constant references to "wandering tribes", "pygmies", and "rain forests"', but he comments simply that these descriptions are used to make the social explorer sound as adventurous and hardy as his counterpart overseas.[34] There is much more to it than this. The terminology applied to non-white 'races' and to the working- or under-classes is often interchangeable, as several commentators have noticed.[35] So it is at once true and yet not enough to write, as Keating does, that

> [t]he upsurge of interest in the East End of London during the 1880s and 1890s had at hand a ready-made contrast between East and West which could be used to refer simultaneously to both London and the Empire, and this

became so popular that it led to what can almost be considered a sub-genre of exploration literature.[36]

This makes the process sound too automatic. Further, while Keating rightly claims that the imagery of exploration was 'clearly as important to the romance as to the realistic novel and social documentary' and operated on a metaphorical and literal level, I think he is wrong to assert that its emphasis is 'totally different'. According to Keating, the 'realist, the journalist and the sociologist … draw the reader's attention to neglected areas of contemporary life', but the writer of romance 'employed the same imagery in order to escape from the present, or, if he had a point to make of direct contemporary relevance, to set up a process of extrapolation that the reader was expected to follow through'.[37] In fact, as I hope my discussion of Wells, Wilde, and MacDonald will make clear, the writers of romance and other forms of fiction were concerned just as directly with those present conditions. They were not escaping, but offering vantage points from which those neglected areas could be seen more clearly, from a different perspective.

Elaine Showalter has observed that: 'The ends of centuries seem not only to suggest but to intensify crises.'[38] Given this fact and the perception of critical states it is not surprising that the fin de siècle should be so rich in the types and number of textual travels: characters must journey between conditions if crisis is to be registered, let alone resolved.[39] Showalter goes on to comment that: 'In periods of cultural insecurity, when there are fears of regression and degeneration, the longing for strict border controls around the definition of gender, as well as race, class, and nationality, becomes especially intense.'[40] The conservative longing for inviolable demarcation zones is only one side of the story, for it depends upon the desire to transgress, and this desire may exist overtly in others or latently in oneself. Whichever applies, the metaphor of travel provides a way through, be it by passport or illegal entry. Like metamorphosis, 'itself a process of exchange in which "body" connects the two forms',[41] travel also affords the perfect opportunity to consider two or more states at once, even if this is not the acknowledged aim. Beastly travels permit the metaphoric contemplation of migration, naturalisation, and transformation.

Metaphors, money, and Marx

Since I wish to view these processes not as unchanging psychic tendencies, but as historically inflected, an outline of some of the events from 1885 to 1900, suggesting their significance for fictional travels, should now be provided, together with statements on the role of money in effecting change.

'Until the 1870s', writes David Cannadine, 'there was an exceptionally high correlation between wealth, status, and power, for the simple reason that they were all territorially determined and defined.'[42] In the literature that I shall be examining, the collapse of this correlation and the loss of this definition are expressed by gaps between appearance and meaning and by a confusion of shapes and places. It is especially apt, then, that Cannadine should describe his historical survey of the aristocracy's decline as 'this *monstrous* and overbearing enterprise',[43] for the social and political changes that he records are very often reflected in representations of monstrosity. This process is not, of course, unique to the period. But the details of what it reflects are. Tracing the etymology of the word 'monster', Marina Warner writes that it *'resonates with the word for "to show"* monstrare*, influenced by* monere *"to warn", thus implying a portent, a warning'.*[44] What it is that is shown and warned about will vary from one time to another.

Observing that '[a]s the last quarter of the nineteenth century opened, the traditional, titled, landowners were still the richest, the most powerful and the most well-born people in the country',[45] Cannadine calculates that in 1880 more than 60 per cent of the land of the British Isles was owned by fewer than 11,000 people who held estates of over a thousand acres.[46] From 1875 and over the next seventy years, British landowners suffered a loss of economic and political control. The new fortunes that were made during the rapid rise of the international plutocracy, notably in the United States, were, for example, in business and industry, not from agricultural land; they were, in other words, 'in more liquid form'[47] – a term that suitably conveys the fluidity of the social order.

Karl Marx wrote of 'the change in form or the metamorphosis of commodities through which the social metabolism is mediated'.[48] He used this image to describe the process by which labour transforms itself into a product, which then becomes a commodity when it is exchanged for money. At this stage, the opposite forms of the commodity as use-value and exchange-value confront each other. 'These antagonistic forms of the commodities', stated Marx, 'are the real forms of motion of the process of exchange' (p.229). A further transformation occurs when the money that is handed over for a commodity is itself exchanged for a commodity. This transaction also results in a change of role for the original seller of the commodity, who now becomes a buyer. Indeed, as Marx pointed out, '[b]eing a seller and being a buyer are therefore not fixed roles, but constantly attach themselves to different persons in the course of the circulation of commodities' (p.206). Additionally, Marx wrote of the 'personification of things and the reification of persons' in modern society (p.1054).[49]

Whether Marx's account simply employs a metaphor or whether capitalism has, in fact, naturalised the processes he describes to such an extent that we have lost sight of transformations that actually underpin the economy may be debatable. What seems surer is that metamorphosis helps us to understand what is involved in the ownership and transfer of property. According to Marx, if exchange is to occur at all, then 'a change of form [in the commodity] must always occur'. Change is inherent in the process: 'the conversion of a commodity into money is the conversion of money into a commodity' (p.203). These dynamics of exchange ensure that transaction always involves transformation. They also involve motion. If this is the normal way of things in capitalist societies, then it is easy to see how moments of economic and social crisis will generate intense and worried attention to both the metamorphosis and the movement. A particular focus is likely to be money and the relationship of people to it; not just because money may be lost or gained at such times, but because so much is invested in it. It is 'all other commodities divested of their shape, the product of their universal alienation'. It is 'the absolutely alienable commodity' (p.205). Neither the commodity nor the role of its producer or seller is fixed. Indeed, Marx assumes that the 'complete metamorphosis of a commodity, in its simplest form, implies four *dénouements* and three *dramatis personae*' (p.206). Transformation thus seems intrinsic to a description of the economy, whether that term is meant metaphorically or literally.

Marx's views have, of course, been widely criticised. Yet, in an essay that outlines the opposing ideas of Marx and Adam Smith and that notes the 'very large number of intermediate positions' held by those such as Georg Simmel, two of Marx's latter-day critics, Jonathan Parry and Maurice Bloch, write that: 'what all these different strands in our cultural tradition appear to agree about is that – whether for good or ill – money acts as an incredibly powerful agent of profound social and cultural transformations'.[50] Parry and Bloch argue that the role of money as an agent has been exaggerated. They doubt that it has the intrinsic power often ascribed to it. There is not, they claim, such a gulf between the significance of money in capitalist and pre-capitalist societies or between monetary and non-monetary economies as is usually assumed. Marx's writings, they imply, are marred by a mistaken assumption of universal rules and features. Instead '[n]ot only does money mean different things in different cultures, but ... it may mean different things within the same culture' (p.22). Whether or not one accepts Parry and Bloch's thesis, their proposition is testament to the power and pervasiveness of the idea they are countering: money as a force for transformations. Even they see money not as having any 'fixed and immutable meaning' (p.22), but as having its meaning 'situationally defined' *and* 'constantly re-negotiated' (p.23).

The perception of a connection between money (or property) and transformation is strong. Late nineteenth-century images of bestiality both link to enduring concerns and are culturally and historically specific. Before proceeding to discuss intellectual influences on the shape of beasts of the 1880s and 1890s, I shall first consider economic, political, and social factors, for 'in the Victorian age money is a potent source of cultural anxiety' and '[o]f the enormous corpus of Victorian fiction, there is barely a single novel whose contents remain untouched by money'. Money has been described as 'the text beneath the text', exerting such power that 'from *Our Mutual Friend* to *Capital* ... it even seems to possess a will of its own, accomplishing changes in the social world without human agency'.[51] A theme throughout *Beastly Journeys* will be the growing sense of alarm at a widening disjunction between moral, social, and financial worth; an apprehension of a mismatch between where and what one is and where and what one should be. Simon James is right to point out that novelists such as Dickens, Gaskell, Gissing, and Wells 'were concerned that existing structures of social relations were failing to adapt to the rapidly changing nature of their economic base, that economic value and social or moral value could not coincide'. James makes an interesting point, too, about the effect of this on literary style, observing that 'money remains the site where realism and romance frequently compete'.[52] We shall bear this in mind when we look at transforming genres. Here it is sufficient to note that this was a period in which the emergence of literary forms that we now take for granted was a response to the economic conditions of the time.

Keating notices the development of the short story, first in the United States and then in Britain, but perhaps pays insufficient regard to the material reasons for its rise, which was rooted in the production of the literary magazines and journals of the US.[53] He does, however, remark on the proliferation of literary forms, many of them admixtures and transformations of related genres, during these years. Thus, for example, 'Wells's short stories and romances drew indiscriminately on elements of horror, supernatural, psychological, fantastic and adventure fiction.'[54]

Keating also observes that certain narrative journeys into the past, such as Haggard's *She* (1887), besides those into the future, bear a kinship with science fiction, as do Kipling's experiments with non-realistic literary forms, including those tales such as '.007' and 'Wireless', in which his interest in technology showed itself to be anthropomorphic. There was also the birth and spread of the invasion novel, on which both Kipling and Wells drew.[55] Genres were transforming, along with the social conditions that stimulated them. Neetens notices that '[o]f the 188 Victorian novels of working-class life listed by Keating, over two thirds were published between 1880 and 1900'.[56]

These conditions affected authors directly. Published writing is property, too; professional authors write for money. The Society of Authors was founded, on Walter Besant's initiative, in 1883 and, among other causes, campaigned for the acceptance in the US of a copyright act.[57] Authors are labourers, as Keating reminds us:

> In urging that authors should unite to oppose the unfair practices of publishers, the Society of Authors was at one with the wider changes in the 1880s and 1890s that saw the growth of trade unionism ... No less than the dockworkers and matchgirls, authors were being urged to gain strength for a battle against their 'employers', the publishers and editors ... Enemies of the Society were eager to point out, and rightly so, that if it succeeded it would be, in all but name, a trade union.[58]

These years also gave birth to the professional literary agent, one of the first of whom – A. P. Watt – acted for Wells and also on behalf of George MacDonald (the latter the subject of Chapter Four of this book).[59]

Lost property

Since '[p]ossession of property ... was portrayed in novels of the *fin de siècle* as a potent source of social and psychological disorder',[60] it seems important to look at what was happening to property and its possession. In particular, the focus of what follows will be on London – that 'strangely mingled monster',[61] as Henry James called it. Political and literary discourse of the late nineteenth century is saturated with changes of shape.[62] The metaphors used by historians a century later to describe the consequences of these material shifts repeat the imagery then current. Property 'was a cluster of complex and chameleon-like ideas', and there was 'a metamorphosis in the part played by property in political conflict', wrote one historian in 1993.[63] It might fairly be objected that this proves nothing beyond a similarity in the figures of speech used both then and now to communicate what was happening in society at the end of the nineteenth century, but metaphors can be particularly revealing, and this one of transformation is especially powerful and persistent.

According to Cannadine, it is from the 1880s onwards that the 'circumstances and consciousness [of the patricians] changed and weakened'. Cannadine attributes this change in large part to the 'sudden and dramatic collapse of the agricultural base of the European economy' and to its political and social consequences – one feature of which was the agitation that led to the extension of the franchise.[64] His view is that '[t]he age of the masses had superseded the age of the classes. At the same time that the economy became global, politics became democratized.'[65] If this diagnosis seems too sanguine, Cannadine does not overstate the anxieties created in the minds of the upper and middle classes by the pressure for these democratising changes. As Neville Kirk puts it: 'the newly enfranchised masses were believed to pose a serious threat to property and to the balance of power and status'.[66] Moreover, 'by the end of the nineteenth century Britain had become "unquestionably a working-class nation"'.[67] Harrison notes that '[a]lthough the middle class and aristocracy set the tone and fashion of the later nineteenth century, about 75 per cent of the population belonged to the working class'.[68] 'In 1901 "about 85 per cent of the total working population were employed by others, and about 75 per cent as manual workers".'[69] More than seven million people – 46 per cent of the workforce – were employed in manufacturing, mining, and building.[70]

The picture we have is of an uneasy and reluctant accommodation by the old of the new. The established and threatened power evolves strategies for the containment of that which challenges it. Central to this policy is the sense of a directed mobility that is arranged in order to prevent a larger, uncontrolled movement. In the words of one historical survey of the period:

> Without some fresh influx of wealth the nobility as a class would have been hard pressed. But from the 1880s new peerages were granted to men whose fortunes had been made in trade and industry ... There was also an

increase in the number of new baronetcies and knighthoods, most of which went to businessmen and manufacturers. The top echelons of industry and commerce were thus assimilated into the ruling elite, and second and third generation brewers or millowners graduated easily via the public schools and the Universities of Cambridge and Oxford into high society.[71]

The passing of the 1884 to 1885 Reform Acts had increased the number of people able to vote to about five million. Most of these were working men, but these *were* men: suffrage was denied to women until 1918 and even the measures of 1884 to 1885 still left only about 28 per cent of the United Kingdom's population above the age of twenty qualified to vote.[72] Nevertheless, the 'patrician dominance of the lower house soon vanished for ever as a result',[73] and

> the Third Reform Act created a new and very different representational structure for the whole of Great Britain and Ireland, in which the cities and the suburbs were pre-eminent, and in which a working-class electorate possessed the dominant voice ... [T]he more representative and democratic the Commons became, the more anachronistic and unacceptable the House of Lords appeared by comparison.[74]

All the same, '[t]he gap between Salisbury, the political leader of his country, and the mass of post-1884 voters whom he supposedly led, could hardly have been greater', and '[d]espite the continuing existence of an aristocratic elite most late Victorians no longer thought of themselves as living in a primarily aristocratic nation'. If there was a growing perception of a movement away from aristocratic rule, this does not mean that the middle class felt secure. It was 'far from homogeneous', and the process of accommodating new members risked leaving the door open for unwanted intruders and errant insiders.[75] Beneath the surface confidence of the middle class lay deep insecurity. The reasons for this are manifold: political, economic, intellectual, and psychological.

The class instability I have been describing coincided with challenges abroad to Britain's imperial power. Since the discourses of race and class were (and are) closely linked in any case, it is hardly surprising that they should come together at this critical period. As Neetens argues, '[b]ourgeois representations of the working class can indeed be understood as intimately linked to the properly colonial discourses produced in the service of Britain's imperial enterprise overseas.'[76] Images of the savage and primitive were applied to members of the working class and unemployed – the latter being a word that 'with reference to the surplus of casual labour in London especially, was coined in the 1880s'.[77]

The extension of the franchise under the 1884 Act has been described as giving

> dramatic political form to the wider cultural and social democratisation which confronted the professional classes with a deeply disturbing problem of social identity, as the boundaries between the lower bourgeoisie and their inferiors became increasingly blurred.[78]

Wim Neetens's account of this problem of social identity and blurred boundaries fits the confusion that is evident in the texts that I shall discuss in the following chapters. In these works, journeys between two types of creature or state symbolise the disturbance of borders between classes (and between genders and sexualities). Changes to the physical body reflect modifications to the social body. As these tended towards encroachment and conjunction, so the narratives of the time stressed similar perceptions of invasion, commingling, and expulsion. A cartoon from the January 1884 issue of *Punch* illustrates this nicely, with the wolf of Socialism accosting a Little Red Riding Hood figure. This is a threat not only of attack, but of ingestion: the wolf saying to himself 'ALL THE BETTER TO EAT YOU, MY DEAR'.[79] The reworking of the famous fairy tale shows the importance of examining such images in their context, rather than taking them as timeless expressions of psychological Othering.[80] My chapter on George MacDonald's fairy tales will explore the rootedness of his fantastic worlds in the realities of late nineteenth-century society. My reading of this material, as of many of the texts discussed in the present volume, is influenced by the work of Chris Baldick, who writes of how 'the myth of Frankenstein registers the anxieties of the period inaugurated in the twin social and industrial revolutions in France and Britain'. Baldick concedes the necessity of psychological interpretations, but insists that 'it is of little help to reduce the story of Frankenstein and his monster to a conflict of psychic structures if this means abstracting it from the world outside the psyche, with which the myth engages'.[81] Class – 'the central faultline of nineteenth-century life'[82] – is crucial. Baldick notes that after the French Revolution, 'Burke announces the birth of the monster child Democracy, while Paine records the death of the monster parent Aristocracy.'[83] Burke and Paine were writing almost a century before the writers considered here, but the imagery and issues survived. Lord Brabourne's fear of the 'devouring spirit of democracy' was held by many of his rank, and Disraeli and Lord Salisbury saw the Liberal victory in the general election of 1880 as 'portending a "serious war of the classes"'.[84] In the

1885 election, seventy Liberal MPs who were returned were pledged to abolish the upper house.[85]

So, class conflict and social change marked this period. The 1880s 'saw the third great upsurge of trade unionism in the nineteenth century, and a new orientation of British labor'.[86] Throughout the decade, '[a]gitation for a Labour Party had been gathering strength'.[87] The Independent Labour Party was founded in 1893. Between 1888 and 1892, trade union membership had doubled to over one-and-a-half million,[88] though by the mid-1890s, 'adverse economic conditions and a fierce employer counter-attack had halved the new unionist upsurge' of these years.[89] In 1884, 80,000 people attended a meeting in Hyde Park held by the London Trades Council; a later demonstration for reform attracted 120,000. In 1885, a demonstration of the Social Democratic Foundation in Hyde Park was suppressed by the police. The demonstrators then broke windows in Pall Mall.[90] On 13 November 1887 – 'Bloody Sunday' – a meeting in Trafalgar Square to demand justice for Ireland, organised by the Federation despite police prohibition, broke up in violence. 'Violence and counter-violence continued.' In 1888, a workman was killed by the police. The Socialists held a great procession for his funeral.[91] In that same year, the match girls struck. The year 1889 saw gas workers win an eight-hour day and gain a small increase in wages without having to go on strike, as well as witnessing the great dock strike in August. This latter, writes Lynd, 'ushered in the full tide of the new unionism'.[92] In 1893, two coal miners were killed by troops at Featherstone during a bitter dispute that lasted for four months.[93] By the 1890s, the strike, having been deprecated even until the 1880s by union leaders and employers, 'was coming to be regarded as an indispensable means of enforcing labor demands'.[94] But these disputes were not straightforward symptoms of conflict between classes. As Lynd puts it, '[t]he dockers' strike signalized a new kind of alliance between labor and certain sections of the middle class';[95] she quotes the *Annual Register* for that year, observing that 'for quite the first time the sympathy of the middle-classes at home, and even in the Colonies, was with the men and against the masters'.[96] These labour disputes contributed to the fact that in the 1880s '[m]en became more sharply aware that institutions are man-made and, therefore, changeable'.[97] In Lynd's view, the decade

> was a period of education and preparation, of accustoming people to new ways of seeing England and of interpreting relations among men … It did not bring social revolution, but it helped to make ready the way for it.[98]

The literature of the time reflects and helps facilitate those new ways of seeing. Because, in the 1880s, '[a]ccepted institutions and accepted philosophies were being sharply challenged by changes in economic conditions',[99] contemporary narratives will show those established systems under threat.

Darwinism

The previous pages have outlined the social and economic habitats of the beasts of the 1880s and 1890s that will stalk the remaining chapters, but the shape of these creatures was formed by intellectual developments also, especially by those of Darwin, who 'himself revolutionized the concept of form'.[100] 'Darwin's theory of the mutability of species struck at the normative thinking that made of monsters deviations from Platonic or ideal form.'[101] Post-Darwinian images of the beastliness of 'man' have different connotations from those that preceded them. The beasts that prowl these pages are not those of the Middle Ages, Renaissance, Enlightenment, or Romantics,[102] even if there is some continuity between them. From Darwin we see that

> the human being is no longer the prototype of ideal form in its unity, its originality, its integrity, and its perfection. Hybrid and even teratoid, as it were, in both body and mind, it contains little bits and traces of other animals ... aspects of male and female, and primitive instinctual glimmers suffused throughout its civilized behaviour.[103]

Darwin's theories focused attention on diachrony: on movement through time. He made it impossible to claim finiteness or summation. As Beer observes, evolutionism is a theory 'which does *not* privilege the present, which sees it as a moving instant in an endless process of change' (*DP*, p.13). Richter puts it thus:

> The principle of evolution is dynamic: forms change and develop into other forms ... The close biological affiliation of bodies means that each organism retains the memory of its past.[104]

Looking at beings meant looking at process:

> Any change in structure and function, which can be effected by small stages, is within the power of natural selection; so that an organ rendered, through changed habits of life, useless or injurious for one purpose, might be modified and used for another purpose. An organ might, also, be retained for one alone of its former functions. (*OS*, p.381)[105]

Mutability is key. Darwin draws a comparison with written language: 'Rudimentary organs may be compared with the letters in a word, still retained in the spelling, but become useless in the pronunciation, but which serve as a clue for its derivation' (*OS*, p.382). Since 'the chief part of every living creature is due to inheritance; and consequently, though each being assuredly is well fitted for its place in nature, many structures have no very close and direct relation to present habits of life' (*OS*, p.152), one might wonder, to extend Darwin's simile, when particular words will become obsolete and disappear from our vocabulary. So it might be with those who no longer fulfil a useful social function.

Darwin's theory of evolution not only stressed the modification of form, but also employed metaphors of economy in its communication. Indeed, as the introduction to a collection of essays on *The Origin of Species* points out, 'the theory of natural selection is consistently and explicitly cast as a theory of political economy in nature'.[106] In *The Origin of Species*, Darwin wrote:

> Nothing is easier than to admit in words the truth of the universal struggle for life, or more difficult – at least I have found it so – than constantly to bear this conclusion in mind. Yet unless it be thoroughly ingrained in the mind, the whole economy of nature, with every fact on distribution, rarity, abundance, extinction, and variation, will be dimly seen or quite misunderstood. (*OS*, p.47)

There is a neat symmetry to Darwin's use of economic images in describing the biological world, since his own theories about this would be adapted by others – notably Herbert Spencer – and applied to the social and economic realm. Even if the idea of the economy of nature is only a figure of speech (though it is surely more than that), the concept of physical alteration was literal enough. Towards the end of the century, Darwinism would combine with the social and political anxieties outlined above to intensify fears about the future shape of things. Most obviously, Darwinian thought was taken by some to reduce the possibility of human agency (though it also allowed for the beneficial results of improving the environment). For Darwin, 'Natural Selection ... is a power ... as immeasurably superior to man's feeble efforts, as the works of Nature are to those of Art' (*OS*, p.47). The stories of beastly journeys are ones of the human – civilisation, culture, art – cowed by the animal; by the irruption of nature. Max Nordau, a 'convinced Darwinian', identified progress as 'the effect of an ever more rigorous subjugation of the beast in man'.[107] Wilde, of course, challenged this view (and was a particular target of Nordau). Richard

Ellmann's summary of Wilde's view – 'Wilde had always held that the true "beasts" were not those who expressed their desires, but those who tried to suppress other people's'[108] – illustrates Wilde's method of taking conventional imagery and subverting it.

Darwin may have carefully avoided making any direct reference to the consequences of his theory for humans in *The Origin of Species* (though not in the later *Descent of Man*), but the economic metaphors mean that the inference can be drawn. Beer points out that '[t]he exclusion of any discussion of man did *not* prevent his readers immediately seeing its implications for "the origin of man and his history"' (*DP*, p.59). As if this were not threatening enough, natural selection involved intergenerational as well as situational or environmental conflict:

> As natural selection acts solely by the preservation of profitable modifications, each new form will tend in a fully-stocked country to take the place of, and finally to exterminate, its own less-improved parent-form and other less-favoured forms with which it comes into competition. Thus extinction and natural selection go hand in hand. (*OS*, p.127)

The social consequences of Darwin's theory of natural selection become a little more apparent when he writes of how 'if any one species does not become modified and improved in a corresponding degree with its competitors, it will be exterminated' (*OS*, p.76). For species, we might well read classes. Certainly, this is the interpretation upon which Social Darwinists' adaptations of natural selection depended. The worrying message is that failure to modify will result in extermination, but that in any case progress depends on struggle and in that struggle the least fit will expire: 'natural selection acts by life and death, – by the survival of the fittest, and by the destruction of the less well-fitted individuals' (*OS*, p.148).

Struggle, extermination, transmutation, and the influence of the environment, with metaphors of nature and the economy used interchangeably, are the principal elements of Darwinism that help distinguish late nineteenth-century representations of beastliness and animality from earlier treatments. The emphasis on change was deeply unsettling. True, sometimes Darwin seems optimistic about the effects:

> Natural selection will modify the structure of the young in relation to the parent, and of the parent in relation to the young. In social animals it will adapt the structure of each individual for the benefit of the whole community; if the community profits by the selected change. What natural selection cannot do, is to modify the structure of one species, without giving it any advantage for the good of another species. (*OS*, p.64)

But at other times, the threat of extinction faced by forms that are no longer useful reverberates in ways that alarmed many of Darwin's contemporaries. It is difficult not to interpret the following passage in terms of social class:

> [N]atural selection is continually trying to economise every part of the organisation. If under changed conditions of life a structure, before useful, becomes less useful, its diminution will be favoured, for it will profit the individual not to have its nutriment wasted in building up a useless structure. (*OS*, p.111)

Wells's *The Time Machine* investigates a future world where exactly this has happened: the leisure-class Eloi have, physically and figuratively, lost their stature. Years of existence without useful toil have turned them into effete and decorative specimens. The fearful result for class relations is something the tale explores, as Chapter Three, on Wells (whom Beer does not mention in her otherwise excellent book on the effects of evolutionary thought upon narrative structure in literature), will show.

Perhaps as worrying to Darwin's readers would have been his proclamation that 'the appearance of new forms and the disappearance of old forms … are bound together' (*OS*, p.282). While this may lead to progression, it ensures destruction also: 'The extinction of old forms is the almost inevitable consequence of the production of new forms' (*OS*, p.299). Clearly, this language can be applied to other spheres besides the biological. Those that I shall concentrate on in this book are the sociocultural, political, and literary. We have seen something of the first two already in this introduction. The significance for literature of Darwin's ideas about the replacement of old forms by new is evident in Raymond Williams's formulation of 'complex relations between what can be called dominant, residual, and emergent institutions and practices'. These exist '[a]t any particular point', and the key to their analysis is 'investigation and identification of the specific places these occupy within an always dynamic field'. Of course, Williams is writing more under the conscious influence of Marxist than Darwinist thought, but they cannot always be easily separated (as *The Time Machine* shows) and the connections between the social and biological are in any case made in the metaphors applied to both. What also links them is the sense of instability. Williams reminds us that 'any historical analysis, when it centres on a date, has to begin by recognizing that though all dates are fixed, all time is in movement'.[109] The same is true of species. Evolution depends on the chance mutation of a specimen, which, proving advantageous to survival, is preserved as a characteristic in its descendants. The key is transformation; the mutations carry the old and anticipate the new.

To compare physical and literary forms in this regard is not fanciful. Indeed, Darwin's writing has itself been seen to embody his theories. According to Jeff Wallace, *The Origin of Species* displays a 'tension between the familiar and the absurd, tradition and revolution, in its own form'.[110] At least one commentator has compared the textual variations of *The Origin of Species* (six editions published between 1859 and 1872) with 'organic evolution'.[111] Darwinism itself changed shape.[112] Peter Keating notes that

> it was not always Darwinism itself that exercised the minds of novelists: it tended to enter British fiction as a re-import, returning to its native land in various guises and modifications, fitting itself easily into Schopenhauerian pessimism, French naturalism, and Nietzschean elitism.[113]

What is more, Darwin conceives of the imagination as bringing together the past and present to shape something new. Raymond Williams quotes him as writing (in 1871):

> Imagination is one of the highest prerogatives of Man. By this faculty he unites, independently of the will, former images and ideas, and thus creates brilliant and novel results.[114]

Williams develops this idea, using others, also, to argue that imagination has a past, present, and future. From Darwin and Associationist psychology and psychoanalysis, he derives the 'sense of imagination as working on the past to create some new present'. In 'ideas of divination' and 'different and more rational bases', imagination is turned towards the future, 'towards foreseeing what will or could happen'. And imagination operates in the present by enabling us to 'understand what it is like to be in some other contemporary condition: bereaved, unemployed, insane'.[115] Admittedly, Williams then makes a distinction between imagination and the process of writing fiction, using a term he employed earlier in the criticism of novels and which he now applies to his own experience of literary creativity, 'structures of feeling', to describe the latter. This distinction notwithstanding, Williams's comments on dominant, emergent, and residual forms and on the tenses of the imagination parallel Darwin's about evolutionary time and natural selection. That is, historical process and the environment modify forms, whether physical, literary, or social.

The relationship between Darwinism and narrative form has been examined by Beer, who, observing that '[w]hen it is first advanced, theory is at its most fictive' (*DP*, p.3), notices that Darwin 'sought to appropriate and to recast inherited mythologies, discourses, and narrative disorders. He was telling a new story, against the grain of the language available to tell it in' (*DP*, p.5). His 'ideas profoundly unsettled the received relationship between fiction, metaphor, and the material world' (*DP*, p.31). Beer notes the 'two-way traffic' of ideas, metaphors, myths, and narrative patterns between scientists and non-scientists as the former 'drew openly' in their texts 'upon literary, historical and philosophical material as part of their arguments' and general readers were able to turn directly and respond to the primary works of scientists (*DP*, p.7). According to Beer, the influence of evolutionary theory upon the nineteenth-century novel was such that it affected not only theme but organisation. So, for example,

> [a]t first evolutionism tended to offer a new authority to orderings of narrative which emphasised cause and effect, then descent and kin. Later again, its eschewing of fore-ordained design ... allowed chance to figure as the only sure determinant. (*DP*, p.8)

Evolutionism was 'rich in contradictory elements which can serve as a metaphorical basis for more than one reading of experience' (*DP*, p.9). Remarking that 'the concepts of metamorphosis and of transformation were organised in nineteenth-century fiction by [a] third, crucial, term ... Development', Beer argues that '[m]etamorphosis and development offer two radical orders for narrative: the tension between the two orders and the attempt to make them accord can be observed in the organisation of many Victorian fictions. Causal relations preoccupy novelists and biologists alike' (*DP*, p.112).

Much of the literature of the late 1880s and 1890s expresses newness in old forms (the urban poetry of John Davidson being an example). Some of it was shockingly and dangerously new. Sturgis reminds us that Henry Vizetelly, the publisher who introduced (in translation) the novels of Emile Zola to England, was jailed in 1888 for six months on charges of obscenity following the publication of *The Earth*. Although '[t]he unflinching naturalism of [Zola's] works, many chronicling in explicit terms the bestial degradation of working-class existence, had from the start provoked scandal, publicity and, of course, sales',[116] Vizetelly's company was bankrupted after his conviction.

Animals, humans, and in-between

Humans may have been labelled as beasts, but the process also happened in reverse and met at intermediate states, too. Perceptions of animal attributes in humans were mirrored by the ascription of human traits to animals.[117] Harriet Ritvo has emphasised the ways in which nineteenth-century classifications of the animal world justified the hierarchy of, and among, humans. For example: 'The dichotomy between domesticated animals and wild animals was frequently compared to that between civilized and savage human societies', and '[w]hen animals stood for foreigners, the hierarchy of nature was apt to be presented in the stark, violent terms of conquest.'[118] Descriptions of animals favoured those that 'displayed the qualities of an industrious, docile and willing human servant', so that 'subordination to human purposes transfigured and elevated the animal itself'. On the other hand, 'the worst not only declined to serve, but dared to challenge human supremacy' (p.17), just as beastly people threatened the social and moral order. Ritvo observes that '[t]he concomitant of the praise heaped on animals that knew their places and kept happily to them was the opprobrium endured by less complaisant creatures' (p.21). The same applied to assessments of people. 'For both animals and people a distinguished lineage divided those with hereditary claims to high status from arrivistes', writes Ritvo (p.61), who suggests that the activities of the Kennel Club (founded in 1873)

> expressed the desire of predominantly middle-class fanciers for a relatively prestigious and readily identifiable position within a stable, hierarchical society ... The identification of elite animal with elite owner was not a confirmation of the owner's status but a way of redefining it. (p.104)

After *The Origin of Species*:

> The emerging continuity between animals and people made it even easier to represent human competition, and the social hierarchies created by those who prevailed, in terms of animals ... Animals became the types not just of domestic servants and other laborers, but of the exotic peoples that Europeans subjugated in the course of the nineteenth century. (pp.40–41)[119]

According to Ritvo:

> Darwin may have transformed the relation between human beings and other animals in principle, but the egalitarianism he had suggested by including humankind among the beasts had little practical effect, even on the thinking of naturalists. More influential was the notion of the survival of 'the vigorous, the healthy and the happy', which seemed to justify and

even celebrate human ascendancy. Animals remained the symbols of various orders within human hierarchies, as well as the victims of human control. (p.41)

But there is no single view of Darwin, whose ideas were, in any case, open to continual reinterpretation, even by himself. That was so in the nineteenth century, and it is as true now. Beer notes that '[William] Paley, Darwin, and [Charles] Kingsley all take particular delight in the processes of transformation, though the ideological patterns that they perceive vary profoundly.'[120] Kingsley, like Darwin, 'move[d] away from the Paleyian model, in which the young through all its transformations, strives *backwards* to become the parent type' and proposed instead 'the value of change, mutation, the new beginning – and this is part both of his Darwinian and his socialist thinking'.[121] Whereas Ritvo writes that 'Darwin speculated that the wildness often shown by hybrids of domestic species had the same cause as the wickedness that characterized human half-breeds' (p.16), Darwin himself was, according to Beer, 'bent on re-emphasising community'. His theory's support for monogenesis placed him in the camp of those who believed that all 'races' had a common origin and were related. This belief was in opposition to those – the polygenists – who maintained that the 'races' were separate and who wished to emphasise their separateness from the Caucasian. 'The idea of a common progenitor gave an egalitarian basis to theories of development, whether of races or of species' (*DP*, p.117).[122] Beer stresses that Darwin took 'considerable pains – not always successfully – to avoid legitimating current social order by naturalising it' (*DP*, p.58). She points out that among the multiplicity of stories inherent in evolution were the contradictory ones of equality and domination:

> Whereas the story of man's kinship with all other species had an egalitarian impulse, the story of development tended to restore hierarchy and to place at its apex not only man in general, but contemporary European man in particular – our kind of man, to the Victorians. (*DP*, p.114)

In Beer's view:

> One of the most disquieting aspects of Darwinian theory was that it muddied descent, and brought into question the privileged 'purity' of the 'great family'. In terms of the class organisation of his time this is clearly a deeply unpalatable view.
>
> ... The utopian drive in Darwin's thinking declares itself in the levelling tendency of his language, which always emphasises those elements in meaning which make for community and equality and undermine the

hierarchical and the separatist. Darwin's rejection of special creation leads him to an enhanced evaluation of all life and to an emphasis on deep community. So classification becomes not an end in itself but an arrested moment in a long story. Taxonomy and transformation are set in tension. (*DP*, pp.63–64)

The tension between taxonomy and transformation well describes the situation in which the beastly journeys of this book are made: the threat posed by the creatures that are caught up in these narratives arises from their slipping out of place. Their misshapenness makes them difficult to label. The literature discerns the transformation and attempts to describe and capture it.

Intermediacy – the occupation of a position between classifications – also bothers Nordau and those with similar views. Tracing a link between degeneracy and the 'originators of all the *fin-de-siècle* movements in art and literature' (p.17), Nordau observes that '[q]uite a number of different designations have been found for these persons. Maudsley and Ball call them "Borderland dwellers" – that is to say, dwellers on the borderland between reason and pronounced madness' (p.18). Nordau then discusses the 'lower stages' of degeneracy, in which

> the degenerate does not, perhaps, himself commit any act which will bring him into conflict with the criminal code, but at least asserts the theoretical legitimacy of crime; seeks, with philosophically sounding fustian, to prove that 'good' and 'evil,' virtue and vice, are arbitrary distinctions; goes into raptures over evildoers and their deeds; professes to discover beauties in the lowest and most repulsive things; and tries to awaken interest in, and so-called 'comprehension' of, every bestiality. (p.18)

The higher or fully-fledged degenerates lack the 'sense of morality and of right and wrong. For them there exists no law, no decency, no modesty' (p.18). Clearly, the states of travel and bestiality are connected in the mind of the degenerate-hunter. Even the journeying of the creative mind is distrusted: the degenerate 'rejoices in his faculty of imagination … and devotes himself with predilection to all sorts of unlicensed pursuits permitted by the unshackled vagabondage of his mind' (p.21). Wagner and the 'morally insane' 'vagabond' Whitman, whose fame rests on his 'bestially sensual pieces' (p.231), are attacked by Nordau for their incapacity to submit their 'capriciously vacillating thoughts' to regular form (p.232). Nordau turns to animal metaphors to convey and condemn the comportment of those whom he regards as criminals, decadents, and mentally diseased. For example: 'In the degenerate with disturbed equilibrium consciousness has to play the part of an ape-like mother finding excuses for the stupid and naughty tricks of a spoiled child' (p.111). And 'he who places pleasure above discipline, and impulse above restraint, wishes not for progress, but for retrogression to the most primitive animality' (p.554). We are close to Freud's notion of the id here – a resemblance that reminds us that Freud drew on the same sets of metaphors. Sometimes the criticism of animal-like behaviour is directed at literary characters: 'The sole characteristic distinguishing these [Ibsen's] Lövborgs, Ekdals, Oswald Alvings, etc., from beasts is that they are given to drink' (p.405). At other times and often simultaneously it was directed at the creators of these characters. So, when Nordau finds in Ibsen a 'revolt against the prevailing moral law, together with a glorification of bestial instincts', his contempt for this 'egomaniacal anarchist' (p.356) is one that many of his contemporaries felt as they railed against literary naturalism – 'the premeditated worship of pessimism and obscenity' (p.497) – for indulging in the vices it purported to show.

Beastly sex

While the social body was experiencing the changes outlined above and in Chapter One, the sexual body was undergoing an often shocking crisis. Elaine Showalter writes that:

> The 1880s and 1890s, in the words of the novelist George Gissing, were decades of 'sexual anarchy,' when all the laws that governed sexual identity and behavior seemed to be breaking down … During this period both the words 'feminism' and 'homosexuality' first came into use, as New Woman and male aesthetes redefined the meanings of femininity and masculinity.[123]

Among the many episodes of sexual scandal were rumours of a homosexual circle centred on the Foreign Minister, Lord Rosebery (rumours stoked by Lord Queensberry, whose eldest son, Lord Drumlanrig – the brother of Wilde's lover, Lord Alfred Douglas – committed suicide on 18 October 1894 and had been suspected of involvement in the circle); the divorces of Sir Charles Dilke and Captain Parnell; and the Cleveland Street Affair, in which upper-class men (including Prince Albert Victor, second-in-line to the throne) were implicated in the activities of a male brothel.[124] Earlier in 1870, the trial of Ernest Boulton and Fredrick Park for conspiracy to commit sodomite acts had received much newspaper attention. Besides legal cases concerning the provision of information on birth control and measures for the control of sexual disease, three other episodes were especially prominent: the investigation of child prostitution by the journalist W. T. Stead, whose article 'The Maiden Tribute of Modern Babylon' in 1885 resulted in his imprisonment; the murders committed between the end of August and November 1888 by Jack the Ripper; and the trials of Oscar Wilde in 1895.

We need to take note of the changing conceptions and relations of gender against which these three sexual scandals took place. Cohen argues that:

> As an integral part of the emergence of mass journalism in the late nineteenth century, the coverage of sexual scandals was instrumental in articulating sexual behavior as an element of class and national identities and conversely in unifying class and national identities in relation to normative appraisals of sexual behavior.[125]

As Sally Ledger remarks, '[g]ender was an unstable category at the fin de siècle'.[126] Apart from the growing visibility of homosexuality, which reached its apogee with the trials of Wilde, there was the '*fin de siècle* phenomenon' of the New Woman,[127] who had 'a multiple identity', was 'as a concept ... riddled with contradictions', and excited not only the opposition of many men, but also differences of opinion between women as to who or what constituted her. She was also associated, at this critical moment of endings and beginnings, with modernity. Not only was her identity multiple and contradictory, but her texts were varied also: 'The New Woman writing was aesthetically diverse: it was as if no single form was capable of assimilating the range of experience which the New Woman writers wished to articulate.'[128]

Ledger comments:

> It is no coincidence that the New Woman materialised alongside the decadent and the dandy ... It was the perceived connections between the New Woman and decadence that meant the fate of the New Woman was inextricably linked to the public disgracing of Oscar Wilde.[129]

And '[w]hat most obviously linked the New Woman with the Wildean decadents of the 1890s was the fact that both overtly challenged Victorian sexual codes'.[130]

One should not lose sight of the economic context of these shifts and crises. The growing calls for women's rights, including the passing of the Married Women's Property Acts in 1870 and 1882, helped erode the image of woman's separate sphere that lay beyond the material and economic realm. Of course, for working-class women, economic engagement had been a grim and necessary reality, but the movement towards some kind of independence for women helped foster a view of them as economic beings and entities in their own right.[131] The property acts have been described as carrying through 'one of the great reallocations of property in English history', and the 1882 Act 'demanded an end to the old doctrine of the legal unity of husband and wife'.[132] In 1891, 'an Act was passed which denied men "conjugal rights" to their wives' bodies without their wives' consent'.[133]

Wim Neetens's comments on the place of women point to the importance of the socio-economic context:

> The idea of woman's separate sphere was an integral part of Victorian bourgeois ideology: an economically and sexually innocent, 'spiritualised' femininity was seen as the necessary mitigating complement able to influence and redeem the ruthless amorality of capitalist logic, identified as masculine ... Bourgeois femininity functioned as a locus for the non-utilitarian, humane values ousted from the public sphere by the cash nexus and committed to the private circle of the bourgeois drawing-room, where the idea of the family assumed a new dimension.[134]

As Neetens suggests, middle-class feminine domesticity was, in fact, the culmination of, rather than the counter to, capitalism. The accoutrements and signifiers of it were bought by money and were markers of status; the values it embodied were class-based. Nonetheless, the intrusion of the wilderness into the realm of the feminine or the abdication of this exalted position by the New Woman shows crisis. Calls to 'reaffirm the importance of the family as a bulwark against sexual decadence' bear witness to the extent to which it was felt to be under threat and its role as shelter.[135] These were not only questions of individual morality or even national propriety; they implied, on a larger scale, the fate of Empire: 'many Englishmen regarded the homosexual scandals of the 1880s and 1890s, up to Oscar Wilde's trial, as certain signs of the immorality that had toppled Greece and Rome'.[136] As Joseph Bristow puts it: 'If the [Wilde] trials prove anything, it is that effeminacy and empire at this point stood in violent opposition.' The effeminate style that Wilde emblematised, which 'represented a distinctly late nineteenth-century apprehension of the male homosexual', ran counter to the state's 'promulgation of a hegemonic ideal of Englishness'. Such was, and continued to be, the antipathy to this new effeminacy that 'homoerotic writing after 1885 constantly defines itself against the predominant assumption that to be a man-loving man necessarily meant that one was weakened, morally and physically, by the taint of effeminacy'.[137] Once again, there is a confusion of conditions that are normally regarded as separate or even opposite. The effect of male effeminacy upon animal imagery is discussed in Chapter Five on Wilde, whose greater sin was to embrace members of the working class; to be 'feasting with panthers'.

There is a direct relationship between the legislation and fiction. Keating writes:

> Just as the Married Women's Property Acts rendered inoperable one of the standard plots of eighteenth and nineteenth-century fiction by making the financial manipulation of women no longer a sinister (and legal) motive for marriage, so, in a more general sense, the expanding democratic institutions of the 1880s and 1890s … created freer forms of social and sexual relationships which destroyed the novelist's traditional reliance on home-based courtship and marriage.[138]

While this is more apparent in the difficult relationships between parents and children, it

> also affects every other aspect of fiction. In, for example, the ways that characters in novels move around the city streets, whether going to work, college, restaurant, pub, or just taking a walk. In the novels of Gissing, Wells, Bennett, Joyce and Lawrence, there is a degree of individual freedom – of movement and choice – which simply does not exist in fiction of an earlier period, and indeed could not exist because the social conditions which provide the novelist's raw material did not themselves exist. The increasing openness of society at the close of the nineteenth century and the increasingly open narrative forms of early modern fiction go hand in hand.[139]

Similarly, '[f]rom the mid-1890s – inspired by Hardy, Meredith, and the New Woman novelists, and by the social reality of more easily available separation, divorce, and birth-control methods – irregular sexual relationships moved to a central place in British fiction'.[140]

These sexual and gender perceptions and shifts have been written about by a number of critics and theorists, but the presence of the beast in the sexual scandals seems to have been less remarked upon. Of all the metaphors of beastliness, the sexual connotations are those that are probably most likely to seem timeless. That is to say, the idea of animal lust may seem to be no more characteristic of 1880s and 1890s Britain than of any other period or culture. But context matters. Thus when Nordau writes of the 'love of those degenerates who, in sexual transport, become like wild beasts' (pp.181–182), he is referring to characters in Wagner that 'behave like tom-cats gone mad' and 'reflect a state of mind in the poet which is well known to the professional expert. It is a form of Sadism' (p.181). Nordau's comments are aimed at degenerate art and they belong to his age. Zola was perhaps the prime target. Of him, Nordau writes:

> That he is a sexual psychopath is betrayed on every page of his novels. He revels continually in representations from the region of the basest sensuality ... His consciousness is peopled with images of unnatural vice, bestiality, passivism, and other aberrations, and he is not satisfied with lingering libidinously over human acts of such a nature, but he even produces pairing animals. (p.500)

In Nordau, as in others of his type, there seems to be a perverse delight in the detail of what he finds disgusting.

With or without overt moralising, appalled fascination is apparent in most of the narratives studied in the present volume. The chapters that follow explore the entwining of material circumstances and the metaphors of beastliness and journeys within a range of texts. They proceed in the spirit of George MacDonald's remark that without the influence of the imagination, 'no process of recording events can develop into a history'.[141] Their argument is that through the combination of animal and travel imagery the narratives throw light on the society that generated them and are best approached through knowledge of that society, so that the stories they tell can be understood in both their historical and imaginative aspects. The confusion of shape that the texts describe and their own experiments with form reflect the conditions that produced them. Vint's observation that '[f]requently cultural representations of animals ... will tell us little about the animals themselves and much about the ways animals become caught up in human ideology' may be aptly extended to the animal metaphors on exhibition here.[142]

In Chapter One we shall examine the urban habitat, with figures of various beasts populating an array of fictional and non-fiction narratives about the city. Chapter Two probes the threat from invaders assuming the shape of a bat and beetle in novels by Bram Stoker and Richard Marsh, both published in 1897. Chapter Three considers H. G. Wells's use of the distancing techniques of time travel, space travel, and shipwreck to pose social, political, and ethical questions about contemporary society. Chapter Four concentrates on animal motifs in the fantastic worlds of George MacDonald. Chapter Five looks at the often subversive deployment of animal imagery in both the person and writings of Oscar Wilde. The conclusion to the volume conducts a post-mortem and contemplates the legacy of this extraordinary corpus, whose edgy sense of complicity and self-interrogation has largely given way to the derogation of others for the purposes of exclusion or confinement.

Notes

1 Georg Lukács, 'Narrate or Describe?', in *Writer and Critic and Other Essays* (London: Merlin Press, 1978), p.147, my emphasis.
2 Peter Keating makes this point in *The Haunted Study: A Social History of the English Novel 1875–1914* [1989] (London: Fontana Press, 1991), p.1, while acknowledging both the drawbacks and usefulness of periodicity (p.2).
3 Keating, *The Haunted Study*, p.2.
4 Keating, *The Haunted Study*, pp.142, 143, 155, 158.
5 John Davidson, 'A Northern Suburb' [1897], reprinted in R. K. R. Thornton, ed., *Poetry of the 'Nineties* (Harmondsworth: Penguin, 1970), p.64.
6 Chris Baldick, writing of an earlier period, has made a similar connection, suggesting that: 'The representation of fearful transgressions in the figure of physical deformity arises as a variant of that venerable cliché of political discourse, the "body politic".' Chris Baldick, *In Frankenstein's Shadow: Myth, Monstrosity, and Nineteenth-Century Writing* (Oxford: Clarendon Press, 1987), p.14. My readings of the texts and myths discussed in *Beastly Journeys* are influenced by Baldick's approach, and his ideas are further discussed below, but my focus differs from his, and I depart from some of his interpretations.
7 Max Nordau, *Degeneration* [1892], translated from the second edition of the German work [1895], with an Introduction by George L. Mosse (Lincoln, NE: University of Nebraska Press, 1993), pp.xiv, 5. The first quotation is from Mosse's introduction.
8 Helen Small, 'Introduction', in Walter Besant, *All Sorts and Conditions of Men* [1882] (Oxford: Oxford University Press, 1997), p.xv. Small then immediately acknowledges the limitations of the novel's transgressions by remarking that 'the metamorphoses remain clearly a matter of costume drama'. But this qualification affects only Besant's treatment of the changes, not their existence or connection with property.
9 Besant, *All Sorts and Conditions of Men*, p.90, my emphasis.
10 Gillian Beer, *Darwin's Plots: Evolutionary Narrative in Darwin, George Eliot and Nineteenth-Century Fiction* [1983] (London: Ark, 1985), p.141.
11 Quoted in Marina Warner, *Fantastic Metamorphoses, Other Worlds: Ways of Telling the Self* (Oxford: Oxford University Press, 2002), p.1.
12 Warner, *Fantastic Metamorphoses*, pp.16, 17, 18.
13 Wim Neetens, *Writing and Democracy: Literature, Politics and Culture in Transition* (London: Harvester Wheatsheaf, 1991), p.69.
14 For Warner, the 'encounter with the Americas seems … one of the most transformative experiences of history' (*Fantastic Metamorphoses*, p.19).
15 Warner, *Fantastic Metamorphoses*, p.74.
16 Warner, *Fantastic Metamorphoses*, p.19.
17 Warner, *Fantastic Metamorphoses*, pp.18–19.
18 See my 'White Apes at the Fin de Siècle', in Tim Youngs, ed., *Writing and Race* (London: Longman, 1997), pp.166–190.
19 Keating, *The Haunted Study*, p.133.
20 Irving Massey, *The Gaping Pig: Literature and Metamorphosis* (Berkeley, CA: University of California Press, 1976), p.17.

21 Massey, *The Gaping Pig*, pp.3–15.
22 Nordau, *Degeneration*, pp.1–2.
23 Simon Dentith, *Society and Cultural Forms in Nineteenth-Century England* (Basingstoke: Macmillan, 1998), p.181.
24 Matthew Sturgis, *Passionate Attitudes: The English Decadence of the 1890s* (London: Macmillan, 1995), pp.1, 2.
25 Sturgis, *Passionate Attitudes*, p.2.
26 Adam Phillips, *Darwin's Worms* (London: Faber and Faber Limited, 1999), p.37. Phillips is quoting Frederick Burckhardt and Sidney Smith from their edition of *The Correspondence of Charles Darwin*, vol. 2 (Cambridge: Cambridge University Press, 1986).
27 Phillips, *Darwin's Worms*, p.126.
28 On this latter, see Stephen D. Arata, 'The Occidental Tourist: *Dracula* and the Anxiety of Reverse Colonization', *Victorian Studies* 33, 4 (Summer 1990), 621–645.
29 See my discussion of the tale later in this book and Tim Youngs, 'Stevenson's Monkey-Business: *The Strange Case of Dr. Jekyll and Mr. Hyde*', in Peter Liebregts and Wim Tigges, eds, *Beauty and the Beast: Christina Rossetti, Walter Pater, R. L. Stevenson and their Contemporaries* (Amsterdam and Georgia: Rodopi, 1996), pp.157–170.
30 This work was, in fact, written by W. T. Stead, using Booth's notes. See Gertrude Himmelfarb, *Poverty and Compassion: The Moral Imagination of the Late Victorians* [1971] (New York, NY: Vintage Books, 1992), p.220.
31 Raymond Williams, *The English Novel from Dickens to Lawrence* (London: The Hogarth Press, 1984), p.16.
32 Gillian Beer, reminding us that Darwinism represented continuities, as well as breaks, with existing perceptions, identifies the 'sense that everything is connected, though the connections may be obscured' as giving 'urgency to the enterprise of uncovering such connections'. Beer, *Darwin's Plots*, p.47. Beer notes that Dickens, for whom 'this form of plotting was crucial' (p.27), was one of Darwin's 'most frequently read authors' (p.8).
33 Peter Keating, 'Introduction', in Peter Keating, ed., *Into Unknown England 1866–1913: Selections from the Social Explorers* (Manchester: Manchester University Press, 1976), p.13 (pp.11–32). And see his discussion of Sherlock Holmes as an explorer. Keating, *The Haunted Study*, p.365.
34 Keating, *Unknown England*, p.15.
35 One of many examples is Christopher Herbert, *Culture and Anomie: Ethnographic Imagination in the Nineteenth Century* (Chicago, IL: University of Chicago Press, 1991), Chapter Four: 'Mayhew's Cockney Polynesia', pp.204–252.
36 Keating, *Unknown England*, p.20.
37 Keating, *The Haunted Study*, p.350. I would not wish to criticise Keating unfairly. *The Haunted Study* is a detailed and valuable work.
38 Elaine Showalter, *Sexual Anarchy: Gender and Culture at the Fin de Siècle* (New York, NY: Viking, 1990), p.2.
39 I limit myself here to narratives that do not deal with actual journeys. I have dealt with the reflection of contemporary crises in travel narratives *per se* in the final three chapters of my *Travellers in Africa: British Travelogues, 1850–1900* (Manchester: Manchester University Press, 1994).
40 Showalter, *Sexual Anarchy*, p.4.

41 Massey, *The Gaping Pig*, p.51.
42 David Cannadine, *The Decline and Fall of the British Aristocracy* (London: Macmillan, 1996), p.16.
43 Cannadine, *Decline and Fall*, p.xvi, my emphasis.
44 Marina Warner, *No Go the Bogeyman: Scaring, Lulling and Making Mock* (London: Chatto & Windus, 1998), p.242, italics in original.
45 Cannadine, *Decline and Fall*, p.xiv.
46 Cannadine, *Decline and Fall*, p.9, Table 1.1. He later quotes contemporary figures, showing that '[o]ne-quarter of the land of England and Wales was owned by 710 individuals, and nearly three-quarters of the British Isles was in the hands of less [i.e. fewer] than five thousand people' (p.55).
47 Cannadine, *Decline and Fall*, p.91. Cannadine also quotes Balfour's remark of 1909: '"the bulk of the great fortunes are now in a highly liquid state ... They do not consist of huge landed estates, vast parks and castles, and all the rest of it"' (p.91). The precarious nature of the new wealth receives attention in US author William Dean Howells's novel, *A Hazard of New Fortunes* (1890).
48 Karl Marx, *Capital: A Critique of Political Economy*, vol. 1, introduction by Ernest Mandel, translated by Ben Fowkes (London: Penguin Books, in association with *New Left Review*, 1990), p.199. The original was first published in 1867. Further page references will be to volume 1 of the 1990 edition and given parenthetically.
49 Quoted by Baldick, *In Frankenstein's Shadow*, p.107. (I have corrected 'people' to 'persons' in Baldick's quotation from Marx.) Baldick mentions this quotation in the context of a discussion of Dickens's animation of things and his representation of characters' mechanical repetitions. (Baldick is also drawing on Dorothy Van Ghent, 'The Dickens World: A View from Todgers's', *Sewanee Review* lviii (1950), 417–438.)
50 Jonathan Parry and Maurice Bloch, 'Introduction: Money and the Morality of Exchange', in J. Parry and M. Bloch, eds, *Money and the Morality of Exchange* (Cambridge: Cambridge University Press, 1989), p.3. Further page references will be given parenthetically.
51 Simon J. James, *Unsettled Accounts: Money and Narrative in the Novels of George Gissing* (London: Anthem, 2003), pp.4, 2, 7, 4.
52 James, *Unsettled Accounts*, pp.5, 3.
53 Keating, *The Haunted Study*, pp.39, 42.
54 Keating, *The Haunted Study*, p.358.
55 Keating, *The Haunted Study*, pp.358–359. I discuss Wells's *The War of the Worlds* in Chapter Three.
56 Neetens, p.65.
57 Keating, *The Haunted Study*, pp.27–30.
58 Keating, *The Haunted Study*, p.47.
59 Keating, *The Haunted Study*, p.71.
60 Jose Harris, *Private Lives, Public Spirit: Britain 1870–1914* [1993] (London: Penguin Books, 1994), p.97.
61 Henry James, 'London', quoted in Walkowitz, *City of Dreadful Delight*, p.15.
62 Cannadine's choice of verb in describing the fate of the aristocracy from the 1880s is also apt: it was, he writes, 'in the process of dissolving itself' (p.89). Although this description seems to combine wish-fulfilment with charity, it is a peculiarly fitting phrase, given the loss of shape that is so important a feature of the texts

that I shall be examining. In particular, we might bear it in mind when we turn to Dracula.
63 Harris, *Private Lives, Public Spirit*, pp.96, 118.
64 Cannadine, *Decline and Fall*, pp.24, 26.
65 Cannadine, *Decline and Fall*, p.26.
66 Neville Kirk, *Change, Continuity and Class: Labour in British Society, 1850–1920* (Manchester: Manchester University Press, 1998), p.183.
67 Kirk, *Change, Continuity and Class*, p.143. Kirk is quoting from R. McKibbin, *The Ideologies of Class: Social Relations in Britain 1880–1950*.
68 J. F. C. Harrison, *Late Victorian Britain 1870–1901* (London: Fontana Press, 1990), p.67.
69 Kirk, *Change, Continuity and Class*, p.143. Kirk quotes from J. Benson, *The Working Class in Britain 1850–1939*.
70 The figures are from Benson, *The Working Class in Britain*, cited in Kirk, *Change, Continuity and Class*, p.144.
71 Harrison, *Late Victorian Britain*, pp.30–31.
72 For this and more information, see Harrison, *Late Victorian Britain*, pp.22–24. Those who were still excluded from the vote included, apart from women, male householders who had occupied premises for less than a year, domestic servants residing at their employers' residences, and sons living with their parents. See Harrison, p.24.
73 Cannadine, *Decline and Fall*, p.27. Cannadine concedes that after the 1880 election, the House of Commons was still dominated by landowners, but quotes the *Times*, reporting on 24 August 1883 that: "'Members have been heard … during the last few weeks asking whether it was any longer an assembly of gentlemen'" (p.188). After the 1885 election, they constituted less than a third of the House, instead of just over a half: 'For the first time ever, the patricians had ceased to be a majority element in the lower house: their numerical supremacy was gone for good' (p.189).
74 Cannadine, *Decline and Fall*, p.36.
75 Harrison, *Late Victorian Britain*, pp.33, 49, 50.
76 Neetens, *Writing and Democracy*, p.66.
77 Neetens, *Writing and Democracy*, p.36. Neetens is here drawing on Gareth Stedman Jones, *Outcast London* (1971).
78 Neetens, *Writing and Democracy*, p.37.
79 *Punch*, 26 January 1884. The cartoon is reproduced by Cannadine (*Decline and Fall*, p.38), though he does not follow up the bestial theme.
80 I would therefore want to shore up the second part of Marina Warner's sentence against its contradictory first part: 'Fairy tales may contain eternal, psychological insights that can cross borders and span historical periods, but they are articulated within economic and social circumstances which modify their messages.' (See Warner, *No Go the Bogeyman*, p.319.) Those so-called eternal psychological insights are, of course, identified and interpreted as such in historical moments using cultural tools. If they are judged to possess these universal qualities, the judgement tells us more about the critic's and audience's need for transcendence that lends stability.
81 Baldick, *In Frankenstein's Shadow*, pp.5, 7. Baldick also notes that the meaning of 'monster' has metamorphosed. In pre-nineteenth-century usage, which persisted into the nineteenth century, the connotation of monster was also moral in reference

and '[l]ong before the monster of Frankenstein, monstrosity already implied rebellion, or an unexpected turning against one's parent or benefactor' (p.13). There is something of that implication in post-Darwinian monsters, too. Also relevant to the present study is Baldick's reminder that the monsters of classical mythology are commonly 'composed of ill-assorted parts' (p.13).

82 Dentith, *Society and Cultural Forms*, p.53.
83 Baldick, *In Frankenstein's Shadow*, p.21.
84 Cannadine, *Decline and Fall*, p.38. The contemporary bestial imagery infects even modern-day commentaries on the period: Cannadine, discussing protests in Hyde Park against the House of Lords, refers to a 'monster gathering' (p.41).
85 Cannadine, *Decline and Fall*, p.43.
86 Helen Merrell Lynd, *England in the Eighteen-Eighties: Toward a Social Basis for Freedom* (London: Oxford University Press, 1945), p.238. Lynd identifies the first period as the 1830s and the second as the first half of the 1870s (p.238, unnumbered footnote).
87 Lynd, *The Eighteen-Eighties*, p.292.
88 Lynd, *The Eighteen-Eighties*, p.289.
89 Kirk, *Change, Continuity and Class*, p.167.
90 Founded in 1881 by H. M. Hyndman, the Social Democratic Federation was 'the only avowed Marxist organization in England'. Lynd, *The Eighteen-Eighties*, p.379.
91 Lynd, *The Eighteen-Eighties*, p.283. The preceding details are taken from Lynd, p.282.
92 Lynd, *The Eighteen-Eighties*, p.277.
93 Kirk, *Change, Continuity and Class*, p.167.
94 Lynd, *The Eighteen-Eighties*, p.266.
95 Lynd, *The Eighteen-Eighties*, p.283.
96 *Annual Register*, n.s. 1889, p.177, quoted in Lynd, *The Eighteen-Eighties*, p.287. It is important to note Jones's argument that this middle-class support was a result of the strike leaders' successful emphasis on their strikers' self-discipline, which was why 'middle-class London viewed the mounting wave of strikes, not with feelings of apprehension, but with feelings of relief. There could have been no more pointed contrast between the riots of 1886 and the strikes of 1889.' Gareth Stedman Jones, *Outcast London: A Study in the Relationship between Classes in Victorian Society* [1971] (Harmondsworth: Penguin Books, 1976), p.316.
97 Lynd, *The Eighteen-Eighties*, p.425, my emphasis. Lynd's book was published in 1945, hence its gendered language.
98 Lynd, *The Eighteen-Eighties*, p.424.
99 Lynd, *The Eighteen-Eighties*, p.6.
100 Margot Norris, *Beasts of the Modern Imagination: Darwin, Nietzsche, Kafka, Ernst, and Lawrence* (Baltimore, MD: The Johns Hopkins University Press, 1985), p.15.
101 Norris, p.41. Darwin wrote that: 'By a monstrosity I presume is meant some considerable deviation of structure, generally injurious, or not useful to the species.' Charles Darwin, *The Origin of Species by Means of Natural Selection*, last (sixth) edition [1872] (London: Watts & Co., n.d.), pp.31–32. (I have used this edition, since it is the closest to my period of study and contains the final revisions. Darwin died in 1882.) Further page references will be given parenthetically as *OS*.
102 Beer identifies a distinction between Ovid's idea of metamorphosis ('"Omnia mutantur, nihil interit." Everything changes, nothing dies') and evolutionary

theory. The latter required extinction, whereas metamorphosis 'bypasses death ... the essential self transposed but not obliterated by transformation' (Beer, *Darwin's Plots*, p.111). Further page references to this work will be given parenthetically as *DP*.

103 Norris, p.40.
104 Virginia Richter, *Literature after Darwin: Human Beasts in Western Fiction, 1859–1939* (Basingstoke: Palgrave Macmillan, 2011), p.9.
105 'This preservation of favourable individual differences and variations, and the destruction of those which are injurious, I have called Natural Selection, or the Survival of the Fittest.' (*OS*, p.59)
106 Jeff Wallace, 'Introduction: Difficulty and Defamiliarisation – Language and Process in *The Origin of Species*', in David Amigoni and Jeff Wallace, eds, *Charles Darwin's The Origin of Species: New Interdisciplinary Series* (Manchester: Manchester University Press, 1995), p.9.
107 Nordau, *Degeneration*, pp.xvi, 560. (The first quotation is from Mosse's introduction.)
108 Richard Ellmann, *Oscar Wilde* [1987] (London: Penguin, 1988), p.406.
109 Raymond Williams, 'Forms of English Fiction in 1848', in *Writing in Society* (London: Verso, n.d.), p.150.
110 Wallace, 'Introduction: Difficulty and Defamiliarisation', p.2.
111 Peter J. Vorzimmer, *Charles Darwin: The Years of Controversy: The Origin of Species and its Critics 1859–1882* (Philadelphia, PA: Temple University Press, 1970), quoted in Wallace, 'Introduction: Difficulty and Defamiliarisation', p.15. For a brief discussion of some of the revisions, see pp.17–19 of Jeff Wallace's 'Introduction'. For full details, consult Morse Peckham, ed., *The Origin of Species by Charles Darwin: A Variorum Text* (Philadelphia, PA: University of Pennsylvania Press, 1959).
112 See also Peter J. Bowler, *The Eclipse of Darwinism: Anti-Darwinian Evolution Theories in the Decades around 1900* (Baltimore, MD: Johns Hopkins University Press, 1983).
113 Keating, *The Haunted Study*, pp.111–112.
114 Quoted in Raymond Williams, 'The Tenses of Imagination', in *Writing in Society*, p.260.
115 Williams, 'The Tenses of Imagination', p.260.
116 Sturgis, *Passionate Attitudes*, p.70.
117 Sherryl Vint refers to debates in Human-Animal Studies (HAS) over appropriate terminology for 'humans collectively as distinct from non-human beings. Many people reject the terms "human" and "animal" as already ceding too much anthropocentrism and reinforcing a boundary whose deconstruction is precisely the point of much of this work.' Acknowledging that 'the distinction of human versus non-human is sometimes used' and that she occasionally employs it, Vint opts mainly for 'the terms "human" and "animal" while recognising their limitations'. Sherryl Vint, *Animal Alterity: Science Fiction and the Question of the Animal* (Liverpool: Liverpool University Press, 2010), p.228, n.2.
118 Harriet Ritvo, *The Animal Estate: The English and Other Creatures in the Victorian Age* (Cambridge, MA: Harvard University Press, 1987), pp.16, 17. Further page references will be given parenthetically.
119 And not only of exotic peoples. See, for example, Jean-Yves Le Disez, 'Animals as Figures of Otherness in Travel Narratives of Brittany, 1840–1895', in Glenn Hooper

and Tim Youngs, eds, *Perspectives on Travel Writing* (Aldershot: Ashgate, 2004), pp.71–84.
120 Beer, *Darwin's Plots*, p.130.
121 Beer, *Darwin's Plots*, p.133. For more on Kingsley, see Beer, pp.136–138.
122 Beer, *Darwin's Plots*, p.117. On monogenism and polygenism, as well as on the place of Darwinism in nineteenth-century racial thinking more generally, see George W. Stocking, Jr., *Victorian Anthropology* (New York, NY: The Free Press, 1987).
123 Showalter, *Sexual Anarchy*, p.3.
124 For a brief account of this, see Ed Cohen, *Talk on the Wilde Side: Toward a Genealogy of a Discourse on Male Sexualities* (New York, NY: Routledge, 1993), pp.121–125.
125 Cohen, *Talk on the Wilde Side*, p.121.
126 Sally Ledger, *The New Woman: Fiction and Feminism at the Fin de Siècle* (Manchester: Manchester University Press, 1997), p.2.
127 Ledger, *The New Woman*, p.1.
128 Ledger, *The New Woman*, pp.1, 16, 10, 27, 187.
129 Ledger, *The New Woman*, p.94.
130 Ledger, *The New Woman*, p.95.
131 For the relationship between Feminism and Socialism at this time, see Ledger, *The New Woman*, esp. pp.37–50.
132 Elizabeth K. Helsinger et al., *The Woman Question: Society and Literature in Britain and America, 1837–1883* (3 vols), vol. 2: *The Woman Question: Social Issues, 1837–1883* (Manchester: Manchester University Press, 1983), p.22. The authors write of the 1870 Act that it 'was fraught with compromise and contradiction' (p.21). The 1882 Act, on the other hand, 'provided that a married woman might keep all real and personal property that was hers at the time of marriage or acquired later … [S]he was able to dispose of her separate property in a will or convey it to her husband.' (pp.21–22)
133 Ledger, *The New Woman*, p.11. On developments in women's educational provision and opportunities, see Ledger, p.17.
134 Neetens, *Writing and Democracy*, p.107.
135 Showalter, *Sexual Anarchy*, p.3.
136 Showalter, *Sexual Anarchy*, p.3.
137 Joseph Bristow, *Effeminate England: Homoerotic Writing after 1885* (Buckingham: Open University Press, 1995), pp.11, 2, 9, 10.
138 Keating, *The Haunted Study*, p.186.
139 Keating, *The Haunted Study*, p.186.
140 Keating, *The Haunted Study*, p.196.
141 George MacDonald, 'The Imagination: Its Functions and its Culture' [1867], in *A Dish of Orts* [1893] (Whitethorn, CA: Johannesen, 1996), p.16.
142 Vint, *Animal Alterity*, p.45.

CHAPTER ONE

City Creatures

Strange ways of thinking

This chapter examines images of beasts and bestiality in selected fictional and non-fictional writing about the city produced during the second half of the 1880s and 1890s. Some of the texts will be better known than others, but the concentration on animal imagery should provide a new approach to even the most familiar of these and is quite distinct from commentaries on naturalism. The focus will be on London, since the main themes explored in this study are evident in the literature set in the capital; in particular, the East End looms especially large. However, it is important to recognise that different cities have their own characteristics and stories to tell.[1] In London, the population had grown from 1,873,676 in 1841 to 4,232,118 a half century later. The figures represented an increase in the proportion of the population of England and Wales from 11.75 per cent to 14.52 per cent. At the same time, other cities had expanded: in 1837, there were five cities throughout England and Wales with populations of 100,000 or more; in 1891, there were twenty-three cities.[2] Briggs notes that '[a]s the cities grew, the separation of middle-class and working-class areas became more and more marked' (p.64), and social segregation, then, as now, 'induces strange ways of thinking about other human beings. The fear of the city, like other kinds of fear, was often a fear of the unknown' (p.62). Although true, Briggs's words understate the extent to which the different classes rubbed shoulders. As we saw in the introduction, Raymond Williams has shown how the creation of what he calls the 'crisis of the knowable community' in the mid-nineteenth century led novelists such as Elizabeth Gaskell and, above all, Dickens to show how various representatives of the social order were brought into close proximity with one another.[3]

Bestial language infects the literature of the time. It is present in far more cases than are offered here. William Fishman's study of the East End in the late 1880s quotes a number of examples, among them Ben

Tillett's memory of the daily struggle of the unemployed to obtain work at the docks:

> Coats, flesh and even ears were torn off. The strong literally threw themselves over the heads of their fellows and battled ... through the kicking, punching, cursing crowds to the rails of the 'cage' which held them like rats – mad human rats who saw food in the ticket.[4]

Tillett's description could just as well belong to the narrative of a late nineteenth-century realist or naturalistic novel. Indeed, the first chapter of Arthur Morrison's *A Child of the Jago* (1896) relates how 'Old Jago Street lay black and close under the quivering red sky; and slinking forms, as of great rats, followed one another quickly between the posts in the gut by the High Street, and scattered over the Jago.'[5] The reduction of humanity to a desperate animalistic competition for survival is shared by both documentary and imaginative writing. What both forms have in common in this context is a journalistic urge to record the plight of the destitute and the precariousness of those who, for the moment, exist just above the breadline (a noun whose first print usage the *OED* dates to 1900 in the US). Fishman also quotes Beatrice Webb's view of loafers as 'low looking, bestial, content with their own condition'.[6] Thomas Jackson, a Methodist preacher and philanthropist, witnesses a drunken woman carried away by police, 'shrieking and cursing; a dehumanised thing, as morally insensate as the beasts that perish, and far less clean'.[7] Margaret Harkness, writing in *A City Girl* (1887), observes that '[m]en who at other times were civil and pleasant enough, became like wild beasts the night after they received their wages'.[8] In a novel published two years later, Harkness remarks that 'in these days animals are better off than slum children'.[9]

For all the writing on the working and underclasses, we must apply to the larger situation what Fishman notes of attitudes towards the workhouse in particular, that: 'The tragedy is the absence of any written text from the paupers themselves, who lacked either the ability or the desire to write.'[10] Like the colonised, the urban poor are inscribed in the discourse of others, without the means to represent themselves, except through interview. They are framed by spectators. Their lack of voice deepens their brutishness and increases the apprehension felt by those who look on, scared of the fragility of the barriers between them. Yet, the compulsion to observe was inescapable, as Anne Humpherys attests:

> The Victorians themselves were fascinated and intermittently horrified by their developing urbanization; for them, the issue was almost always how

to 'see' the inarticulate lower classes that crowded into both the industrial cities and the metropolitan center of London, and through this seeing, to rationalize and control urbanization and its effects.[11]

At the end of the nineteenth century, the urban environment contained the threats of social and psychological disintegration and contamination. The resulting anxieties about decline and corruption not only inform the writings of the period, but shape them, too. We shall see in the next chapter how they alter the template of the Gothic. For now, the focus is on journalism, realism, and naturalism. Before moving on we should note that what follows is not simply a beastly parade. The creatures on which we gaze are made what they are by the deforming effects of capitalism, even if the texts that represent them sometimes fall short of recognising the fact. To understand them one needs to see them as moulded by their milieu. Central to determining their shape is money, which, as David Harvey puts it, 'becomes the mediator and regulator of all economic relations between individuals; it becomes the abstract and universal measure of social wealth and the concrete means of expression of social power'.[12] Harvey argues that 'the very existence of money as a mediator of commodity exchange radically transforms and fixes the meanings of space and time in social life and imposes necessities upon the shape and form of urbanization'. He contends that in the 'urban processes under capitalism ... confusion, conflict and struggle are a normal condition' and there 'is an underlying process that precludes liberation from the more repressive aspects of class-domination and all of the urban pathology and restless incoherence that goes with it'.[13] Placing money (or its lack) at the heart of our readings allows us to enhance our understanding of the literary reflection of this phenomenon and, especially, the ghastly consequences of impecuniousness.

Changing hands: *The Strange Case of Dr. Jekyll and Mr. Hyde*[14]

Money is at the root of Stevenson's famous tale of *The Strange Case of Dr. Jekyll and Mr. Hyde*. Since part of the horror of Hyde is his ape-like appearance, then we must try to recover something of the impressions that such imagery evoked for readers at the time. When Hyde is described as manifesting 'ape-like fury' in trampling to death Sir Danvers Carew, Member of Parliament,[15] then plainly something much more interesting is going on than a simple exposition of the struggle between good or evil or the return of the sexually repressed or the anti-social conduct of a secret alcoholic – all of which interpretations are commonly advanced. Stevenson's tale was published just two years after the 1884 Reform Act, which had been preceded by increasing agitation by, and on behalf of, the disenfranchised. Unrest did not cease with the passing of the Act. There were riots in Trafalgar Square during the year of *The Strange Case of Dr. Jekyll and Mr. Hyde*'s publication, most famously on 8 February after a severe winter during which the depression of the mid- to late 1880s was at its height. Twenty thousand people, mostly unemployed dock and building workers, had gathered there.

Gareth Stedman Jones has written fascinatingly of the 'deep-rooted' and 'comprehensive' social crisis of the 1880s.[16] According to Jones, '[t]he cyclical depression of 1884–7 was both more prolonged and hit a far broader spectrum of occupations than the slumps of 1866 and 1879'.[17] It 'greatly accentuated an already endemic condition of under-employment, and the hard winters that accompanied it intensified distress to chronic proportions'.[18] While the rich were generally able to preserve their physical separation from the poor, the 'poor themselves were becoming more closely crammed together regardless of status or character',[19] contributing to increased discontent among the 'respectable working class', as the actual and metaphorical distance between them and the casual poor or 'residuum' diminished. The residuum was considered dangerous not only because it was seen to be degenerate, but because 'its very existence served to contaminate the classes immediately above it'.[20] From 1883 onwards, newspapers and journals were 'full of warnings of the necessity of immediate reform to ward off the impending revolutionary threat'.[21] Jones cites, as an example, Samuel Smith's warning in 1885 that '[t]he proletariat may strangle us unless we teach it the same virtues which have elevated the other classes of society'.[22]

This was not, of course, the only kind of disruption in London at the time. On 24 January 1885, Fenians exploded three bombs simultaneously at Westminster Hall, the Houses of Parliament, and the Tower of London.[23] (And it is well known that the Irish were often referred to as beasts, including apes.)[24] Abroad, events had recently heightened the sense of a crisis of authority, with the death of General Gordon in Khartoum also occurring in 1885.

Jones characterises the predominant feeling of the 1880s among the intellectual and propertied classes as 'not guilt but fear'.[25] At this time, accounts of 'Outcast London' exhibited little sympathy or empathy:

> The poor were presented as neglected, and even to a certain extent exploited … But they did not emerge as objects of compassion. They were generally

pictured as coarse, brutish, drunken, and immoral; through years of neglect and complacency they had become an ominous threat to civilization.[26]

Such attitudes accompanied the rise of the discourse of urban degeneration. It was seen as inevitable that as a result of their environment the poor would become 'brutalized and sexually immoral', seeking the alcoholic and salacious entertainments offered by pubs, music-halls, and prostitutes. Darwinian thinking encouraged the idea that this 'adapting down' to one's surroundings would have increasingly deleterious effects through the generations. However, in a significant twist, it was thought by some that beneficial legislation and improvements in medical science and sanitation had controverted Darwinian laws, allowing for the survival and growth of the unfit.[27] This begs the question of what constitutes unfitness, and it is this question, involving notions of social, physical, and moral health, that helps make so many of the popular texts of the late nineteenth century so engagingly troublesome.

It is interesting that Jones includes as one of the middle-class responses to the social crisis of the 1880s that of the social imperialist. He quotes from Lord Brabazon's *Social Arrows* (1886):

> Let the reader walk through the wretched streets ... of the Eastern or Southern districts of London ... should he be of average height, he will find himself a head taller than those around him; he will see on all sides pale faces, stunted figures, debilitated forms, narrow chests, and all the outward signs of a low vital power.[28]

The importance of this kind of image lies in its kinship with Hyde and similarly with the Morlocks of Wells's *The Time Machine* (1895). David Punter nicely sums up the various concerns at play here and what they have in common when, considering the 'decadent Gothic' of the fin de siècle, of which he lists *The Strange Case of Dr. Jekyll and Mr. Hyde*, *The Picture of Dorian Gray*, *The Island of Doctor Moreau*, and *Dracula* as the most potent examples, he writes:

> they are all concerned in one way or another with the problem of degeneration, and thus of the essence of the human. They each pose, from very different angles, the same question, which can readily be seen as a question appropriate to an age of imperial decline: how much, they ask, can one lose – individually, socially, nationally – and still remain a man? One could put the question much more brutally: to what extent can one be 'infected' and still remain British?[29]

Punter's reading is astute, for he also suggests, rightly, that 'Hyde's behaviour is an urban version of "'going native'".[30] It is hardly surprising, given the similarities of the language applied to subordinated social and racial groups and the common identity of the controlling force in both cases, that a disturbance in one sphere should find its echoes in the other.

Utterson, the lawyer, may have trouble defining Hyde, who 'gave an impression of deformity without any namable malformation' (p.13), but the impression is conveyed to the readers through racial and bestial terms. Hyde has a 'savage laugh' (p.13); he is, to Poole, a 'masked thing like a monkey' (p.37); he plays, according to Jekyll, 'apelike tricks' (p.61) and exhibits 'apelike spite' (p.62); he displays, as we have seen, 'ape-like fury' in killing Carew (p.19); he gives a screech 'as of mere animal terror' (p.38) when cornered in the laboratory, and his hand is 'lean, corded, knuckly, of a dusky pallor, and thickly shaded with a swart growth of hair' (p.54). In the manuscript, he is described as behaving with a 'mixture of cowardice and savagery'.[31] He drinks 'pleasure with bestial avidity' (p.53). It is true that he is also 'pale and dwarfish' (p.13), but much like Wells's Morlocks in *The Time Machine* ten (or rather several thousand) years later, the shock comes with the idea of a white ape – a creature that haunts popular texts with increasing menace during the fin de siècle as biological theories of degeneration combine with political fear regarding the socially repressed and a growing obsession with the psychological unconscious to effect agitated inspections of the subterranean and interior. Utterson thinks it 'madness' or a 'disgrace' that in the event of Jekyll's death or disappearance for longer than three months (p.9), Hyde should stand to inherit Jekyll's 'quarter of a million sterling' (p.20). Like his real-life counterparts, Utterson endeavours ever more frantically to maintain an identification of name with wealth; of social with financial status. Mr Enfield, too, relates how, after witnessing Hyde trampling on a young girl, he and the attendant doctor

> told the man we could and would make such a scandal out of this, as should make his name stink from one end of London to the other. If he had any friends or credit, we undertook that he should lose them. (p.5)

In other words, a social death is resolved upon. The idea of credit in the dual sense of money and morality is prominent here. Hyde should be deprived of financial and social worth. Enfield goes on to recall how 'we screwed him up to a hundred pounds for the child's family':

> The next thing was to get the money; and where do you think he carried us but to that place with the door? – whipped out a key, went in, and presently came back with the matter of ten pounds in gold and a cheque for the balance on Coutts's, drawn payable to bearer, and signed with a name that

I can't mention, though it's one of the points of my story, but it was a name at least very well known and often printed. The figure was stiff; but the signature was good for more than that, if it was only genuine. (p.6)

The suspicious Enfield accepts Hyde's offer to remain with him until the banks open in the morning and has him stay the night in his (Enfield's) chambers where the doctor and the girl's father also join them. In the morning, Enfield tells Utterson, 'I gave in the cheque myself, and said I had every reason to believe it was a forgery. Not a bit of it. The cheque was genuine' (p.6). Since Stevenson has gone to some trouble to record the details of the cheque and its encashment, it can hardly be irrelevant to notice that '[b]y the middle of the 'eighties private banking was becoming almost extinct in England',[32] as provincial bankers lost their influence to the London money market, and that

> [i]ndividual banks were losing any claim to independent status and stability. At the same time 'personal character' ceased to be valid security for loans and overdrafts when the old local bankers, with their individual knowledge of all their clients, were replaced by distant directors whose lack of such knowledge compelled them to confine their loans within hard and fast rules. A structure of big finance was emerging along with the growth of big business.[33]

The relevance of this lies in Enfield's (and the reader's) doubt that personal character counts in the case just related. There is a strong feeling, even after Enfield has been reassured the cheque is genuine, that there can be no proper correspondence between Hyde, who is 'really damnable', and Jekyll, who is 'the very pink of the proprieties' (p.6), leading Enfield to the conclusion that this must be a case of blackmail. The confusion over character and wealth thus becomes increasingly apparent the more Enfield and Utterson try to explain it. The more they rely on outmoded ideas of a match between physical wealth and personal quality, the less able they are to comprehend the actual state of affairs between them.

Stevenson's tale feeds directly into arguments over what constituted the 'gentleman'. We hear these anxieties in Poole's plaintive cry to Utterson: '"O, sir ... do you think I do not know my master after twenty years?"' We gauge the extent of this crisis by our knowledge that Poole, indeed, fails to recognise 'that thing' – Hyde – as his master (p.36). Poole does not know his master after twenty years, just as many in society were no longer sure who their masters were.

Jekyll's statement tells us he was

> born ... to a large fortune, endowed besides with excellent parts, inclined by nature to industry, fond of the respect of the wise and good among my

fellow-men, and thus, as might have been supposed, with every guarantee of an honourable and distinguished future. (p.48)

In this, we must see him as representative of his class. When he proceeds to explain his fall, I am less interested in its particular aspect (which in the manuscript version is hinted much more heavily to be homosexuality,[34] and, of course, 1885 was the year of the Labouchere Amendment) than in the fact of his decline, which ought to be taken as a reflection of the condition of many of his class. Jekyll's statement tells us:

> With every day, and from both sides of my intelligence, the moral and the intellectual, I thus drew steadily nearer to that truth by whose partial discovery I have been doomed to such a dreadful shipwreck: that man is not truly one, but truly two. I say two, because the state of my own knowledge does not pass beyond that point. Others will follow, others will outstrip me on the same lines; and I hazard the guess that man will be ultimately known for a mere polity of multifarious, incongruous and independent denizens. (pp.48–49)

This declaration needs careful reading. It is common for readers of the tale and viewers of the films based on it to take Jekyll and Hyde as different personalities, albeit hosted by the same body. This is understandable, as Stevenson is caught in the paradox of physically projecting and thereby separating the conflicting components of the same person. (Jekyll refers to his consciousness of the 'perennial war among my members' [p.48].) Such a reading might further be encouraged by Jekyll's reference to what he calls the 'thorough and primitive duality of man' (p.49). But scrutiny of his remarks soon reveals that his crisis is brought about by his desire to separate the elements that are at war within him. His explanation of this is crucial, so I quote it here at length:

> I saw that, of the two natures that contended in the field of my consciousness, even if I could rightly be said to be either, it was only because I was radically both; and from an early date, even before the course of my scientific discoveries had begun to suggest the most naked possibility of such a miracle, I had learned to dwell with pleasure, as a beloved daydream, on the thought of the separation of these elements. If each, I told myself, could but be housed in separate identities, life would be relieved of all that was unbearable; the unjust might go his way, delivered from the aspirations and remorse of his more upright twin; and the just could walk steadfastly and securely on his upward path, doing the good things in which he found his pleasure, and no longer exposed to disgrace and penitence by the hands of this extraneous evil. It was the curse of mankind that these incongruous faggots were thus bound together – that in the agonised womb of consciousness these polar

twins should be continuously struggling. How, then, were they dissociated? (p.49)

The story of Jekyll is the story of his ultimate failure to separate and keep apart these elements. It is not particularly rewarding to read this failure in terms of morality – whether in a general Christian, specific Calvinist, or broad philosophical sense – or as an allusion to a particular vice. If we look again at Stevenson's use of the word 'polity' in the earlier quotation, then we surely have to review the passage against the social background. Whatever the dangers of taking Jekyll's statement at face value, the ideas that emerge from it seem to point unmistakably to the social changes and disturbances that were taking place at the time. Jekyll's statement can be taken as a grudging recognition that the polity, the state, consists of all its classes and that to try to keep them apart will lead, in fact, to a destructive imbalance. It hardly gives a welcome embrace to democracy, but in that it is in keeping with several other exclamations of the era. The important point is that it acknowledges the futility of attempting to continue the suppression of the baser side of oneself, of what Jekyll calls the 'lower elements in my soul' (p.50). Here, as elsewhere, the socially respectable and privileged self stands for the social body at large.

Our introduction to Jekyll's house shows very clearly the threat to his social decline, either from his own fall or from contamination by his surroundings:

> Round the corner from the by-street there was a square of ancient, handsome houses, now for the most part decayed from their high estate, and let in flats and chambers to all sorts and conditions of men: map-engravers, architects, shady lawyers, and the agents of obscure enterprises. One house, however, second from the corner, was still occupied entire; and at the door of this, which wore a great air of wealth and comfort, though it was now plunged in darkness except for the fan-light, Mr. Utterson stopped and knocked. (p.14)

This evocation of corruption and decline is a more dramatic sign of threatened and changed identities than the transmutation of Jekyll into Hyde, which, after all, merely personifies the larger alteration already implicit in the narrative. The ancient, handsome houses are not just decayed and not only divided, but are let to 'all sorts and conditions of men' (p.14). The square shows in microcosm the changes that many saw happening in late nineteenth-century society. The old families have moved out, unable any longer to afford their mansions. Their property has been split up to accommodate those from a 'lower' station. Baseness – that is, lowness and vulgarity – is what surrounds Jekyll's now-isolated house, whose tenuous hold on grandeur is apparent when we are told that it '*wore* a great *air* of wealth and comfort', as if, like a garment, it can be shaken off or pulled away (p.14, my emphasis). We can hardly have a more visible representation of the shifting power relations than this, unless it be the description of Hyde's home in its 'dismal quarter of Soho', which to Utterson seems 'like a district of some city in a nightmare' as

> the fog lifted a little and showed him a dingy street, a gin palace, a low French eating-house, a shop for the retail of penny numbers and two-penny salads, many ragged children huddled in the doorways, and many women of many different nationalities passing out, key in hand, to have a morning glass; and the next moment the fog settled down again upon that part, as brown as umber, and cut him off from his blackguardly surroundings. This was the home of Henry Jekyll's favourite; of a man who was heir to a quarter of a million sterling. (p.20)

This last sentence is surely meant as a more frightening incongruity than that which sees Hyde take over Jekyll's body. The prospect of the gentleman's fortune ending up in such a squalid environment was a greater horror for Stevenson's well-to-do contemporaries than the fantastic metaphor of Jekyll's transformation.

The identification of the beastly Hyde with the unruly elements of mass society that challenge the position of Jekyll and his peers has been made before. In a richly suggestive essay,[35] Patrick Brantlinger and Richard Boyle have interpreted the story as an allegory of an artist's feelings of contamination at having to write for an undiscerning public. They quote from a letter written by Stevenson to Edmund Gosse in 1886, in which he declares:

> I do not write for the public; I do write for money, a nobler deity; and most of all for myself, not perhaps any more noble, but both more intelligent and nearer home.
>
> Let us tell each other sad stories of the bestiality of the beast whom we feed ... I do not like mankind; but men, and not all of these – and fewer women. As for respecting the race, and, above all, that fatuous rabble of burgesses called 'the public,' God save me from such irreligion! – that way lies disgrace and dishonour. There must be something wrong in me, or I would not be popular.[36]

Brantlinger and Boyle claim that it was in part due to his 'deep-rooted ambivalence' towards the literary marketplace that Stevenson 'responded ambivalently' to *The Strange Case of Dr. Jekyll and Mr. Hyde* (which he claimed to have written to meet the bills of Byles the butcher).[37] We might recall here Hyde's words to Enfield and the doctor after they have witnessed his trampling of the girl: "'If you choose to make capital out of this … I am naturally helpless'" (pp.5–6). Stevenson himself made capital out of this, selling, according to one report, 40,000 copies of his tale within six months of its publication. It has been seen as the first of his stories to win widespread popularity with adults and children. Indeed, Andrew Lang wrote of how Stevenson 'wins every vote, and pleases every class of reader'.[38]

'nother way out: The Jago

Let us consider – as an example of the effects of the lack of money – the case of the young child, Dicky Perrott, in Morrison's *A Child of the Jago*. Dicky turns increasingly to thieving after stealing a watch from a distinguished visitor to the area. The timepiece is taken from Dicky by his father, Josh, who administers a beating, because of his wife's displeasure at her son's slide into criminality. Dicky is offered coffee and cake by Aaron Weech – owner of Weech's coffee shop – but it becomes apparent after he has consumed them that Weech, who has heard of and knows all about Dicky's theft, has not given him the refreshments out of sympathy and goodness as on first appearance, but expects payment for them, knowing full well that Dicky can only pay what he owes by bringing him stolen goods. Of this revelation, the narrator exclaims: 'Each for himself? Come, he must open his eyes' (p.41). Dicky learns lessons from his experience and so can we. The only collective action manifested in his locale is in support of one's own clan in fights against rival groups. Otherwise, it is – to use another animal expression – a dog-eat-dog world (the first use of which phrase the *OED* dates to 1822).

In the Jago the normal order is inverted. Cake and coffee are not expressions of sympathy, but are the means of entrapment into further criminality. The man who does not hit his wife and the family who take some pride in their accommodation are strange anomalies. The Ropers, the family across the way from the Perrotts and from whom Dicky opportunistically purloins a clock, are described by the narrator as being

> disliked as strangers because they furnished their own room, and in an obnoxiously complex style; because Roper did not drink, nor brawl, nor beat his wife, nor do anything all day but look for work; because all these things were a matter of scandalous arrogance, impudently subversive of Jago custom and precedent. (p.44)

Similarly, the Ropers' flat displays, in the eyes of Dicky and his neighbour Old Fisher, 'a monstrous absence of dirt' (p.46). Fisher walks into the open door and steals unemployed cabinetmaker Roper's old tools. In the world of the Jago, stealing, violence, and squalor are the norm; honesty and clean-living are the signs of non-conformity. In such passages, the effect of the narrative depends upon an irony that connects the narrator and audience with the world of the Jago by an inversion of shared values. That is to say, in these instances, the narrative works by assuming that the narrator and readers have similar codes of behaviour and that the readers recognise the distance between the narrator and the people whose outlook he describes as though he were straightforwardly explaining it. We shall return to this idea of simultaneous narrative proximity and distance, since it is often identified as a problem or contradiction in realism and naturalism. Suffice to say here that whatever the text's intention, the effect is to emphasise the humanity of the narrator and author in comparison with the animality of those who are paraded before us.

When some of the old houses are cleared, the animal analogies accrue. The wreckers expose

> the secret dens of a century of infamy ... letting light and air at last into the subterranean basements where men and women had swarmed, and bred, and died, like wolves in their lairs; and emerging from clouds of choking dust, each man a colony of vermin. (p.98)

The difficulty for realist or naturalistic writers is to convey the brutishness of the conditions of the underclasses while evoking some sympathy for them. They may be depicting repulsive characters, but writers such as Morrison and Gissing wish to move readers to an understanding of the plight of the impoverished and destitute without softening the effects of environment through plot contrivances that offer amelioration impossible in real life. Dicky is told by old Beveridge that the Bag of Nails, where they see all manner of criminals, is

> the best the world has for you, for the Jago's got you, and that's the only way out, except gaol and the gallows. So do your devilmost, or God help you, Dicky Perrott – though he won't: for the Jago's got you! (p.63)

The repetition of the phrase 'the Jago's got you' forces home the entrapment. Dicky nearly finds a way out when Sturt helps him obtain a shop assistant's job, but he is sacked when Weech, annoyed by Dicky's growing independence from him, lies to the shopkeeper and plants the idea in his head that Dicky planned to steal from him. Dicky's unexplained dismissal sees him turn to full-time crime as the only way to support himself and his family, especially after his father is sentenced to five years imprisonment for house-breaking and, on his release, murders Weech in revenge for betraying him to the police and causing Dicky to lose his job.

If there is no real escape for the beasts, they need at least to be protected from the extremes of their wild ways. Father Henry Sturt, the vicar who makes his way into the Jago (and who is modelled on Father Arthur Osborne Jay, Vicar of Holy Trinity, Shoreditch), a 'well-dressed stranger' exuding 'so bold a confidence', is presented as being 'like a tamer among beasts'. This simile occurs when he disperses a mob attack on the Ropers' flat, during which he 'flung them back, commanded them, [and] cowed them with his hard, intelligent eyes' (p.49), but it applies to his role more generally. However, his efforts are largely ineffective. He wins the respect of the locals and they accordingly exercise restraint in front of him, but the forces operating on them are too oppressive and their lifeways too entrenched for him to achieve anything more than light change.

The tragedy of the Jago is that opportunities for both travel and change are limited. The only exit is to other parts of London for thieving. Those who journey to it are fleeting visitors and often the victims of crime within it. Parts are no-go areas for the police. When alteration does occur, it is usually a turn for the worse. Thus, for example, when Josh hacks with a knife at Weech's face and then below his chin, '[t]he bubbling Thing dropped in a heap, and put out the flaring candle' (p.158). The transformation here is from a lying, manipulating dealer in stolen goods to an inhuman object. Dicky's exhortation to Father Sturt – 'Tell Mist' Beveridge there's 'nother way out – better' (p.173) – occurs when he is dying, after having been stabbed by Bobby Roper in a fight between Jago and Dove-Lane factions. Death seems the only release, but it is unaccompanied by any narrative sense of consolation. Dicky's final words illustrate another kind of transformation in *A Child of the Jago*: that of the English language itself. Morrison represents the broken dialect of the slum-dwellers in ways similar to his US counterpart, Stephen Crane, in *Maggie* (1893) and, indeed, comparisons were drawn between them. In his dying sentence, Dicky's truncated words match his stunted physique – his growth is arrested at five feet, two inches – and his restricted intellectual development and cultural appreciation. To say this is not to endorse any judgement of dialect as inferior to Standard English, but to make the point that the bluntness of the speech with its missing syllables fits the neighbourhood with its missing facilities. The voice of the narrator is in Standard English – a problem associated with much realism and naturalism, since it signals the narrator's position apart from the other characters. The distance between narrator and characters is underlined by the difference in speech codes, suggesting a gulf in social class and experience. This is often seen as a flaw in such writing: if the characters are determined by their environment, why not the narrator? In Morrison's case, it appears from extra-textual evidence that his life underwent transformation of a kind not open to his characters. (The nearest exception is Kiddo Cook, who, under Sturt's encouragement, works up to having a stall, gets married, and moves into one of the new county council dwellings.) Introducing a modern edition of the text, Peter Miles notes that although Morrison was 'not frank' in print about his background,[39] he 'was a working-class boy from Poplar who, there is every reason to suppose, grew up in the East End as [the] son of an engine-fitter in the docks'.[40] Miles observes that 'there exists little evidence to counter an impression of Morrison as a man who no longer felt the need to write when he could well afford not to, as someone who in later years had found his own fairly comfortable "way out"'.[41] That way out was made possible largely by his success as a dealer in Japanese and Chinese art.

The dichotomous nature of British (more specifically, English) society, and the two-faced conduct it leads to in some, is also exposed by Bernard Shaw. In his preface to *Widowers' Houses* (1892), explaining why it appears with two other works under the title 'Plays Unpleasant', he states:

> the average homebred Englishman, however honorable and goodnatured he may be in his private capacity, is, as a citizen, a wretched creature who, whilst clamoring for a gratuitous millennium, will shut his eyes to the most villainous abuses if the remedy threatens to add another penny in the pound to the rates and taxes which he has to be half cheated, half coerced into paying. In Widowers' Houses I have shewn middle-class respectability and younger son gentility fattening on the poverty of the slum as flies fatten on filth. That is not a pleasant theme.[42]

Here Shaw takes the language of the bestial and reverses it, applying it to those who would normally apply it to others. The loathsome in this case are the excrement-feeding rich, who gorge themselves on the poor. Monstrosity is found not in the habits or appearance of the poor, but in the airs and pretences of the rich. In exposing the exploitation Shaw may escape the charge levelled at Morrison by Kevin Swafford: that *A Child of the Jago* portrays the grotesque, but shows nothing of its larger causes.

Swafford alleges that '[t]he most important ideological objective of the novel is to dissociate any clear connection between West End prosperity and East End poverty by substituting effects for causes'.[43] According to Swafford, Morrison's novel neglects to make any critique of capitalism and thus fails to direct attention to the factors responsible for the slum conditions. Shaw, on the other hand, bluntly declares:

> I must, however, warn my readers that my attacks are directed against themselves, not against my stage figures. They cannot too thoroughly understand that the guilt of defective social organization [lies] ... with the whole body of citizens whose public opinion, public action, and public contribution as ratepayers, alone can replace Sartorious's slums with decent dwellings, Charteris's intrigues with reasonable marriage contracts, and Mrs. Warren's profession with honourable industries guarded by a humane industrial code and a 'moral minimum' wage.[44]

By such strategies Shaw confronts his audience, disclosing their complicity, but he seems at the same time to acquire authority himself through performing the role of truth-teller, which has him occupying a space between the parties.

Missing link

> I ain't a man ... I ain't nobody. Sometimes I says to myself as I'm 'the missing link,' as I'll come back again as a dog or something. Not but that I'd rather be a dog than a midget ... I'm worse off than a dog now, for folks aren't afraid of dogs, but they won't come nigh me if they can help it ... I've spent my life travelling about to be looked at. I'm tired of it, captain. I don't want to come back again.[45]

So, bitterly, speaks the 'midget' to Captain Lobe of the Salvation Army in Margaret Harkness's 1889 novel *Captain Lobe* (later reprinted as *In Darkest London*). These remarks come just after the 'midget' has asked Lobe if he thinks he, the 'midget', has a soul. The scene occurs in a 'penny gaff' on Whitechapel Road. The road is the 'most cosmopolitan place in London' (p.13). In that respect the district has itself undergone a transformation, and the narrator is scornful of those who refuse to accept the change:

> among the foreigners lounges the East End loafer, monarch of all he surveys, lord of the premises. It is amusing to see his British air of superiority ... He is looked upon as scum by his own nation, but he feels himself to be an Englishman, and able to kick the foreigner back to 'his own dear native

land' if only Government would believe in 'England for the English,' and give all foreigners 'notice'. (*IDL*, p.13)

The narrator realises that there can and should be no changing back: the 'Hottentot', Jewesses, Algerian, Indian, Italian, Russian, Polish Jew, and German are as much a part of Whitechapel Road as the East End loafer, who has his West End counterpart: 'In the West End they haunt the clubs; in the East End they hang around the public-houses' (*IDL*, p.13).

The 'midget' recalls only one other kind face apart from the Captain's that he would like to see when he is dying – that of a lady who did not shrink from shaking his hand: 'She said nothing but I could tell she was sorry for me, and often as I lies awake I think of her!' (*IDL*, p.16). The sentiments recall those of 'the Elephant Man', Joseph Merrick, when similarly the recipient of unflinching but sympathetic acknowledgement. Merrick, now known to have been suffering from neurofibromatosis, was discovered by the surgeon Sir Frederick Treves in 1884 being exhibited as the 'Elephant Man' in London for money by a showman. Treves later recalled that:

> Painted on the canvas [outside the building] in primitive colours was a life-size portrait of the Elephant Man. This very crude production depicted a frightful creature that could only have been possible in a nightmare. It was the figure of a man with the characteristics of an elephant. The transfiguration was not far advanced. There was still more of the man than of the beast. This fact – that it was still human – was the most repellent attribute of the creature. There was nothing about it of the pitiableness of the misshapened or the deformed, nothing of the grotesqueness of the freak, but merely the loathing insinuation of a man being changed into an animal.[46]

Treves goes on to write of how, when he secured a private viewing, he found 'the creature' huddling to 'warm itself'. The 'hunched-up figure was the embodiment of loneliness'. When the showman (Tom Norman), 'speaking as if to a dog', commanded his exhibit to stand up,

> [t]he thing arose slowly and let the blanket that covered its head and back fall to the ground. There stood revealed the most disgusting specimen of humanity that I have ever seen ... at no time had I met with such a degraded or perverted version of a human being as this lone figure displayed. (p.191)

Treves's description of the man who would come under his care contains mixed animal metaphors, as if further to demonstrate the confusion of classification: Merrick's right arm 'suggested the limb of the subject of elephantiasis', his right hand 'was large and clumsy – a fin or paddle rather than a hand', and '[f]rom the chest hung a bag of ... repulsive flesh ... like a dewlap suspended from the neck of a lizard' (p.192). Treves would refer to one of Merrick's keepers as 'the vampire showman' (p.200). His assertion that Merrick had been 'housed like a wild beast' (p.194) and 'dragged from town to town and from fair to fair as if he were a strange beast in a cage', exposed in his 'nakedness and hideous deformities' to a 'gaping crowd who greeted him with such mutterings as "Oh! what a horror! What a beast!"' (p.198), made more poignant the 'overwhelming tragedy of his life', the full extent of which Treves only realised 'when I came to know that Merrick was highly intelligent, that he possessed an acute sensibility and – worse than all – a romantic imagination' (p.194). The description may recall Frankenstein's monster.

According to Treves's record, a further change in Merrick's condition occurred, and it is one whose cause reinforces gender stereotypes. Although Treves suggests that Merrick had an idealised view of women, it is he himself who demonstrates one. When 'a friend of mine, a young and pretty widow' accepts Treves's invitation to 'enter Merrick's room with a smile, wish him good morning and shake him by the hand', the effect upon Merrick, who 'told me afterwards that this was the first woman who had ever smiled at him, and the first woman, in the whole of his life, who had shaken hands with him', is such that '[f]rom this day the transformation of Merrick commenced and he began to change, little by little, from a hunted thing into a man' (p.202).

Another agent of transformation in Merrick's life was, of course, Treves himself, who, by his own account, rescued his patient from a life of vagabondage:

> he had been moving on and moving on all his life. He knew no other state of existence. To him it was normal. He had passed from the workhouse to the hospital, from the hospital back to the workhouse, then from this town to that town or from one showman's caravan to another. He had never known a home nor any semblance of one. He had no possessions. His sole belongings, beside his clothes and some books, were the monstrous cap and the cloak. He was a wanderer, a pariah and an outcast. That his quarters at the hospital were his for life he could not understand. (pp.199–200)

Like Merrick, Harkness's midget is exhibited for curious paying audiences, but dressed so that he can play Napoleon.

Lobe 'loved his Whitechapel people' (*IDL*, p.19), but found that '[m]onstrosities were a trial to his faith'. He does not want to place himself above God by turning away from them in disgust, but admits 'I feel all of a creep. I wonder if they're men or beasts!' The midget is, he knows, a man, 'and yet *he* feels himself to be a missing link or something' (*IDL*, p.21). Lobe resolves to ask the general's advice.

The 'monstrosities' function here in typical fashion: they force inspection of the states between which they lie (which, of course, is also a function of travel). In Harkness's novel they direct attention to the social poles associated with humanity and bestiality. Thus,

> [t]here is in every one of us a deeply seated love of cruelty for its own sake, although the refined only show it by stinging words and cutting remarks. So let no one think the scum worse than the rest. The scum is brutal, the refined is vicious. (*IDL*, p.21)

Going through 'some of the worst streets in the metropolis', Lobe finds himself in a square into which, at midnight,

> the public-houses that flanked its entrance vomited forth their cargoes of depravity and vice, and the air rang with the oaths of women who sell their babies for two shillings or eighteen pence, and with the curses of men lower than the beasts but for the gift of speech. (*IDL*, p.24)

Amongst those public-houses 'congregated the lowest dregs of the East End populace', ready to rob drunken sailors, who would be lured by a 'vampire dressed in a gaudy skirt' (*IDL*, p.24). Harkness does not, as some authors of the time do, wholly detach the observer from the observed. She emphasises social connections in her writing, and social movement reveals the unsettledness. As in *The Strange Case of Dr. Jekyll and Mr. Hyde* and Henry James's *Washington Square* (1880), there is a sense of social character changing:

> Legend says that years gone by the square was inhabited by 'real gentry.' 'Middling folks' live in it at present – people who own small factories or large shops, who are in trades or business. These 'middling folks' talk of the 'lower classes', and it is difficult to say whereabouts in the social scale 'middling folks' come exactly. Certainly the upper ten have nothing to do with them ... It suffices to say that 'middling folks' bestow old clothes and soup on 'the poorer classes,' just as 'the real, gentry' visit 'the deserving poor' when down in the country, and give donations to charities during the season in London. (*IDL*, pp.24–25)

The changing relationships and the inadequacy of part-time charity both suggest the dislocation that needs to be fixed. In this place, within a room close to the roof in a house on the right-hand side of the square lives Ruth, an orphan, who has been brought up by her father's foreman. The latter was made, by her father's will, sole trustee of his property on condition that he look after her. At the age of eighteen, Ruth was to inherit her father's business: Weldon & Co.'s cocoa-nut chip factory.

Lobe wonders about Ruth joining the Salvation Army – 'These slum saviours were of all classes … and worked day and night among the scum of London' (*IDL*, p.31) – but thinks she is too young and delicate (*IDL*, p.33). Nevertheless, Ruth decides that she wishes to dedicate herself to the Army's service (*IDL*, p.42), though she will later be told by the Salvation Army superintendent James Cooke that she should sort out her problems with her trustee, Mr Pember (later called by the narrator 'the serpent' [*IDL*, p.101], before she can become a slum saviour [*IDL*, pp.85, 87]). Questioning other female workers, she is told of the conditions faced by themselves and the people they help. They receive the worst treatment not from men, but from women, who 'are more like demons than human beings' (*IDL*, p.45). Juxtaposition again underpins the reality and enables the moral:

> I have worked in Whitechapel, but I have never seen anything to equal what I see in these streets. And what makes it so terrible to me is the fact that, not a mile away, people are enjoying every luxury. This whole slum could be cleared away in a fortnight if people had a mind to do it. (*IDL*, p.45)

So says the eldest of the 'slum saviours' who instructs Ruth. The younger remarks on the lack of Christian principles demonstrated by the local rich, who do not feed, drink, clothe, or visit the poor. Her statement that '[a]nimals could teach the people about here many a lesson' seems directed at those who live in filth, '[b]ut, then, how can one tell these people that they ought to keep clean when they are starving?' (*IDL*, p.45) The idea of animals educating people illustrates my argument: in literature and other cultural forms of the time beastly avatars assist contemporaries's recognition of, and attempts to, understand social and intellectual movements.

Harkness's treatment of those who 'sink into the scum of London' is remarkable. She does not recoil from their persons so much as from the system that has made them thus. When she commands her readers to '[l]ook at the thousands of men [at the dock gates] who fight for work, who struggle like wild beasts for the contractors' tickets', she also instructs us to '[r]emember that a million men throughout the United Kingdom are out of work'. At the same time, she warns of the consequences of not working to improve the situation. She notes that while other people assume they have soldiers and policemen to protect them, they are unaware that 'policemen went in the dark hours of the night to a well-known Socialist, and begged him to take part in their last demonstration' and forget that 'soldiers are beginning to ask, "What will become of *me* when my short period of service is over and I leave the army?"' These people do not want to be conscious of the dangers open to themselves from the large army of the unemployed; from the

> seething mass of discontent that is even now undermining the whole of society. Only those who go amongst them, who know them intimately, are aware of the bitter hatred which they express for 'the upper classes,' the angry feelings which they smother while ladies and gentlemen roll by in carriages. (*IDL*, p.55)

A more optimistic vision of the relationship between the classes is presented when the lady who has acknowledged the 'midget' is taken by Lobe once more to visit him. Asked if she thinks he has a soul, because he is 'afraid of coming here again as a dog or something', she replies that he should not be afraid:

> Things are changing fast. Social conditions are becoming different. Barriers are breaking down, and classes are amalgamating. By the time you come back all men will be brethren ... People will put you first then, if you come into the world handicapped. (*IDL*, pp.65–66)

Assured by her kiss, the 'midget' feels that he must be a man and have a soul: she would not have kissed him were he a missing link. Harkness combines a humanist response with a call for material change. When her narrator describes the 'human insects' (*IDL*, p.69) that swarm around the poor district, there is not the same contempt, resignation, or distancing that is a feature of naturalistic writing of the time. Rather, the concern is to remedy the social system that has rendered them less or other than human. True, they are still described in animalistic terms, but the clear message is that in order to prevent the damaging effects of further transformations of people, the social structure and social attitudes must be changed. It is a message that is underlined by the sympathetic doctor who forsook a future in the West End with a name for himself in order to help those starving in the East End, to which he has now become tied, 'a modern Prometheus, bound to the rock by the woes of his fellow-men' (*IDL*, p.75). The doctor quotes Engels on the condition of the poor and says were he younger, he would enter politics and be 'a constitutional socialist, using all lawful means to improve the condition of the working man' (*IDL*, p.77). He thinks that '[t]he West End is bad, or mad; not to see that if things go on like this we must have a revolution' (*IDL*, p.154); that the people of the East End, where everyone is starving, will one day 'walk westwards, cutting throats and hurling brickbats, until they are shot down by the military'. He refers dismissively to the 'pretty stories about the East End made up by Walter Besant' (*IDL*, p.154) that people prefer to read rather than hear the truth, but if they ignore the latter, they will be in danger.

Similarly, Jane Hardy – the labour-mistress at Ruth's factory – tells her of her Socialist sympathies when Ruth reports for work. Animal imagery is used once again to convey the point as she remarks of the girls who work there that '[t]he best thing that could happen to [them] just now would be a leetle pressure of the finger and thumb on the windpipe when they're just born, and don't feel any more than young kittens' (*IDL*, p.92). There are, she believes, 'too many of 'em, and they only add to competition, which, as the Socialists say, is playing the devil with us at present' (*IDL*, p.92). Her attitude may not carry absolute authorial or even narrative endorsement – she believes in 'combination, fighting the upper classes, and justice' (*IDL*, p.90) – but has to put her principles in her pocket as she has her mother to keep and will 'never take on a Jewess', because '[t]he East End is just overrun with foreign people, and that makes matters worse for us English' (*IDL*, p.95). Her hatred of capitalists seems focused on Mr Pember, whom she might have loved, but who withdrew once he saw that he was dear to her and whom she now blames for her childlessness (p.140). Yet the condition of the miserable girls, whom Ruth encounters 'jabbering and scolding like young magpies' (*IDL*, p.90), is one that requires remedy: 'They had only just escaped from the Board school; but many of them had faces wise with wickedness, and eyes out of which all traces of maidenhood had vanished' (*IDL*, p.90). They work standing from seven in the morning till seven at night for half a crown a week and without holidays (*IDL*, p.98). Jane Hardy's comment to Ruth – '[y]ou can't form an opinion about the hands … until you have witnessed their environment' (*IDL*, p.107) – might just as well be uttered by Harkness to her readers. Hardy's acknowledgement of their social conditions and personal situation entails an understanding of prostitution: 'Virtue is easy enough when a woman has plenty to eat, and a character to keep, but it's quite a different thing when a girl is starving' (*IDL*, p.113). Harkness declines to blame people for circumstances over which they have no control. If they are brutalised by their life, they are not themselves wholly at fault, though she does not entirely absolve them from personal responsibility. Again, animal imagery conveys this point as we are told that at the docks people would sometimes say to Lobe 'it's just no good, Salvation … I can't get no work, so I may as well make a beast of myself, and forget God made a man of me at the beginning' (*IDL*, p.145). They repent, but are hopeless cases once drink gets hold of them (pp.145–146) and come 'to take pleasure in their filthy existence' (p.171).

By contrast, the Jews 'had not the down-trodden look of our Gentile population, which, seems to enjoy crouching and whining instead of asserting itself with sturdy independence'. They have 'long-suffering faces, but they have hope written on their features instead of that despair which seems to sodden English East End men and women' (*IDL*, pp.166–167). Their religiousness and sense of community seem to account for this: 'Charity offers him [the Jew] no premium for idleness; so the chosen people hang together, the rich help the poor, and every Jew finds a friend on the Jewish Board of Guardians' (*IDL*, p.167). Harkness is engaged here in her own effort of transformation, aiming to counter negative stereotypes of the Jew. Her purpose becomes clearer still when her narrator presents the death-bed confession of a blood-thirsty slaughterhouse man who murdered a woman and then, a Gentile, hid among the Jews (pp.168–169). Although the man confesses to having murdered only one woman, it seems plain that Harkness intends to challenge anti-Semitic views of Jack the Ripper as a Jew. (The Ripper's murders took place in the second half of the year in which the novel is set – the year before the book's publication. There is also a suggestion that the continual slaughtering of beasts made the man like a cannibal, thirsting for human blood.)

After the death of 'Napoleon the midget', Lobe and the lady who had visited the deceased discuss Socialism. The lady tells him: 'I believe in the principles of Socialism; but, like every one else, I get tired of seeing so little accomplished' (*IDL*, p.129). She is unimpressed by the inability of Socialists to work together, but sees that '[s]ocialism is growing every day' and believes that '[a]t present its most hopeful sign is an embryonic labour-party' (*IDL*, p.132).

The doctor despises social climbing, which 'always ends in moral degradation'. He would 'rather be fettered to the people with iron chains, than wear the gilded livery of a West End physician' (p.157). It is more important to him that one should do real work and leave one's mark than be talked about.

Harkness resists the false comfort of the pastoral. When thousands of people travel by train to Kent for hop-picking,

> [t]hey are … cheaper to carry about than dumb beasts, for they can be packed closer together, and if one or two are suffocated on the journey no one claims damages … the death of a hop-picker matters to no one. (*IDL*, p.171)

Once picking, though in better spirits, 'their conversation was about the last East End murder, and their songs had the filthiest choruses; nature did not purify their thoughts, as Captain Lobe had expected ...' (*IDL*, p.181).

The people are 'more like beasts than human beings'; '[t]hey come out of the holes they call homes, and the public-houses, to enjoy themselves in truly bestial fashion' (*IDL*, p.196). It is a slum saviour who interrupts their 'woman-baiting' to remind them '[y[ou are men and women, you are not wild beasts' (*IDL*, p.200), telling them to go home and not kill the half-naked woman whom they are taunting and manhandling.

Sordid struggle

In George Gissing's *The Nether World* (1889), bestiality is linked to both class and race. The narrator tells us of the protagonist, Clem Peckover, that

> the broad joviality with which she gloated over the prospect of cruelties shortly to be inflicted, put her at once on a par with the noble savage running wild in woods. Civilisation could bring no charge against this young woman; it and she had no common criterion.[47]

Clem is described as 'showing really remarkable skill in conveying pieces of sausage to her mouth by means of the knife alone' and possessing 'Red Indian scent' that allows her to detect others' feelings (p.7). The racialised foreignness of aspects of her appearance also introduces temporal difference: 'Her forehead was low and of great width; her nose was well shapen, and had large sensual apertures; her cruel lips may be seen on certain fine antique busts' (p.8). The animality equates to a loss of femininity: 'Clem would have liked dealing with some one with whom she could try savage issue in real tooth-and-claw conflict' (p.8). Later, we are told of her 'savage kind of admiration' for Bob Hewett (p.36).

Travel, such as it exists for creatures like those in Morrison's, Harkness's, and Gissing's novels, is rarely voluntary. They have little choice but to obey the natural forces of their environment – in this case, economic forces. A famous example from across the Atlantic is Theodore Dreiser's *Sister Carrie* (1900), the beginning of which has its central character, Carrie Meeber, going by train to Chicago – a city whose 'many and growing commercial opportunities gave it widespread fame which made of it a giant magnet, drawing to itself from all quarters the hopeful and the hopeless', with the metaphor of the magnet forcing the idea of a lack of free will or resistance.[48] Chicago pulls people in from the Midwest and beyond. In most of the texts with which *Beastly Journeys* is concerned, the bulk of the characters are already resident in their environs and have little hope of escape. Usually, they are part of a swarm or crowd or (in the Jago) they hunt in packs or fight territorial or kinship battles. In *The Nether World*, for example, John Hewett exclaims:

> If any man had said as much as a rough word to me, I'd a gone at him like a bulldog. I felt like a beast. I wanted to fight, I tell you – to fight till the life was kicked an' throttled out of me! (p.22)

When the characters in these novels do journey as individuals it is along routes prescribed to their kind, so that they act instinctively and with little or no free will. For such beasts, transformation is impossible: they possess neither the means nor the stimulus. The only options are stasis or further degeneration, which latter is a matter of degree rather than an alteration of form.

Gissing's narrator shows glimpses of their humanity. When he does so, it is in the context of momentary release from thralldom. Thus,

> [i]t was the hour of the unyoking of men. In the highways and byways of Clerkenwell there was a thronging of released toilers, of young and old, of male and female. Forth they streamed from factories and workrooms, anxious to make the most of the few hours during which they might live for themselves. (p.10)

The lack of leisure time is reflected in the common linguistic reduction of the workers to the useful parts of their body: their designation as 'hands'. Gissing writes: 'Wealth inestimable is ever flowing through these workshops, and the hands that have been stained with gold-dust may, as likely as not, some day extend themselves in petition for a crust' (p.11). Through striking images such as these, Gissing communicates the cost of having such people service our society. Just as in Wells's *The Time Machine* (which we shall examine in Chapter Three), the brutish Morlocks (the descendants of the proletariat and subterranean toilers) labour for the comfort of the Eloi (the descendants of the middle- and upper-classes), so the denizens of the Nether World, with little scope for their own enjoyment, produce the wealth that benefits others, then as now. Sprinkling the metaphor of gold dust and letting it fall in contrast with the basic necessity of a piece of bread, Gissing juxtaposes the two classes and makes the connections that are normally kept hidden shockingly evident. In the Nether World of Clerkenwell, not only the people but even the buildings themselves suggest the 'sordid struggle for existence' (p.51). External conditions and, in some, instincts that a more comfortable existence might keep in check combine to effect the degradation of the people who live there. Thus, for example, we are told of Clara, in relation to Sidney Kirkwood:

> The disease inherent in her being, that deadly outcome of social tyranny which perverts the generous elements of youth into mere seeds of destruction, developed day by day, blighting her heart, corrupting her moral sense, even setting marks of evil upon the beauty of her countenance ... Like a creature that is beset by unrelenting forces, she summoned and surveyed all the crafty faculties lurking in the dark places of her nature; theoretically she had now accepted every debasing compact by which a woman can spite herself on the world's injustices. Self-assertion; to be no longer an unregarded atom in the mass of those who are born only to labour for others; to find play for the strength and the passion which, by no choice of her own, distinguished her from the tame slave. (p.86)

Beyond the question of the character transformations (or lack of opportunity to bring about change) is the role of the author. In John Goode's words: 'Gissing is a novelist: that is, he is a specific kind of literary producer, transforming specific material in determined conditions of production.'[49] Goode makes the important point that Gissing does not simply represent what he sees. Rather, as a writer, he undertakes work that employs genre to mutate London life into fiction that is informed by ideology and material conditions. This is true not only of Gissing, but of all literary realists, and not only of all literary realists, but of all writers. We need more reminding of the fact with realists, because they purport to show life as it really is. As Goode implies, with Gissing there is even more of a temptation to think so, because his gritty portraits are unalleviated by sentimentalism or plot twists that detract from the sense of fidelity to life.[50] Sloan may be right to claim of Gissing that '[t]he brutal accuracy of his account of working-class life in Clerkenwell introduced a new kind of realism to the English public',[51] but Goode reminds us that the absence of sentimentality and contrivance does not mean a lack of mediation. Indeed, the author's social position and ideology need more attention. In Gissing, as with other realist and naturalistic authors, the narrator observes a distance between himself (it usually is a he) and his characters. That gap allows the narrator to rise above the animal condition of his subjects. Whether that distance marks a contradiction and flaw in the view of an overarching determinism or whether it grants an external position from which one can view and criticise the circumstances on display is a question that has been debated in studies of naturalism.

The Minotaur and the frightened lambs

It is in the context of women's propulsion into the economic realm that W. T. Stead's exposé of child prostitution should be seen. Against the background of thwarted proposals to raise the age of consent from thirteen to sixteen and scandals such as the uncovering in 1882 and farcical prosecution in 1885 of Mrs Jefferies for running brothels that catered for wealthy and celebrated clients,[52] Stead 'decided to prove that children could be bought and sent into enforced prostitution by doing it himself'.[53] Having been introduced by Benjamin Waugh to a seven-year-old and a four-year-old girl, both of whom had been lured into brothels and raped, Stead determined to act and use his newspaper for the cause.[54] He recruited Rebecca Jarrett, a 'reformed prostitute, brothel keeper and procuress',[55] to obtain a girl for him. With the help of her old friend Nancy Broughton, Jarrett bought thirteen-year-old Eliza Armstrong for five pounds, had her virginity confirmed by a doctor, and had her taken to France. A good part of the horror of Stead's report lay in the commoditisation of girls. Stead's monster is the Minotaur. Invoking classical Greece, Stead recalls the myth of how Athens was compelled to send to Crete every nine years seven youths and seven maidens, all of whom 'were flung into the famous Labyrinth of Daedalus, there to wander about blindly until such time as they were devoured by the Minotaur, a frightful monster, half man, half bull, the foul product of an unnatural lust'.[56] From Ancient Greece Stead switches his gaze to modern London, where '[t]his very night … and every night, year in and year out, not seven maidens only, but many times seven … will be offered up as the Maiden Tribute of Modern Babylon'. They were maidens this morning, but tomorrow 'will find themselves within … the maze of London brotheldom'. Developing his classical metaphor for rhetorical and social impact, Stead continues: 'The maw of the London Minotaur is insatiable.' Yet London, Stead claims, does not care for the fate of its 50,000 prostitutes. Stead is 'not without hope that there may be some check placed upon this vast tribute of maidens … which is nightly levied in London by the vices of the rich upon the necessities of the poor' (I, p.2), but he asks that if the sacrifice of maidenhood must continue, its victims should at least be of an age at which they can understand their situation and loss and therefore sacrifice willingly, rather than through coercion or ignorance:

> That is surely not too much to ask from the dissolute rich. Even considerations of self-interest might lead our rulers to assent to so modest a demand.

For the hour of Democracy has struck, and there is no wrong which a man resents like this ... the fathers and brothers whose daughters and sisters are purchased like slaves, not for labour, but from lust, are now at last enrolled among the governing classes – a circumstance full of hope for the nation, but by no means without menace for a class ... unless the levying of the maiden tribute in London is shorn of its worst abuses ... resentment, which might be appeased by reform, may hereafter be the virus of a social revolution. It is the one explosive which is strong enough to wreck the Throne. (I, p.2)

Distinguishing between sexual immorality and sexual criminality, Stead makes clear that his concern is with the latter, which he classifies as follows:

I. The sale and purchase and violation of children.
II. The procuration of virgins.
III. The entrapping and ruin of women.
IV. The international slave trade in girls.
V. Atrocities, brutalities, and unnatural crimes. (I, p.2)

Explaining that he writes from personal knowledge, Stead describes how he spent four weeks with two or three coadjutors 'oscillat[ing] between the noblest and the meanest of mankind, the saviours and the destroyers of their race, spending hours alternately in brothels and hospitals, in the streets and in refuges, in the company of procuresses and of bishops'. This 'strange, inverted world ... was the same, yet not the same, as the world of business and the world of politics' (I, p.2). At best, one wanders in a Circe's isle,

[b]ut with a difference, for whereas the enchanted in olden time had the heads and the voices and the bristles of swine, while the heart of a man was in them still, these have not put on in outward form 'the inglorious likeness of a beast,' but are in semblance as other men, while within there is only the heart of a beast – bestial, ferocious, and filthy beyond the imagination of decent men. (I, p.3)

Stead recounts his discovery of a former brothel-keeper who proves to him that she can procure girls – including a thirteen-year-old – for three pounds. He does not proceed with the transaction, but has a 'thoroughly trustworthy woman' go with the ex-brothel-keeper to a 'bad house' where a girl is purchased for two pounds plus a sovereign when she is proved a virgin. The girl, grown nervous and suspicious when told she will be taken to the country, escapes (I, p.5).

Class is a factor throughout. The former brothel-keeper has told Stead that '[p]retty girls who are poor, and who have either no parents or are away from home, are easiest picked up' (I, p.4). Stead relates how, though he has been inquiring in the East End, he learns of a house in the West End 'kept apparently by a highly respectable midwife, where children were taken by procurers to be certified as virgins before violation, and where, after violation, they were taken to be "patched up", and where, if necessary, abortion could be procured'. The house stands 'imperturbably respectable in its outward appearance, apparently an indispensable adjunct of modern civilization, its experienced proprietress maintaining confidential relations with the "best houses" in the West-end'. The proprietress says, 'Oh, Mr. — is a gentleman who has a great penchant for little girls. I do not know how many I have had to repair after him' (I, p.5). The discrepancy between the respectable exterior and disreputable interior is the architectural equivalent of the condition symbolised by Dr Jekyll and Mr Hyde and signifies a duality that runs through so many narratives of these years. 'Anything can be done for money, if you only know where to take it' (I, p.6), writes Stead in a comment that testifies to the power that has transformed the state of things and contributed to the disparity between social exterior and inner secret.

Stead tells the tale of thirteen-year-old Lily (Eliza), who was sold by her alcoholic parents for three pounds, plus two pounds to be paid once her virginity was certified. Taken to 'a house of ill-fame', she is put to bed, drugged, and locked in with her purchaser. After a short silence 'there rose a wild and piteous cry – not a loud shriek, but a helpless, startled scream like the bleat of a frightened lamb' (I, p.6). This scene, Stead writes, occurred in a 'well-known house, within a quarter of a mile of Oxford Circus' (II, p.1). Stead deplores the fact that a child becomes a woman at thirteen in the eyes of the law and can dispose of her virtue then, three years before she can dispose of other valuables (II, p.1). He is appalled by the ignorance of the girls: 'It is one of the greatest scandals of Protestant training that parents are allowed to keep their children in total ignorance of the simplest truths of physiology, without even a rudimentary conception of the nature of sexual morality' (II, p.2). His simile of the lamb evokes a Christ-like innocence and sacrifice, while casting himself as protector.

Stead relates his dealings with the outwardly respectable Miss X and Miss Z, whose 'systematized business' is the procuring of virgins (II, p.3). From Miss Z, Stead solicits a virgin of around fourteen-years-old for five pounds plus a doctor's fee. He is told by Miss X and Miss Z that one of their friends, an unnamed doctor, takes three girls (age sixteen or over) for his own use each fortnight at between five pounds and seven pounds a night. From these two women, Stead orders five virgins to distribute among his friends for five pounds a head, plus doctor's fees. He is brought nine girls, four of whom a doctor (in whom Stead has confided) certifies as virgins.

Reporting the rarity of street girls under thirteen and his own inability to obtain a prostitute under that age, though 'there is no doubt as to the existence of a vast and increasing mass of juvenile prostitution' (III, p.2), Stead calls for the raising of the age of consent to sixteen. At a villa in North London he is shown a young-looking fourteen-year-old, in whom there 'still lingered the timid glance of a frightened fawn'. And he is told of 'a monster now walking about who acts as a clerk in a highly respectable establishment' (III, p.2). The clerk is fifty-years-old and has ruined children for years, but cannot be prosecuted, because the girls are thirteen-years-old.

Stead writes that:

> I have at this moment an agreement with the keeper of one of the houses near Regent Street to the effect that she will have ready in her house, within a few hours of receipt of a line from me, a girl under fourteen.

He tells the story of Emily, 'a child-prostitute who, at the age of eleven, had for two years been earning her living by vice in the East-end' and explains that, legally, abduction is only an offence if a girl is in the custody of her father at the time of her abduction (III, p.3).

Class scandal again rears its head when Stead mentions a brothel in St. John's Wood, which is rumoured to be patronised by 'at least one Prince and one Cabinet Minister' (8 July, p.5). And he refers to a '[w]ealthy Mr. —', whose 'whole life is dedicated to the gratification of lust' and whose name he constantly came across '[d]uring my investigations in the subterranean realm'. It was 'actually Mr. —'s boast that he has ruined 2,000 women in his time' (III, p.5).

It is an inverted world that Stead exposes; and one in which the police cannot be trusted. Stead's weeks of night-prowling have convinced him that talk of the scandalous state of the streets is greatly exaggerated. Indeed, he records his 'respect and admiration for the extraordinarily good behaviour of the English girls who pursue this dreadful calling' (IV, p.3). The Criminal Law Amendment Bill was passed in August 1885, but Stead was charged with, and found guilty of, abduction, because Liza's step-father had not given his permission for his daughter to be taken. He was also found guilty of assault and sentenced to three months' imprisonment.

Man monster

The bestial epithets attached to Jack the Ripper are the least surprising of the cases presented in this chapter. Combining animality with race and vampirism, *The Star* described the Ripper as 'half-beast, half-man'; a 'ghoul-like creature who stalks through the streets of London, stalking down his victim like a Pawnee Indian ... [who] is simply drunk with blood, and he will have more'.[57] Judith Walkowitz reproduces an illustrated page of the *Police Illustrated News* for 17 November 1888 that reports 'THE SEVENTH HORRIBLE MURDER BY THE MONSTER OF THE EAST-END'[58] and she also quotes from the *Daily Telegraph* of 14 September 1888, which referred to the 'man monster who stalks the streets in search of fallen women'.[59] Walkowitz cites contemporary reports linking the Ripper with a Gothic creature, werewolf, and vampire, ogres and monsters.[60] According to Walkowitz, the murders 'triggered off a set of psychosexual and political fears that resounded, in different ways, across the social spectrum'.[61] To be triggered, those fears had to be already present and primed. Walkowitz goes on to apply an analysis based on postmodern theories of fragmentation and the body,[62] but she finds the origin of those fears in movements and divisions of the fin de siècle. Observing of the capital that '[t]he opposition of East and West increasingly took on imperial and racial dimensions, as the two parts of London imaginatively doubled for England and its Empire', she notes that at the end of the nineteenth century, 'journalistic exposés highlighted this geographic segregation, impressing on Londoners the perception that they lived in a city of contrasts, a class and geographically divided metropolis of hovels and palaces'.[63] At the time, the Ripper murders could be 'shaped ... into a story of class conflict and exploitation',[64] as suspicions about the murderer's identity 'shifted from the East End to the West End' and 'representations of the Ripper oscillated from an externalized version of the Other to a variation of the multiple, divided Self'.[65] In fact, writes Walkowitz, it was Stead who was the first journalist to notice the sexual origins of the murders, to make comparisons with Stevenson's *The Strange Case of Dr. Jekyll and Mr. Hyde* (1886), and to suggest, after first assuming that the murderer belonged to the slums, that the Ripper, who had an uncontrolled sexual appetite for blood, may be of a more 'respectable' station.[66] Because of their context, the killings are emblematic of the contrasts, juxtapositions, and encounters that characterise representations of the 1880s and 1890s. Whitechapel, as Walkowitz and others note, was an impoverished area on the edge of the East End, but adjacent to the financial district, the City, and accessible from the West End. Indeed, its working-class entertainments attracted rich young men from the West End, who enjoyed what we would now call 'slumming'.[67] It is eastward through 'this grey, monstrous London of ours, with its myriads of people, its sordid sinners, and its splendid sins' that Wilde's Dorian Gray heads, 'soon losing my way in a labyrinth of grimy streets and black, grassless squares' before he reaches the 'absurd little theatre' at which he sees and is drawn to young actress Sibyl Vane.[68] Indeed, the *OED*'s examples of 'slumming', in the sense of visiting slums, date from the 1880s.

A point made by Walkowitz about the Ripper murders may throw further light on the significance of beastly images to those living in the late nineteenth century. She writes that:

> If, traditionally, the 'classical' body has signified the 'health' of the larger social body – of a closed, homogeneous, regulated social order – then the mounting array of 'grotesque,' mutilated corpses in this case represented the exact inverse: a visceral analogue to the epistemological incoherence and political disorientation threatening the body politic during the 'autumn of terror'.[69]

Nowadays some of the horror has been lost and the ghastly misogyny of the murders has been softened by a foggy nostalgia for late Victorian London. In fact, one of the foremost Ripper authorities, Paul Begg, notes that 'very soon after the murders stopped – and probably even as they were being committed – Jack the Ripper passed through a strange transformation from real life murderer to bugaboo of nightmare'.[70] That alteration may have been a way of coping with the terror created by the figure of the Ripper himself, but perhaps lost from view to later generations is the fact that the Ripper gave 'substance and form' to contemporary fears of a 'working class uprising and revolution'. There existed, Begg reports, an anxiety that just as this brutal killer might 'move out of the warren of hovels and alleys' of the Nether World into 'the civilised city', so 'could the diseased savages themselves, espousing socialism, demanding employment and fair wages, education and acceptable housing, and bringing an end to the world as the Victorian middle classes knew it'.[71] Begg quotes from George Bernard Shaw's letter to *The Star* in which Shaw suggests that the Ripper has succeeded more effectively than social reformers in drawing the attention of the wider public and press to conditions in the East End and promoting reform:

> The moral is a pretty one, and the Insurrectionists, the Dynamitards, the

Invincibles, and the extreme left of the Anarchist party will not be slow to draw it. 'Humanity, political science, economics, and religion', they will say, 'are all rot; the one argument that touches your lady and gentleman is the knife'. That is so pleasant for the party of Hope and Perseverance in their toughening struggle with the party of Desperation and Death.[72]

Begg notes that the 'fundamental and far-reaching changes' to the 'social, political and economic structure' of the country was 'frightening' and that by the end of the decade there was a real fear of revolution. The 'social evils' of both the capital and nation 'came to be embodied by the poor, the destitute and the unemployed of the East End', and 'Jack the Ripper came to represent the East End and so to represent all the anxieties of the age.'[73]

Despite the efforts of concerned commentators in the 1880s and 1890s to enlist sympathy for the urban underclass, the pervasiveness of pejorative animal metaphors worked against a general softening of attitudes among those who held power. Journeys into the Nether World tended (with some exceptions) to underline the distance between observer and observed. When that distance looked like being broken down, it was perceived as a threat to social or psychological stability.

In no late nineteenth-century texts are the combination of sex, bestiality, class, and capitalism more evident than in Bram Stoker's *Dracula* and Richard Marsh's *The Beetle*, to which we turn in the next chapter.

Notes

1 On this, see, for example, Asa Briggs, *Victorian Cities* [1963] (London: Penguin, 1968).
2 Briggs, *Victorian Cities*, p.59.
3 Raymond Williams, *The English Novel from Dickens to Lawrence* [1971] (London: The Hogarth Press, 1984), p.16.
4 Ben Tillett, *A Brief History of the Dockers Union* [1910], quoted in William J. Fishman, *East End 1888: A Year in a London Borough among the Labouring Poor* [2005] (Nottingham: Five Leaves Publications, 2009), p.24.
5 Arthur Morrison, *A Child of the Jago* [1896], Peter Miles, ed. (London: Everyman, 1996), p.11.
6 Beatrice Webb, *My Apprenticeship* [1926], quoted in Fishman, *East End 1888*, p.20.
7 William Potter (C. Tirling), *Thomas Jackson of Whitechapel* [1929], quoted in Fishman, *East End 1888*, p.239.
8 Margaret Harkness (as John Law), *A City Girl* [1887], quoted in Fishman, *East End 1888*, p.250.

9 Margaret Harkness (as John Law), *In Darkest London* [1889 as *Captain Lobe: A Story of the Salvation Army*], quoted in Fishman, *East End 1888*, p.152.
10 Fishman, *East End 1888*, p.110.
11 Anne Humpherys, 'Knowing the Victorian City: Writing and Representation', *Victorian Literature and Culture* 30, 2 (September 2002), 602.
12 David Harvey, *The Urban Experience* (Oxford: Basil Blackwell, 1989), p.168.
13 Harvey, *The Urban Experience*, p.165.
14 This section revises and condenses my essay, 'Stevenson's Monkey-Business: *The Strange Case of Dr. Jekyll and Mr. Hyde*', in Peter Liebregts and Wim Tigges, eds, *Beauty and the Beast: Christina Rossetti, Walter Pater, R. L. Stevenson and their Contemporaries* (Amsterdam: Rodopi, 1996), pp.157–170. See also my essay, 'White Apes at the Fin de Siècle', in Tim Youngs, ed., *Writing and Race* (London: Longman, 1997), pp.166–190.
15 Robert Louis Stevenson, 'The Strange Case of Dr. Jekyll and Mr. Hyde', in *Dr. Jekyll and Mr. Hyde, The Merry Men and Other Tales* (London: Dent, 1925), p.19. All further references to this text will be given parenthetically.
16 Gareth Stedman Jones, *Outcast London: A Study in the Relationship between Classes in Victorian Society* [1971] (Harmondsworth: Penguin Books, 1976), p.281.
17 Jones, *Outcast London*, p.281.
18 Jones, *Outcast London*, p.282.
19 Jones, *Outcast London*, p.284.
20 Jones, *Outcast London*, p.289.
21 Jones, *Outcast London*, p.290.
22 Jones, *Outcast London*, p.291. Smith's warning is from his article, 'Industrial Training of Destitute Children', published in *Contemporary Review* in January 1885.
23 Karl Beckson, *London in the 1890s: A Cultural History* (New York, NY: W. W. Norton, 1992), p.18.
24 'The transformation of peasant Paddy into an ape-man or simianized Caliban was completed by the 1860s and 1870s.' See L. Perry Curtis, *Apes and Angels: The Irishman in Victorian Caricature* (Newton Abbot: David and Charles, 1971), p.2.
25 Jones, *Outcast London*, p.285.
26 Jones, *Outcast London*, p.285.
27 This paragraph was drawn from Jones, *Outcast London*, pp.286–287. Jones illustrates the idea of the proliferation of the unfit, with reference to Arnold White's *The Problems of a Great City* [1887].
28 Jones, *Outcast London*, p.308.
29 David Punter, *The Literature of Terror: A History of Gothic Fictions from 1765 to the Present Day* (London: Longman 1996), p.1.
30 Punter, *Literature of Terror*, p.3.
31 See William Veeder, 'Collated Fractions of the Manuscript Drafts of *Strange Case of Dr Jekyll and Mr Hyde*', in William Veeder and Gordon Hirsch, eds, *Dr Jekyll and Mr Hyde after One Hundred Years* (Chicago, IL: Chicago University Press, 1988), p.22.
32 Helen Merrell Lynd, *England in the Eighteen-Eighties: Toward a Social Basis for Freedom* (London: Oxford University Press, 1945), p.44.
33 Lynd, *The Eighteen-Eighties*, p.45.
34 See Veeder, 'Collated Fractions', pp.34–35.
35 Patrick Brantlinger and Richard Boyle, 'The Education of Edward Hyde: Stevenson's

"Gothic Gnome" and the Mass Readership of Late-Victorian England', in Veeder and Hirsch, eds, *Dr Jekyll and Mr Hyde after One Hundred Years*, pp.265–282.
36 Brantlinger and Boyle, 'The Education of Edward Hyde', p.272.
37 Brantlinger and Boyle, 'The Education of Edward Hyde', p.266.
38 Andrew Lang, 'Mr. Stevenson's Works', in *Essays in Little* (London: Henry and Co., 1891), p.35.
39 Peter Miles, 'Introduction', in Arthur Morrison, *A Child of the Jago* [1896], Peter Miles, ed. (London: Everyman, 1996), p.xliv.
40 Miles, 'Introduction', p.xliii.
41 Miles, 'Introduction', p.xxxvii.
42 Bernard Shaw, 'Preface: Mainly About Myself', in *Plays Unpleasant: Widowers' Houses, The Philanderer, Mrs. Warren's Profession* (Harmondsworth: Penguin, 1946), pp.25–26. The preface was written in 1898.
43 Kevin R. Swafford, 'Translating the Slums: The Coding of Criminality and the Grotesque in Arthur Morrison's "A Child of the Jago"', *The Journal of the Midwest Modern Language Association* 35, 2: *Translating in and across Cultures* (Autumn 2002), 53.
44 Shaw, 'Preface', p.27.
45 Margaret Harkness, *In Darkest London* (Cambridge: Black Apollo Press, 2003), pp.15–16. First published as John Law, *Captain Lobe: A Story of the Salvation Army* (London: Hodder and Stoughton, 1889). The novel is set in 1888, though p.132 mistakenly suggests 1886. Further page references will be given parenthetically as *IDL*.
46 From Treves's essay 'The Elephant Man', published in his 1923 book *The Elephant Man and Other Reminiscences*, reproduced in Michael Howell and Peter Ford, *The True History of the Elephant Man* (Harmondsworth: Penguin, 1980), pp.190–210, quoted at p.190. Further page references will be given in the text.
47 George Gissing, *The Nether World* [1889], edited with an introduction by Stephen Gill (Oxford: Oxford University Press, 1992), p.6. Further page references will be given parenthetically.
48 Theodore Dreiser, *Sister Carrie* [1900] (Harmondsworth: Penguin, 1981), p.16.
49 John Goode, *George Gissing: Ideology and Fiction* (London: Vision, 1978), p.14.
50 John Sloan also notes that: 'The novel [*The Nether World*] is completely free of the sentimentalising strain which we find in the "industrial novel" of the 1840s and 1850s, and indeed to some extent in Gissing's own earlier novels on the condition of the people. Absent too is any representative middle-class character through whom the novel might hold out a consolatory vision of refuge or retreat.' See John Sloan, *George Gissing: The Cultural Challenge* (Basingstoke: Macmillan, 1989), p.76.
51 Sloan, *George Gissing*, p.76.
52 Jefferies, whose activities had been uncovered in 1882, pleaded guilty, saving 'herself and her clients the embarrassment of being asked difficult questions. [She] was fined £200, which she paid with cash.' See Paul Begg, *Jack the Ripper: The Definitive History* (London: Longman, 2003), p.118.
53 Begg, *Jack the Ripper*, p.119. For an account of Stead's activities, see, for example, Grace Eckley, *Maiden Tribute: A Life of W. T. Stead* (Philadelphia, PA: Xlibris, 2007), especially Chapter Four.
54 Waugh was Honorary Secretary of the London Society for the Prevention of

Cruelty in 1884. In 1899, he would found the National Society for the Prevention of Cruelty to Children. See Begg, *Jack the Ripper*, p.119.
55 Begg, *Jack the Ripper*, p.119.
56 [W. T. Stead], 'The Maiden Tribute of Modern Babylon' ('The Report of the *Pall Mall Gazette* Secret Commission), Monday 6 July 1885, p.1. The report was published in four parts on 6, 7, 8, and 10 July 1885. Further page references will be given parenthetically, preceded by the part number.
57 *The Star*, 8 September 1888, quoted in Begg, *Jack the Ripper*, p.155.
58 In Judith Walkowitz, *City of Dreadful Delight: Narratives of Sexual Danger in Late-Victorian London* [1992] (London: Virago, 1994), Figure 15, facing p.135. In fact, 'the number of murders committed by Jack the Ripper is disputed'. Begg, *Jack the Ripper*, p.231. There are five so-called canonical victims – i.e. those generally accepted to have been killed by him.
59 Quoted in Walkowitz, *City of Dreadful Delight*, p.168.
60 Walkowitz, *City of Dreadful Delight*, p.197.
61 Walkowitz, *City of Dreadful Delight*, p.198.
62 See, for example, the last full paragraph in Walkowitz, *City of Dreadful Delight*, p.198.
63 Walkowitz, *City of Dreadful Delight*, p.126.
64 Walkowitz, *City of Dreadful Delight*, p.3. Walkowitz concludes her sentence thus: 'and into a cautionary tale for women, a warning that the city was a dangerous place when they transgressed the narrow boundary of home and hearth to enter public space'.
65 Walkowitz, *City of Dreadful Delight*, pp.205–206.
66 Walkowitz, *City of Dreadful Delight*, pp.206–207.
67 Walkowitz, *City of Dreadful Delight*, pp.193–194.
68 Oscar Wilde, *The Picture of Dorian Gray* [1891] (Oxford: Oxford University Press, 1981), p.48. That Gray refers to '[a] hideous Jew', who was 'such a monster' and has 'an enormous diamond … in the centre of a soiled shirt' (p.48) illustrates racial – more specifically, anti-Semitic – Othering.
69 Walkowitz, *City of Dreadful Delight*, p.198.
70 Begg, *Jack the Ripper*, p.x.
71 Begg, *Jack the Ripper*, p.1.
72 George Bernard Shaw, 'Blood Money to Whitechapel', *The Star*, 24 September 1888, quoted in Begg, *Jack the Ripper*, p.2.
73 Begg, *Jack the Ripper*, p.3.

CHAPTER TWO

The Bat and the Beetle

Dracula
'them there animiles'[1]

Although subsequent representations of Dracula have tended to fix his alter ego as a vampire bat, in Stoker's 1897 novel itself the animal analogies are more varied and extensive. Early on, when Jonathan Harker spies Dracula crawling down the wall of his castle, he compares his host's movements with those of a lizard (p.35). Shortly afterwards, Dracula is heard calling to wolves, which seem to answer 'from far and wide' (p.46), and he throws a child to be consumed by them. Five days later, Harker hears the howling of these 'allies' of Dracula, 'almost as if the sound sprang up at the raising of his hand, just as the music of a great orchestra seems to leap under the baton of the conductor' (p.49). The day after this, Harker discovers Dracula in his coffin with blood spilling from his mouth onto his chin and neck: 'he lay like a filthy leech, exhausted with his repletion' (p.51). Indeed, when in Whitby a bat is seen outside Lucy's window (p.89), we are left to infer its connection with the recently arrived Dracula. Much later in the novel, Mina Harker's journal records Van Helsing's explanation that the vampire 'can transform himself to wolf' and that 'he can be as bat' (p.223). He also has 'long, sharp, canine teeth' (p.24). All combine to create this 'monster' (p.51). It is a curious fact that most adaptations of the story pin down its protagonist to just one of these incarnations, as though the full range of shape-shifting in the original is too difficult to deal with.

More worrying than Dracula's bestiality, though, is the beast that he brings out in those around him. As Thomas Bilder, the hapless zookeeper, remarks: 'Mind you ... there's a deal of the same nature in us as in them there animiles' (p.128). It is not simply that Dracula infects those whom he bites, but that he transforms those who observe the changes that result. A startling example occurs when Van Helsing has Dr Seward and Arthur join him in a mission to decapitate Lucy.

The adventure is recounted in the diary of Dr Seward, who records that '[w]hen Lucy – I call the thing that was before us Lucy because it bore her shape – saw us she drew back with an angry snarl, such as a cat gives when taken unawares; then her eyes ranged over us'. The eyes are Lucy's 'in form and colour', but are 'unclean and full of hell-fire, instead of the pure, gentle orbs we knew'. On seeing them, writes Seward, 'the remnant of my love passed into hate and loathing; had she then to be killed, I could have done it with savage delight' (p.197). What alarms is not so much the manifestation of beastliness in the figure most closely associated with it, as the 'ordinary' person's capacity for brutal violence. This is true of many of the texts considered in the present volume. Seward's display of atavism is the more graphic for its contrast with his professional status (his social rank, but, more strikingly, his vocation: he has gone from caring and saving to an urge to kill). His conduct well illustrates what David Glover has written of Stoker's

> constant sense that the divide between the stable and the unstable is itself unstable, that the line cannot be held. Subjects and nations seem to oscillate between modernity and atavism, and no science of race or place quite promises to guarantee the former without the latter.[2]

The degree of instability is such that even the animal correspondences are in flux. We have seen how diverse are the bestial attributes of Dracula, but even the imagery applied to his victims is confused and contradictory. In the passage that I have just quoted, Lucy is described as snarling like a cat; later in the same paragraph, she throws to the ground a child whom she has been clutching and is heard 'growling over it as a dog growls over a bone' (p.197). We could, of course, dismiss this sudden shift from the feline to the canine as the result of a talentless writer's snatching at mixed metaphors. But it would be wrong or at least unhelpful to make such a judgement: the pervasiveness and range of animal similes are perfectly in keeping with the themes of the novel and with the cultural concerns that it addresses and reflects.

While *Dracula* shares with many contemporary texts a morbid fascination with degeneration and atavism marked by the assumption of animal characteristics, it does not settle for the straightforward correspondences that we find in several other works. In keeping with the malleability of its titular character, Stoker's book exhibits the same movement from substance to incorporeality that one observes at the end of *Heart of Darkness*. Dracula, knows Van Helsing, 'cannot flourish without this diet' of 'the blood of the living'. He throws no shadow; he make in the mirror no reflect ... He can come in mist which he create ... but ... the distance he can make this mist is limited, and it can only be round himself. He come on moonlight rays as elemental dust. (p.223)

He can 'become so small' that he can 'slip through a hair-breadth space at the tomb door'. He can, Van Helsing goes on, 'when once he find his way, come out from anything or into anything, no matter how close it be bound or even fused up with fire – solder you call it' (p.223). Van Helsing's broken English itself reinforces this sense of transmutation and dissolution; even the language of narration alters its shape. Such features point to the distinctiveness of *Dracula*, for this is a work in which the very form and structure of its narration bear the ambiguities and instabilities of its theme. David Punter is quite right to point to the formal inventiveness of the book.[3] Apart from Van Helsing's insecure command of English, there is, as many critics have observed, the mix of narrative voices: for example, Harker's journal, Mina Murray's journal, newspaper cuttings, Seward's diary kept on phonograph, letters between Mina and Lucy (some of them unopened), Lucy's diary, and other correspondence, including by telegram, and so on. Not only do these provide multiple perspectives, but they constantly interrupt one another. Each section is short. Many are incomplete. Authority is called into question by the plurality of accounts, but also by the differences in kind: they range from young women's letters to personal journals, from newspaper stories to scientific record. In the character of these sections, too, questions of authority are raised; in this case, of the relative weight of the past and present for '[t]hough alluding to the Gothic devices of lost manuscripts and letters, *Dracula*'s fragments are recorded in the most modern manner: by typewriter, in shorthand and on phonograph'.[4] We might take the latter as an antecedent of what Marina Warner describes as '[t]he ubiquitous electronic voice [that] has become domestic now, the everyday magic of hearing the voice of someone dead or faraway ... [one of the] powerful recent agents of literary metamorphoses'.[5] I shall have more to say about these and other signs of modernity later, but for now I want only to introduce the idea of movement and the struggle between past and present; the proposition that '[m]odernity's progress, threatened by Dracula throughout the novel, is not as secure as its explanations suggest'.[6] The insecurity is reflected in the multiple forms of Dracula as much as in the amorphism of the novel. Botting puts this well when, having described 'Dracula's crossing of boundaries [as] relentless', he writes that

> Dracula's threat is polymorphousness, both literally, in the shapes he assumes, and symbolically in terms of the distinctions he upsets ... Dracula's fluid, shifting and amorphous shape is ... threatening because it has no singular or stable nature or identity.[7]

We may then contradict Van Helsing's assertion that Dracula 'make in the mirror no reflect' and say that, on the contrary, despite his image not appearing in the mirror, he reflects the culture in and of which Stoker is writing.

The range of avatars has been noted by David Glover, who suggests that

> [t]he vampire stands at the threshold between the human and the subhuman and it is entirely appropriate that Dracula and his kind make their mark through their shifting affinities with a variety of nonhuman forms: wolves, lizards, bats, and dogs.

So if we substitute 'straddles' or 'crosses' for 'stands at', then Glover's remark seems quite acceptable. It is not meant as a criticism of Glover's book – which has many interesting things to say about race, politics, and nationalism in Stoker's work – to suggest that the significance of this variety of non-human forms eludes Glover's diagnosis. According to Glover, 'while the vampire's peculiarly perverse polymorphousness is the source of its resistance to representation, making it notoriously difficult to pin down ... its polymorphous perversity is what allows it to proliferate'.[8] Glover seems quickly propelled towards a postmodern view of this lack of definition and consequently misses some of what is really interesting about it. Noticing that 'in Stoker's imagination at least, Dracula's likeness cannot be captured either by painting or photography', Glover observes that

> the vampire continues to reproduce itself in a seemingly endless series of copies, always resourcefully different from previous incarnations, often revising the rules of the game in order to secure a new lease of life, without ever being fully laid to rest.[9]

These interminable metamorphoses contribute to the creature's mythic status. One can feel the temptation to slip into postmodern discourses of simulacra and elusiveness, difference and deferral, but to succumb would be to transport us away from the context of Stoker's writing (something that Glover commendably labours against throughout the rest of his book). The vampire does not resist representation. It encourages it. The assumption of so many forms – and sometimes of no form at all – is what characterises Dracula. The vampire is multiple in shape.

In so many of the texts contemporary with Stoker's novel, there is a relatively straightforward opposition between the human and bestial or the uncomplicated posing of an unanswerable question about where the animal ends and the human begins. *Dracula* is considerably more complex. David Punter judges that 'it belongs securely with *Jekyll and Hyde*, *Dorian Gray* and *The Island of Doctor Moreau*, while transcending all of them in its development of a symbolic structure in which to carry and deal with contradictions'.[10] A vital part of this symbolic structure is the multiplicity of images. In contrast to Stevenson's, Wilde's, and Wells's texts where the symbols are markers of opposites that cause disturbance when they meet, Stoker's narrative has the added confusion of features that dissolve. It does not rest at a simple forcing together of polarities with the predictable tensions, but shows through mutation that no position is fixed. The normal processes of self-construction against otherness do not work, because neither the self nor the other is stable. Unlike contemporary texts in which the civilised may go native, the civilised and the savage cohabit in both the city and pre-industrial worlds. Moreover, the civilised and the wild, the human and the animal, take on several different shapes.

Sometimes, of course, they are without shape. Indeed, one of the most interesting aspects of *Dracula* is the movement between the material and immaterial. Unlike Conrad and Wells, however, Stoker seems unwilling to seek refuge in the metaphysical. It is the material that triumphs. In *Heart of Darkness*, the wilderness enters the house of the Intended with Marlow and makes possible the novella's closing vision of eternal nature into which any specific frame must fit. The material, which stands for the commercial, is nullified and reabsorbed by nature. Conrad, I argue elsewhere, is quite deliberately undermining the power of Henry M. Stanley, making of this much-discussed text a more radical or at least a less complicit one than is very commonly supposed.[11] But Stoker goes even further. *Dracula* does not turn away from the actualities of modern capitalism; the narrative is packed with its signs.[12] What it does do is restore the supremacy of this material world, while leaving open the possibility of future threat. It is the faith in the material that leads to the narrative rejection of Dracula, but the appeal of the immaterial is so great and enduring that we must turn to the spiritual for confirmation. True, we are reminded by Van Helsing that '[o]ur enemy is not merely spiritual', and Van Helsing's warning here is that Dracula 'has the strength of twenty men' (p.232), but the reminder can serve without distortion as an image of the vampire's ability to cross over between nature and civilisation. The travels of, to, and from the vampire are vital to the novel's symbolic structure.

Many critics have recognised the significance of Jonathan Harker's statement at the start of his journal as he journeys through Europe towards Dracula's home: 'The impression I had was that we were leaving the West and entering the East' (p.5). The first border has been crossed. I shall not open up the cultural baggage of West and East here; it has already been thoroughly inspected by Said and those whom he has influenced.

In any event, Stoker reinforces his theme clearly enough. Harker is a newly qualified solicitor, who has been sent out to explain to Dracula the purchase of a London estate. This professional practitioner of the law has researched Transylvania in the British Museum and has 'read that every known superstition in the world is gathered into the horseshoe of the Carpathians, as if it were the centre of some sort of imaginative whirlpool'. Speculating that if this turns out to be the case, his 'stay may be very interesting', Harker soon has 'all sorts of queer dreams' (p.6). A dog howling under his window disturbs his night and prepares us for the range of animal imagery that will follow. After a night's stay at the Golden Krone Hotel, he is warned by his landlady, who learns of his destination and notes that it is the eve of St. George's Day, that 'all the evil things in the world will have full sway' (p.8). Seeing that Harker will not change his plans, she gives him a crucifix, which, Harker writes in his journal, 'as an English Churchman, I have been taught to regard … as in some measure idolatrous' (p.8), though he takes it nonetheless, so as not to alarm or seem rude to her. This is a critical stage in Harker's journey, as he moves from Western rationalism and the rule of law to the supernatural. Harker's crossing of the border happens both physically and symbolically. He has crossed both bodily (by train) and mentally or imaginatively (by dreams and superstition). Again, the border seems to be marked by linguistic disturbance (just as Van Helsing's broken English is the vehicle in which science and superstition ride together).[13] Here, the landlady who hysterically warns Harker not to go to Dracula's castle 'was in such an excited state that she seemed to have lost her grip of what German she knew, and mixed it all up with some other language which I did not know at all' (p.8). The disruption of language marks the territory where the supernatural and rational meet, and the fact or sensation of dreaming marks the cognitive alteration that results from this encounter. Thus when Harker stands at Dracula's door for the first time and states that '[i]t all seemed like a horrible nightmare to me' (p.18), he is expressing much more than a Gothic cliché. His impression is of exactly that mixture of the real and unreal, the rational and fantastic, which gives the book its meaning.

Inside Dracula's castle, Harker discovers the 'vast number of English books ... and bound volumes of magazines and newspapers' from which Dracula has taught himself about the language, society, and culture of England: 'The books were of the most varied kind – history, geography, politics, political economy, botany, geology, law – all relating to England and English life and customs and manners' (p.22). This passage is central to Stephen Arata's shrewd argument that Dracula's reading, which 'provides the groundwork for his exploitative invasion of Britain', is an Occidentalism that 'both mimics and reverses the more familiar Orientalism underwriting Western imperial practices'.[14] Like Glover, Arata stresses the Irish context:

> Dracula is to England as Ireland is to England, but, Dracula is to England as England is to Ireland. In Count Dracula, Victorian readers could recognize their culture's imperial ideology mirrored back as a kind of monstrosity.[15]

(The latter is precisely what Wells has the Martians do in *The War of the Worlds*, as we shall see in the next chapter.) Arata has brought out the importance of the travel motif in *Dracula*. He postulates that it has long been a popular ingredient of the Gothic and by highlighting the ideological elements of travel and disrupting Harker's 'tourist perspective at Castle Dracula', Stoker is calling 'into question the entire Orientalist outlook' and expressing 'a telling critique of the Orientalist enterprise through the very structure of his novel'.[16] Like Van Helsing and the fearful landlady, Dracula speaks in a broken tongue, as becomes increasingly apparent, the more he speaks of England. Describing the many hours of pleasure that his books have given him 'ever since I had the idea of going to London', he asserts that:

> Through them I have come to know your great England; and to know her is to love her. I long to go through the crowded streets of your mighty London, to be in the midst of the whirl and rush of humanity, to share its life, its change, its death, and all that makes it what it is. But alas! as yet I only know your tongue through books. To you, my friend, I look that I know it to speak. (p.22)

The word order of that last sentence reads somewhat awkwardly; in particular, the phrase 'that I know it to speak' suggests a non-native speaker. That impression is confirmed moments later when Dracula continues: 'But a stranger in a strange land, he is no one; men know him not – and to know not is to care not for' (p.23); and even more strongly by his asking Harker, a little later, to 'tell me when I make error, even of the smallest, in my speaking' (p.23). The sense of a middle territory between the known and unknown is as strongly present here as in the language spoken by Van Helsing and the landlady. Moreover, Dracula employs the idea of travel to communicate his progress in English: 'I fear that I am but a little way on the road I would travel. True, I know the grammar and the words, but yet I know not how to speak them' (p.22). In *Dracula*, travel figures both literally and metaphorically. Stoker emphasises his exploration of intermediate states by making those that occupy them indeterminate. Botting, Glover, and other critics have done much to show how contemporary developments in, and responses to, gender roles underlie the threatening shifts in *Dracula* and are, for the time being, settled by the novel's resolution. For example, Alexandra Warwick has proposed that

> [t]he threat that is offered by the de-feminized women is very different from that embodied by men. This is one of the 'dreadfulnesses' of vampirism; the revelation that gender categories are unstable, and a fear that sounded a profound echo in the culture of the 1890s, already shaken by such horrors as the trials of Oscar Wilde and the presence of the New Woman.[17]

Yet the challenges to class positions should not be understated either. Dracula's comment on being a stranger in a strange land has been noted above, but it is framed by him saying:

> Here I am noble; I am *boyar*; the common people know me, and I am master ...I have been so long master that I would be master still – or at least that none other should be master of me. (p.23)

To be an anonymous stranger, he says, is 'not enough for me' (p.23). The narrative attitude to authority is clearly ambivalent here. One can empathise with the fall from power (which was the fate of many members of the British aristocracy during this period), while one recoils from the insatiable taste for it, just as the middle classes (like those represented by Harker and his companions) reacted against their exploitation by those who would suck their blood.

Class and gender cannot be separated when considering the question of authority in the text, though the aim of the discussion that follows is to recover the former. When Dracula momentarily addresses Harker as 'Harker Jonathan', he quickly apologises for his mistake, explaining: 'I fall into my country's habit of putting your patronymic first' (p.25). The effect of this inversion and apology for it is to make the patriarchal nomenclature seem archaic. It distances Britain's social organisation from that of Dracula's country. As Dracula has said shortly before this: 'We are in Transylvania; and Transylvania is not England. Our ways are not your ways, and there shall be to you many strange things' (p.23). What happens is that Transylvanian society seems old-fashioned – the patronym is synecdochical of other customs, with the image of the outmoded concentrated in Dracula himself. The text presents to its British readers the feudal as decaying, and there is hardly any more appropriate literary form in which to do this than the Gothic, with its crumbling castles,[18] its empty chambers, its plain, middle-class protagonists,[19] and its aestheticising of the ruined edifices of a once-solid social structure. In part, there is something of the middle-class farewell to the aristocracy in all this, but the temporal detachment can also work more conservatively, relying on self-satisfaction with the progress that has been made. British readers may assure themselves that feudalism has passed away, but their very contentment with this might mask their resistance against further change (notably against that posed by the New Woman). *Dracula* enacts a social tension as the seemingly dead are brought back to life, apparently to be dispatched again.

For all the text's and its critics' protestations that Dracula casts no reflection, the Count's situation reflects the predicament of the British aristocracy with great clarity: 'I myself am of an old family', he says, 'and to live in a new house would kill me' (p.26). Accordingly, Harker has found an old estate at Purfleet for him to purchase, situated 'on a by-road' (p.25) – that is, off the beaten track. The house, which is 'very large', is, says Harker, 'of all periods back' probably 'to mediaeval times' (p.25). The place 'is surrounded by a high wall, of ancient structure, built of heavy stones, and has not been repaired for a large number of years'. The old oak and iron gates are 'eaten with rust' and even the 'for sale' notice is 'dilapidated' (p.25), as if it will not enter the new, commercial age. Intriguingly, the very name of the estate repeats the motif of a language that has shifted and whose altered state signifies the unsettled condition of its bearer. The estate's name, Harker tells his host, is 'Carfax, no doubt a corruption of the old *Quatre Face*, as the house is four-sided, agreeing with the cardinal points of the compass' (p.25). Language has slipped. The old name has been modified, just as its new occupant will bring it and himself into the new world – a world whose advancements are illustrated by the object that Harker carried with him: a Kodak. Stoker's metonymic use of the brand name as generic – he does not simply write 'camera' – sharpens the impact of the modern. Of the portion of the house that 'looks like part of a keep', Harker has 'taken with my Kodak views of it from various points', for 'I could not enter it, as I had not the key of the door leading to it from the house' (p.25). This area, which Harker cannot access, is the oldest part of the building. Once again, Harker's failure to examine more than its exterior demonstrates the worrying inability of the past and present to accommodate each other. Near to the house, as if to emphasise the consequences of not achieving the right balance, is 'a private lunatic asylum' (p.25). This struggle to incorporate the past and present is largely what the novel is about. The genre of the Gothic is perfectly suited to it, being 'a thoroughly modern genre', but also 'a repository for everything modernity hoped it had left behind', such as 'feudal tyrants, arbitrary rule, cruel punishment, corrupt monks, menaced virgins, and peasants cowering in superstition'.[20]

Although the house can be interpreted as a symbol of one's identity, to privilege psychoanalytic readings of *Dracula* is to risk conspiring with the narrative's conservative way out of the problems that it raises. The novel is less about the commingling of universal desires and fears than it is about the specific situation of the middle classes and aristocracy in the 1890s. Just because the text tries clumsily to resolve these particular problems through blatant recourse to a supernatural immensity does not mean that critics should follow suit. When Dracula tells Harker that '[w]e Transylvanian nobles love not to think that our bones may be amongst the common dead' (p.26), it is a sentiment that is as anachronistic as he who feels it. Such aversion to a democratic repose is disagreeable to Stoker. Harker, too, turns against it once he realises that the Count's 'castle is a veritable prison, and I am a prisoner!' (p.28).

Unwarranted subservience to another is also signalled in Renfield's obeisance to Dracula, whom he calls 'the Master' (p.95). Of course, the Count's supernatural powers are great enough for Renfield to have little choice other than to obey him, but when he 'sniff[s] about as a dog does when setting' (p.95), eats flies (p.109) and birds (p.68), and 'lick[s] up, like a dog' the blood that he has drawn from Seward's wrist by stabbing him (p.132), then the extent of his humiliation is sufficient to suggest that no one should exercise the degree of power that Dracula possesses. In Seward's record of Renfield's illness, however, democratic movement seems to be delimited. Suspecting, as does his attendant, that their patient is suffering from 'some sudden form of religious mania' (p.95), Seward writes in his diary – in what reads like a complaint – that '[h]is [Renfield's] attitude to me was the same as that to the attendant; in his sublime self-feeling the difference between myself and attendant seemed to him as nothing' (pp.95–96).

Unlike most of the texts discussed in the previous chapter, but like Mary Shelley's *Frankenstein*, *Dracula* has survived its era and, like *Frankenstein*, its political elements have largely been exorcised. Fittingly, the story of Dracula is one that has been 'freely adapted into a myriad different forms'.[21] Even by the end of the twentieth century, there had been '[a]round 3,000 vampire or vampire-related films … made so far, and … it seems safe to say that their differences are often more striking than their similarities'.[22] Van Helsing spoke more truly than he knew when he revealed that '[t]he vampire live on, and cannot die by mere passing of the time' (p.222). Yet Dracula's longevity, like Jekyll and Hyde's, has been achieved at the cost of his original habitat: the social and economic factors that moulded him. As Luckhurst remarks with *The Strange Case of Dr. Jekyll and Mr. Hyde* in mind,

> [t]he endless retellings in theatre, film, and television, the constant stream of rewritings and updating, all take us further away from the original until it lies forgotten under the rubble of its imitators.[23]

Dracula was conceived by Stoker in what Luckhurst described as 'an era of modernizing ancient systems'. Stoker himself, who followed his father into the Civil Service, 'was part of this professionalization'.[24] Through his theatre connections, reviewing, and, in particular, his contact with Shakespearean actor Henry Irving, who would invite him to become his business manager at the Lyceum Theatre in London, where he remained as manager from 1878 to 1898, Stoker 'utterly transformed his life'.[25] He also transformed the Gothic, having 'borrowed some of the formal innovations of the … genre' and 'reanimated and redirected [its] tropes to address the burning issues of the day'.[26] Indeed, hailing *Dracula*'s 'fusion of the fake rediscovered manuscript of Gothic convention with the absolutely contemporary world of technological transcription by shorthand, typewriter, telegram, and phonograph', Luckhurst observes that '[t]he text rattles along at the same speed as the *Orient Express*, chasing not only the ancient beast but its own modernity'.[27]

'Oriental to the finger-tips': *The Beetle*

Richard Marsh's *The Beetle* was published in the same year as *Dracula*, but its serialisation began three months before Stoker's novel appeared.

More popular than Stoker's work at the time, but much less familiar than it now, Marsh's book was in its fifteenth printing in 1913, compared with *Dracula*'s tenth.[28] *The Beetle* has much in common with *Dracula*: it is a type of invasion narrative that exhibits reverse colonisation from the East; it is overtly sexual, combining the exotic with the erotic; it has multiple narrators; and class is crucial, as the body politic struggles to expel the alien from its midst.

Since the story is not so well-known, I shall briefly summarise it here. It concerns the arrival in London of a sexually indeterminate worshipper of Isis seeking revenge on politician and future statesman Paul Lessingham. Twenty years previously, while spending time abroad at the age of eighteen, having decided that 'I should learn more from travel than from sojourn at a university' (p.192), Lessingham was seduced and drugged one night in the native quarter of Cairo by a young woman who sang in many languages and whose eyes 'had on me a diabolical effect. They robbed me of my consciousness, of my power of volition, of my capacity to think, – they made me as wax in her hands' (p.194). The 'Woman of the Songs', one of the 'children of Isis',

> wooed my mouth with kisses. I cannot describe to you the sense of horror and of loathing with which the contact of her lips oppressed me. There was about her something so unnatural, so inhuman, that I believe even then I could have destroyed her with as little sense of moral turpitude as if she had been some noxious insect. (p.195)

Lessingham cannot be sure what really occurred and how much he imagined:

> The happenings were of such an incredible character, and my condition was such an abnormal one, – I was never really myself from the first moment to the last – that I have hesitated, and still do hesitate, to assert where, precisely, fiction ended and fact began. (p.196)

The sense of his being caught up in the blurring of boundaries is heightened by his disclosure that he wondered 'if I had crossed the border line which divides madness from sanity' (p.196). Lessingham's confused and liminal state is characteristic of the genre in which his condition is related. Gothic fiction, as Roger Luckhurst observes, 'mixe[s] up categories of life and death, past and present, reason and fancy, wakefulness and dream'.[29] Marsh's novel depends, even more than Stoker's, on the juxtaposition of the fantastic and the real.

Lessingham was held for more than two months in that 'horrible den', scene of 'religious services' in honour of the beetle, which were 'orgies of nameless horrors' (p.197). Unless he suffered from mirages, he was witness to the sacrifice of naked women (including an Englishwoman), who were 'subjected ... to every variety of outrage of which even the minds of demons could conceive' and then burned alive and their ashes consumed (p.197). When one day he finds that the mesmeric power that the woman holds over him has slipped, he is able to throttle her, until

> [o]n a sudden, I felt her slipping from my fingers. Without the slightest warning, in an instant she had vanished, and where, not a moment before, she herself had been, I found myself confronting a monstrous beetle, – a huge, writhing creation of some wild nightmare. (p.199)

The creature dwindles as he stares at it, and he flees.

Lessingham's fiancée is Marjorie Lindon. She is loved by scientist Sidney Atherton, who is hostile towards Lessingham as a result. Marjorie's father is a rich Tory with a sense of his family's importance; Lessingham is on the opposite side of the House and, in Atherton's view, is a Radical. Lessingham first set her pulse racing when she read in the *Times* a report of his speech on the Eight Hours' Bill. The creature kidnaps Marjorie, whom it apparently intends to transport to Egypt for sacrifice. Investigator Augustus Champnell helps track down the creature, who kills unemployed clerk Robert Holt and escapes or dies (its fate is left open) in a train accident in which Marjorie is seriously injured. Marjorie eventually recovers to marry Lessingham (whose real name is concealed by the text in order to reveal his identity, since he and she are now well-known).

The novel is divided into four books. Each is told in the first person and has a different narrator, though we learn at the end that the first book – 'The Surprising Narration of Robert Holt' – was compiled from statements made by Holt to Atherton and Marjorie Lindon. Book II is by Atherton; Book III is told by Marjorie Lindon; Book IV is from the casebook of 'Confidential Agent', the Hon. Augustus Champnell.

Holt's narrative describes his adventures after he has been refused lodging for the night in the casual ward at Hammersmith workhouse. His condition at once reflects the larger state of society. He is now homeless, penniless, friendless, and suffering the ignominy of being turned away from the first casual ward he has approached. He has had only water to drink and a crust of bread to eat over the past three days. Since Holt is newly forced into tramping, we should not be too distracted from the importance of his social transformation by the more fantastic metamorphosis that follows. As Victoria Margree recognises, 'one of the many anxieties with which the novel engages has to do with the changing nature of the social fabric of Britain, especially as this is experienced in urban areas'.[30]

Holt recounts how when he walked away from the workhouse, '[i]n the darkness and the rain, the locality which I was entering appeared unfinished. I seemed to be leaving civilisation behind me' (p.6). He means, on the surface, that he has found an urban wasteland:

> The path was unpaved; the road rough and uneven, as if it had never been properly made. Houses were few and far between. Those which I did encounter, seemed, in the imperfect light, amid the general desolation, to be cottages which were crumbling to decay. (p.6)

Beneath this picture of urban degeneration, it is obvious that a moral wilderness is being drawn. Such a suggestion would be familiar to readers of texts on East End life, but Holt's exit from civilisation marks an entry into the fantastic, so that it is not only social worlds, but artistic realms that are being swapped as well. Their juxtaposition seems typically Wellsian.

In the barren landscape Holt discovers a house on its own. It is detached and twenty or thirty yards away from its nearest neighbour on either side. 'It was one of those so-called villas which are springing up in multitudes all round London, and which are let at rentals of from twenty-five to forty pounds a year' (p.7). It is later described as 'a tumbledown cheap "villa" in an unfinished cheap neighbourhood, – the whole place a living monument of the defeat of the speculative builder' (p.213). At its back there is no yard, garden, or fence, nothing 'to shut off the house from the wilderness of waste land' (p.214). Holt climbs into a downstairs room through an open window, but inside feels an evil presence watching him. In the darkness, he perceives a creature's eyes advancing towards him, quite low down on the floor. The creature reaches his boots and

> with a sense of shrinking, horror, nausea, rendering me momentarily more helpless, I realised that [it] was beginning to ascend my legs, to climb my body. ... It was as though it were some gigantic spider, – a spider of the nightmares; a monstrous conception of some dreadful vision. It pressed lightly against my clothing with what might, for all the world, have been spider's legs. There was an amazing host of them, – I felt the pressure of each separate one. They embraced me softly, stickily, as if the creature glued and unglued them, each time it moved.
>
> Higher and higher! It had gained my loins. It was moving towards the pit of my stomach. The helplessness with which I suffered its invasion was

not the least part of my agony, – it was that helplessness which we know in dreadful dreams …

…

… It reached my chin, it touched my lips, – and I stood still and bore it all, while it enveloped my face with its huge slimy, evil-smelling body, and embraced me with its myriad legs. (pp.11–12)

At that point, Holt is able to shake the creature off and he runs, shrieking, to the window. A light is struck behind him.

Later in the novel, there will be repeated questions about the sex of the creature, but in passages like the one that I have just quoted there seems to be a heavy air of homosexual rape. It is later disclosed that Holt's assailant is female, but that is not apparent at the time and remains uncertain at various stages. What the assault has in common with *Dracula* is the undefinability of the attacker. Holt is unaware of the identity of his violator. It is not just that he cannot see it clearly, but that it is outside his knowledge and experience. It is strange and cannot be categorised.

Another feature shared with Dracula is its connection with the unEnglish. The person who has struck the light behind Holt is a 'foreigner' and has a 'malicious' voice (p.13). There is also what one may read as a sign of Jewishness (as there is in *Dracula*): 'The nose … was abnormally large; so extravagant were its dimensions, and so peculiar its shape, it resembled the beak of some bird of prey' (p.14). Curiously, the nose becomes less grotesque two chapters later when its owner's face changes and becomes younger-looking. But the alteration comes too late to prevent one's detection of an affinity with the anti-Semitism of other texts of the decade, including *Dracula* and *Dorian Gray*. When Holt sees this person lying in a bed, he had rather he had left it 'unseen' (p.13). Holt cannot determine its gender and '[i]ndeed at first I doubted if it was anything human'. His decision that it must be a man seems to be made without foundation other than an untenable belief in gendered qualities and conduct: 'afterwards, I knew it to be man, – for this reason, if for no other, that it was impossible such a creature could be feminine' (p.13). His conclusion is not supported by the other characters in the novel or by the narrative itself. The foreigner's gender remains ambiguous.

In the presence of this being, Holt experiences an unmanning in a number of senses. First, he turns round, 'mechanically, like an automaton'. Second, although resenting it 'with secret rage', he is rendered 'invertebrate' (p.13). Third, though this becomes more apparent later, the foreigner's sexual identity renders Holt's own uncertain in relation to it.

This last point is made more explicit after the creature on the bed has spoken to him. In response to its questions, Holt utters words that come not from his own willpower, but from the creature's:

> What he willed that I should say, I said. Just that, and nothing more. For the first time I was no longer a man; my manhood was merged in his. I was, in the extremest sense, an example of passive obedience. (p.14)

The thing to which Holt is forced to submit is, like Dracula, ageless:

> His age I could not guess; such a look I had never imagined. Had he asserted that he had been living through the ages, I should have been forced to admit that, at least, he looked it. And yet I felt that it was quite within the range of possibility that he was no older than myself, – there was a vitality in his eyes which was startling. It might have been that he had been afflicted by some terrible disease, and it was that which had made him so supernaturally ugly. (pp.13–14)

So, this ancient is both beyond and within the age. He (if he it be) is of, and outside, the place. The suggestion of disease combines physical with moral and spiritual malady. It spreads into the contemporary discourses of degeneration – an impression heightened by the observation that the foreigner seems inhuman – '[t]he cranium, and, indeed, the whole skull, was so small as to be disagreeably suggestive of something animal' (p.14) – and the apparent absence of a chin – the face seems to stop at the mouth, with its 'blubber lips' – creates a deformity that gives the face an 'appearance of something not human'. The eyes, which leave Holt 'enchained, helpless, spell-bound', have 'the bird-like trick of never blinking' (p.14).

Holt's fantastic encounter with the strange creature would not have happened were it not for his unemployment. He has, after all, undergone a transformation himself. When the foreigner asks him 'What are you?' and Holt replies, 'A clerk', his interrogator bites back: 'You look as if you were a clerk' (p.14). (This is followed by the question: 'What sort of clerk are you?'; the reply: 'I am out of a situation'; the scornful response: 'You look as if you were out of a situation'; and the charge that he is a thief, having broken into the house [pp.14–15].) This sharp exchange reveals the knowledge that one is identified with one's job or profession. Without work, one loses one's identity. Holt explains how he came to this end. He swears that he was the victim only of bad luck:

> Misfortune had followed hard upon misfortune. The firm by whom I had been employed for years suspended payment. I obtained a situation with one of their creditors, at a lower salary. They reduced their staff, which entailed

> my going. After an interval I obtained a temporary engagement; the occasion which required my services passed, and I with it. After another, and a longer interval, I again found temporary employment, the pay for which was but a pittance. When that was over I could find nothing. (p.15)

That was nine months ago. Since then, he has not earned any money at all. He has tramped through London in a vain search for work. It is to us that Holt recounts these events. To his questioner he says nothing, though he suspects that the foreigner might have 'read my story, unspoken though it was'. Of course, if Holt is suppressing this account because 'I did not know what it was he wished me to say', he is also suppressing the real reason for his 'descent' (p.15). That reason must be the economic conditions that have led to the financial difficulties of his employers. Holt's attribution of his fall to mere ill fortune ignores these structural difficulties, just as capitalism encourages us to take a person's standing as proof of their personal qualities. (I concede that Holt's insistence that bad luck is solely to blame for his parlous state could be taken as an overemphatic denial of any other cause and so may lead us to speculate about his own culpability. Perhaps he has been guilty of misdemeanours that have cost him his employment, but we can do no more than surmise. Nor should we take his intrusion into the creature's house as evidence of a propensity to thieve: the window was open, the house seemed empty, and he was merely seeking shelter from the heavy rain for the night. In any case, we have already seen from other sources that not only was this an age of unemployment, it was the very period that gave rise to the term.)

It is important to bear in mind the text's – and Holt's – rootedness in specific economic conditions when we survey the more fantastic elements of the narrative. Even more explicitly than in *Dracula*, 'race' informs the description of the conflict between the alien threat and the Londoners who fall victim to it. This is especially so in a scene that astonishes with frank overtones of (male) homosexuality. It occurs straight after Holt has told us (but not voiced to his questioner) the history of his slide into unemployment. The ageless man instructs him bluntly to 'Undress!' (p.15)

> When he spoke again that was what he said, in those guttural tones of his in which there was a reminiscence of some foreign land. I obeyed, letting my sodden, shabby clothes fall anyhow upon the floor. A look came on his face, as I stood naked in front of him, which, if it was meant for a smile, was a satyr's smile, and which filled me with a sensation of shuddering repulsion.
> 'What a white skin you have, – how white! What would I not give for a skin as white as that, – ah yes!' He paused, devouring me with his glances;

then continued. 'Go to the cupboard; you will find a cloak; put it on.' (pp.15–16)

The foreigner then commands him to take food and drink, which he does, 'cramming myself, I believe, like some famished wolf', after which 'that satyr's grin' returns to his instructor's face (p.16). Even without the allusion to the satyr, the reference to homosexuality would be obvious. With it, the 'foreign land' of which the strange voice is reminiscent assumes a (homo)sexual identity.

At the climax of this (third) chapter, an implied homosexual act leaves Holt prone and helpless:

> I looked him in the face, – and immediately became conscious, as I did so, that something was going from me, – the capacity, as it were, to be myself. His eyes grew larger and larger, till they seemed to fill all space – till I became lost in their immensity. He moved his hand, doing something to me, I know not what, as it passed through the air – cutting the solid ground from underneath my feet, so that I fell headlong to the ground. Where I fell, there I lay, like a log. (p.16)

The aftermath of the act is rendered clearly in the following chapter, where animal imagery is deployed to convey Holt's self-disgust. His coercer throws off Holt's covering, leaving him naked once again, and prods him with his fingers, 'as if I had been some beast ready for the butcher's stall' (pp.17–18). And then

> whether I was dead or living, I said to myself that this could be nothing human, – nothing fashioned in God's image could wear such a shape as that. Fingers were pressed into my cheeks, they were thrust into my mouth, they touched my staring eyes, shut my eyelids, then opened them again, and – horror of horror! – the blubber lips were pressed to mine – the soul of something evil entered into me in the guise of a kiss. (p.18)

The homosexual inspection and invasion of Holt provokes feelings of loathing. If we isolate the last clause from the above quotation, the connotation of homosexual desire and revulsion can be seen even more directly. If that were not enough, Holt's description of the person who has felt, prodded, and kissed him as 'this travesty of manhood' makes it almost explicit (p.18). Spoken two years after the trials of Oscar Wilde, the words then uttered by the active partner – 'Dead! – dead! – as good as dead! – and better! We'll have him buried' (p.18) – speak of a social and moral demise as much as a physical one. Holt's uncertainty about whether the sentiment is directed at him or at the person who voices it adds to the sense of shame, corruption, and denial.

The next day there seems to be a repetition of the episode. It is presented as the placing of a hypnotic spell on Holt, but the way in which it is done – with a hand-gesture – and the stirring to life of a previously quiescent Holt portend another bout of homosexual activity:

> He made a movement with his hand, and, directly he did so, it happened as on the previous evening, that a metamorphosis took place in the very abysses of my being. I woke from my torpor, as he put it, I came out of death, and was alive again. I was far, yet, from being my own man; I realised that he exercised on me a degree of mesmeric force which I had never dreamed that one creature could exercise on another; but, at least, I was no longer in doubt as to whether I was or was not dead. I knew I was alive. (p.23)

Holt's metamorphosis is undoubtedly sexual in nature. Even the narrative of hypnosis carries this meaning, being suggested in terms that are both sexual and racial, communicating ideas of submission and inferiority as he is told by the one who has awakened him: 'you are my slave, – at my beck and call, – my familiar spirit, to do with as I will, – you know this, – eh?' And Holt confirms his low position: 'I did know it' (p.23).

It is not only Holt who has undergone a profound alteration or whose change involves a moral judgement. Seeing the man in the bed in the morning, Holt finds him younger, his nose less grotesque, his skin still yellow, but his contours rounded, in possession of a chin, and 'the most astounding novelty' of all

> was that about the face there was something which was essentially feminine; so feminine, indeed, that I wondered if I could by any possibility have blundered, and mistaken a woman for a man; some ghoulish example of her sex, who had so yielded to her depraved instincts as to have become nothing but a ghastly reminiscence of womanhood. (p.22)

Apart from the ambiguity of gender, there is here an unmistakeable condemnation of women's sexuality. Women, the text appears to be saying, ought not to have or exhibit active sexual appetites. Somehow, the deeds to which Holt has been, and will further be, subjected are even more depraved if committed by a woman.

After the person of indeterminate sex has made a slave of Holt, he (I shall call him 'he' as the text continues, for the time being, to refer to him as such) commands him to break into the home of Lessingham. Now it is the body politic, in the form of Lessingham, that is threatened or, more accurately, part of the body politic, since Lessingham will later be represented as himself constituting a threat to the established order in the shape of a traditional – indeed, anachronistic – MP, Lindon.

Lessingham's background is a mystery. He represents a new force in politics: one in which one's forebears are irrelevant. But like some of his celebrated real-life counterparts, Lessingham is a politician with a past; one that will be disclosed to us later.

Holt's tormentor observes tenderly that Lessingham is good to look at: 'He is straight, – straight as the mast of a ship, – he is tall, – his skin is white; he is strong … how strong! – oh yes!' He then gives way to envy and becomes momentarily 'transfigured' by a look of 'savage, frantic longing' (p.25). He accuses Lessingham of being the devil, of falseness and treachery, and promises that the day of vengeance will come. When he tells Holt that he will show him Lessingham's house, '[t]here was about his manner something hardly human; something which, for want of a better phrase, I would call vulpine' (p.26). The man instructs Holt that if Lessingham should discover and obstruct him, he must utter the words: 'THE BEETLE!' As the man speaks these words, the room falls into darkness and Holt feels again the evil presence of the previous night:

> Two bright specks gleamed in front of me; something flopped from off the bed on to the ground; the thing was coming towards me across the floor. It came slowly on, and on, and on. I stood still, speechless in the sickness of my horror. Until, on my bare feet, it touched me with slimy feelers, and my terror lest it should creep up my naked body lent me voice, and I fell shrieking like a soul in agony. (p.28)

The creature retreats, the lamp is illuminated again, and the man lying in bed repeats that he should speak those words if interrupted by Lessingham and that twice will suffice.

Outside the house occupied by the foreigner, Holt realises that '[m]y condition was one of dual personality, – while, physically, I was bound, mentally, to a considerable extent, I was free' (p.30). If the causes of his predicament are unique, his symptoms are not, for we have seen that the split personality is something that afflicts a number of his contemporaries.

Directed by his malevolent guide, Holt beaks into Lessingham's house, study, and bureau, which later he shoots open with a revolver that he has found in the room (leading him to observe that '[s]tatesmen, nowadays, sometimes stand in actual peril of their lives' [p.34]). As Holt grabs a bundle of letters from the drawer he has forced open, Lessingham enters. When Lessingham advances toward him, asking him to hand over the revolver, Holt finds that 'something entered into me, and forced itself from between my lips, so that I said, in a low, hissing voice, which I vow was never mine, "THE BEETLE!"' (pp.36–37). It seems to Holt that the room turns to darkness and evil is present. Lessingham – the normally unflappable statesman – cowers against his bookshelves, transformed. In Holt's words:

> A most extraordinary change had taken place in the expression of his face; in his countenance amazement, fear, and horror seemed struggling for the mastery. I was filled with a most discomforting qualm, as I gazed at the frightened figure in front of me, and realised that it was that of the great Paul Lessingham, the god of my political idolatry. (p.37)

Lessingham's repeated command to Holt to reveal his identity is made in a voice that 'seemed changed; his frenzied, choking accents would hardly have been recognised by either friend or foe' (p.37). He guesses that his intruder is associated with a house in the Rue de Rabagas in Cairo (about which we will learn more later). He attempts to dismiss his time there as 'one of mirage, of delusion, of disease. I was in a condition, mentally and bodily, in which pranks could have been played upon me by any trickster. Such pranks were played. I know that now quite well' (p.38). Driven increasingly anxious and agitated by Holt's continued (forced) silence, Lessingham loses his temper. His discomposure, and the events that have caused it, suggest blackmail. We can hardly infer anything else from his telling Holt: 'Come, I see that you suppose my intentions to be harsher than they really are, – do not let us have a scandal, and a scene, – be sensible! – give me those letters!' (p.41). In a period when political ruin and personal disgrace coincided not infrequently, Lessingham's situation would have readily been identified by readers with some of his celebrated contemporaries. Indeed, Vuohelainen refers to later speculation that Marsh himself 'may have been involved in a financial or sexual disgrace of some kind'.[31] The supernatural elements of the tale do not detract from the immediate political and social setting. At the end of this chapter, Lessingham and some of his servants rush Holt, who repeats the words 'THE BEETLE!' (p.42). The room is filled with darkness and screams. Horror has come into it, and Holt exits, propelled by he knows not what.

Holt returns, or is returned, to his tormentor's room, to 'that chamber of my humiliation and my shame'. He feels again the presence of evil and it is 'as if I had been taken out of the corporeal body to be plunged into the inner chambers of all nameless sin' (p.45). Something flops from the bed and comes at him. Holt screams (screams that he seems to hear sometimes even now, he tells us in a Wellsian aside), and the creature slips and slides back across the floor. The lamp is lit again, and he is stared at by the man on the bed – 'the dreadful cause of all my agonies' (p.45).

Again, that person is hard to place sexually. He asks Holt: '"Are you not well? Is it not sweet to stand close at my side? You, with your white skin, if I were a woman, would you not take me for a wife?"' (p.46). That last question suggests quite strongly that gender identity is both nothing and everything; that a bond exists – whether by force or by desire – and that which is frowned upon by society because it is same-sex would not matter to the participants were it not for society's disapproval. Holt appears to have been an unwilling participant in this relationship and to have been terrorised into and by it, but the instruments of his subjection have been supernatural horror (the beetle) and hypnotic influence, while the causes that are given for his terror seem code for social unacceptability. Both elements are present in a key homosexual text of the previous decade – the anonymous, privately printed novel *Teleny*, published in 1883. In that novel, the narrator, Camille Des Grieux, remarks that 'nothing renders people so superstitious as vice'.[32] The comment carries more significance than its almost casual utterance would indicate, for those who engage in vice are obliged to mask their activities, both physically and linguistically, by employing a kind of code. Operating thus outside the 'normal' conventions, their behaviour and relationships are sometimes communicated and explained via supernatural attraction. For example, the homosexual love that Des Grieux feels for (and practises with) the pianist Teleny is accompanied by a telepathic, mesmeric understanding. Of course, this phenomenon is not unique to homosexual relationships, and the interest in hypnosis, mesmerism, and the occult was widespread and growing at the close of the nineteenth century, but its presence in *Teleny* does establish a connection with *The Beetle* – a connection that, if not intentional, is no less important and, indeed, strengthens the possibility of a reading of Holt's experiences as an initiation into homosexuality. That link is reinforced even further by a common presence of domination and submission.

When Holt's oppressive partner asks him if he would take him if he were a woman, Holt thinks:

> There was something about the manner in which this was said which was so essentially feminine that once more I wondered if I could possibly be mistaken in the creature's sex. I would have given much to have been able to strike him across the face, – or, better, to have taken him by the neck, and thrown him through the window, and rolled him in the mud. (p.46)

Holt cannot physically harm him, because he cannot be sure that he is not a woman.

The man takes Lessingham's letters from Holt and, seeing that they are love letters from Marjorie Lindon, becomes so angry that Holt tells us: 'Never did I suppose that rage could have so possessed a human countenance' (p.47). His 'yellow fangs' show through his parted lips and, while he reads, 'he kept emitting sounds, more resembling yelps and snarls than anything more human, – like some savage beast nursing its pent-up rage' (p.48).

In his 'demoniac' hatred (p.48), the man curses Lessingham and Marjorie Lindon. He then turns his fury against Holt – the 'thief' – and attacks him in a way that implies male rape: 'He leaped, shrieking, off the bed, and sprang at me, clasping my throat with his horrid hands, bearing me backwards on to the floor; I felt his breath mingle with mine and then God, in His mercy, sent oblivion' (p.48).

The next, second, book of *The Beetle* is narrated by inventor and scientist Sydney Atherton (currently experimenting with ingredients for chemical warfare – 'legalised murder' [p.61]), who has declared his love to Marjorie Lindon, only to be told, in confidence, that she is engaged to Paul Lessingham. Her request to Atherton that he support her against the objections that her father will have makes him uncomfortable. Atherton's antipathy to Lessingham is clear and will become more so. He is the one, we will soon learn, who momentarily apprehends Holt as the latter flees Lessingham's house, saying: 'Is that the way to come slithering down the Apostle's pillar? – Is it simple burglary, or simpler murder? – Tell me the glad tidings that you've killed St Paul, and I'll let you go' (p.44). Although Atherton's venom has been made more potent by his jealousy, the names that he sarcastically gives to Lessingham communicate the opposition and subversion of values in this novel. Markers of Christian morality are used abusively.

Another opposition is established in Atherton's narrative: a political one. Marjorie Lindon's father sits on the other side of the House from Lessingham, has 'high-dried Tory notions of his family importance', and a fortune (p.52). Lessingham is a Radical and the differences between him and Lindon reflect the increasingly profound divide between older and newer political and social forces. Along with the Gothic elements of this novel, there is a critical inspection of Lessingham's credentials. Marriage to Marjorie may potentially be a way of reconciling antagonistic camps, but the appearance of the Arab and Atherton's determination to investigate Lessingham's past and the cause of his fear – whether his motives be to reassure himself that Marjorie is not in danger or hope that the match can be broken, leaving the way open for him to marry her – allow an examination of the Radical as statesman, as well as an inquiry into the relevance of the relationship between private and public faces.

In his laboratory, Atherton receives a visit from the Arab in a scene that sets up a conflict between different ways of knowing the world: the scientific and the supernatural or magical. The Arab seems to have gained admittance by hypnotising Atherton's servant, Edwards. Once Atherton removes his (own) protective mask, an image nicely paralleled in the Arab's brushing aside of 'the hanging folds of the hood of his burnoose', he sees more of his visitor's face:

> I was immediately conscious that in his eyes there was, in an especial degree, what, for want of a better term, one may call the mesmeric quality. That his was one of those morbid organisations which are oftener found, thank goodness, in the east than in the west, and which are apt to exercise an uncanny influence over the weak and the foolish folk with whom they come in contact … I was, also, conscious that he was taking advantage of the removal of my mask to try his strength on me, – than which he could not have found a tougher job. The sensitive something which is found in the hypnotic subject happens, in me, to be wholly absent. (p.64)

Atherton's scepticism sets up a confrontation between Western science and Eastern magic. He tells the Arab, whom he sees is a mesmerist, that as a scientist he would like to conduct an experiment or two on him. Backing away, the Arab, who has retorted, 'I am nothing, – a shadow!', has in his eyes a 'gleam … which suggested that he possessed his hideous power to an unusual degree, – that, in the estimation of his own people, he was qualified to take his standing as a regular devil-doctor' (p.64).

The tension between reason and superstition, West and East, intensifies with Atherton's blunt remarks to his visitor:

> 'And, once more, sir, who are you?'
> 'I am of the children of Isis!'
> 'Is that so? – It occurs to me that you have made a slight mistake, – this is London, not a dog-hole in the desert.' (p.64)

The purpose of the Arab's visit has been to tell Atherton that he can help him destroy Lessingham, thus making sure that Marjorie will not marry him.

Straight after the visitor's disappearance, Lessingham calls on Atherton, who wonders at Lessingham's entitlement to be called a gentleman. His doubts may be inspired by jealousy of Marjorie's love for Lessingham, but they are also part of the wider questioning – often self-questioning – concerning the aptness of the title. Atherton notes to himself that Lessingham is

> a man of position, – destined, probably, to rise much higher; a man of parts, – with capacity to make the most of them; not ill-looking; with agreeable manners, – when he chose; and he came within the lady's definition of a gentleman ... And yet–! Well, I take it that we are all cads, and that we most of us are prigs; for mercy's sake do not let us all give ourselves away. (pp.67–68)

If there seems to be a sneer here at the inadequacy of women's definition of a gentleman, there is also an acknowledgement of men's general failure to *be* gentlemen, unless there is understood to be in that condition a disparity between reality and appearance. Certainly, the fact of this, or worry that it *is* a fact, preoccupies much of the literature of the time. And it is reflected in Atherton's remark that Lessingham 'was dressed as a gentleman should be dressed' (p.68), where the emphasis on the modal verb indicates a shallow reliance on appearance.

Unconsciously, perhaps, but significantly nonetheless, the narrative links this social and class uncertainty with scientific uncertainty by immediately following Atherton's musings with Lessingham's remark that: 'I never enter a place like this, where a man is matching himself with nature, to wrest from her her secrets, without feeling that I am crossing the threshold of the unknown' (p.68). Atherton is just one of many scientists in popular novels to be pushing beyond the boundaries of the known and, possibly, the safe. The link between social and natural disquietude is not accidental: changes in the conception of one affected that of the other.

Such changes find their curious reflection in *The Beetle*, as in other texts of the age. Lessingham questions Atherton about the followers of Isis and the possibility of transmigration; specifically, if it is 'absolutely certain that there could be no foundation of truth in the belief that a priest of Isis – or anyone – assumed after death the form of a beetle?' (p.71). This irruption of the supernatural in the scientist's study is barely suppressed. The cult of Osiris and Isis ('one and the same' [p.69]) cannot safely be assumed to be extinct, since Atherton thinks it 'possible, even probable, that, here and there, in Africa ... homage is paid to Isis, quite in the good old way' (p.70). And, on seeing an illustration of the beetle, 'produced apparently by some process of photogravure ... and ... so dextrously done that the creature seemed alive' (pp.72–73), a

> look came on his [Lessingham's] face which, literally, transfigured him. His hat and umbrella fell from his grasp on to the floor. He retreated, gibbering, his hands held out as if to ward something off from him, until he reached the wall on the other side of the room. A more amazing spectacle than he presented I never saw. (p.72)

I am interested not so much in the symbolism of his hat and umbrella falling to the ground (which in a psychoanalytic reading may suggest an unmanning through the drop of these functionally upright accoutrements) as in the reduction of the statesman to a state of animal terror. 'Gibbering' is a breakdown of reason and language that afflicts countless characters in literature of the time. One of the reasons for Lessingham's slide into inarticulacy, beyond the immediate fright he has received from the image of the scarab beetle that reminds him horribly of his supernatural visitor, is that the creature represents a force from which he can hardly free himself. The cause of the scarab's scuttling to London is, we are told, to gain revenge on Lessingham for the murderous destruction that he wrought in making his escape from the captivity in which Isis's followers were holding him in Egypt during his youth. In other words, the beetle stands for the past – his past – and the narrative is really asking whether this statesman-in-the-making can break free of it. The choice of the priest of Isis to symbolise this is especially apt. A leading Egyptologist of the day, E. A. Wallis Budge, would write, four years after *The Beetle*, that: 'The Egyptians believed that a man's fate or destiny was decided before he was born, and that he had no power whatever to alter it.'[33] It was a common observation in anthropological texts of the time that 'primitive' peoples were hopelessly in thrall to their deities and idols. There is clearly a tussle within Lessingham between the dictates of the past and his ability to shape his future; and in this he does, like a true statesman, stand as representative of his age.

So when Atherton helps bring Lessingham round to normality by taking his shoulder and shaking him vigorously and '[m]y touch had on him the effect of seeming to wake him out of a dream, of restoring him to consciousness as against the nightmare horrors with which he was struggling' (p.73), the moment symbolises the suppression of the past and of the supernatural by the modern and science.

Richard Lehan has noted that:

> Fantasy literature in the late Victorian period dealt with the meaning of the past, perhaps because the rate of change during this era was so great that readers desired to get a sense of what needed to be kept at a distance. In these fantasies, the past is often held together by mythic beliefs enforced

through the power of cults. The modern journeyer confronts these beliefs and tries to demystify them.[34]

Lehan does not mention *The Beetle*, but it fits his thesis. Apart from the probability that readers were actually drawn to aspects of the past because they wanted to mitigate some of the effects of the present (hence the interest in antiquity, the primitive, spiritualism, ancient religions, and so on), Lehan has it right, I think. The cult of Isis fits exactly, as do the modern journeyers, if we take those to be the characters that seek and pursue the Beetle and its first London victim – the unemployed clerk who was tramping through the capital in search of a bed.

In this novel and many of its kind, suppression of the past and of the irrational or extra-rational is never entirely effectual. Nor was it in life, as the growing fascination in late Victorian and Edwardian times with spiritualism and the occult testifies. (It still does, of course.) Thus when Atherton holds up in front of Lessingham the picture of the beetle in order to show him that it *is* only a picture, Lessingham trembles and screams that Atherton should destroy it, which the latter has to do before Lessingham can regain some sense of composure.

Texts like these try to work through the problem of the influence of the past by reducing it to a question of personal morality. Atherton asks Marjorie what she knows of Lessingham's private life and when she insists that he is 'incapable of a dishonest thought or action', he advises her: 'don't appreciate any man too highly. In the book of every man's life there is a page which he would wish to keep turned down' (p.78). This ignores the structural and institutional by diverting attention to the individual. In fact, the idea of scandal has everything to do with public matters, since it can only become an issue when there are influential or consensual views on standards of conduct, which are then challenged or broken by people's behaviour: in this case and at this time, people who are politicians, gentlemen, or both. To expose a scandal may be to discover the inadequacy of public standards and ideas of conduct as much as, or rather than, to reveal the failings of an individual. In the late nineteenth century, many of the sexual scandals (in particular) were the result of unrealistic views of conduct and relationships; unrealistic both because they did not truly comprehend the state of society and because they tried falsely to impose irrelevant standards on public individuals.

The Beetle underlines the difference between the public and private face by having Atherton, who has little respect for Members of Parliament, admire Lessingham's performance in the House of Commons. Lessingham's skill and self-command belie the terror he exhibited towards the picture of the beetle. Moreover, the result of his statesman-like speech is that the arguments of others are 'transformed' (p.84). Thus, Lessingham is now the agent, not the victim, of change.

The 'mysterious Egypto-Arabian' (p.95) appears again when Atherton drags Percy Woodville outside his laboratory. Woodville, another unsuccessful suitor of Marjorie's, has accidentally smashed a pallet of Atherton's 'Magic Vapour', which Atherton has been demonstrating to Woodville on a black cat. When the stranger revives the unconscious Woodville by an emphatically narrated kiss of life, we have another strongly (homo)erotic passage, as 'passing his arms beneath his body, [he] extended himself at full length upon his motionless form. Putting his lip to Percy's, he seemed to be pumping life from his own body into the unconscious man's' (p.96). Percy's twitching, his convulsive motions, and the 'rigidity about the muscles of his face' all suggest that this is much more than a kiss of life (p.97).

The man's foreignness is as crucial to this sexual theme as it is to the other forms of threat that he poses. Observing him in the laboratory while Percy recovers outside, Atherton notes:

> The fellow was oriental to the finger-tips ... yet in spite of a pretty wide personal knowledge of oriental people I could not make up my mind as to the exact part of the east from which he came. He was hardly an Arab, he was not a fellah, – he was not, unless I erred, a Mohammedan at all ... So far as looks were concerned, he was not a flattering example of his race, whatever his race might be. The portentous size of his beak-like nose would have been, in itself, sufficient to damn him in any court of beauty. His lips were thick and shapeless, – and this, joined to another peculiarity in his appearance, seemed to suggest that, in his veins there ran more than a streak of negro blood. (p.98)

Swarthy foreigners play an insidious role in colonial fiction and popular invasion narratives of the late nineteenth century. Marsh is evidently depending on a shared understanding of a set of signifiers. The stranger's Egyptian background signals a shiftiness and seediness to British readers. Kelly Hurley makes an interesting point about the particularity of the creature's origin:

> a paranoiac text like *The Beetle* serves to reflect and feed into British suspicion of and contempt for Egyptians during a period of heightened British military activity in Egypt. The perceived inhumanity of the orient becomes a rationale for subjecting it to the humanizing, civilizing process of British colonization ... *The Beetle* inverts the issue of colonization by presenting the East/West conflict in terms of oriental aggression – an oriental incursion,

with white slavery and genocide as its end, into the very heart of London. It then distorts the issue further by representing Egypt as a site not of relatively stable English rule during Lord Cromer's occupation, but of oriental misrule, under which innocent white tourists are kidnapped, tortured, and murdered with impunity. Reversing the territorial actualities, the text transposes the colonized subject into a savage aggressor whose duplicity and desire for mastery swell across the boundaries of the orient into the homeland of civilized England.[35]

Hurley's political historicism is welcome, and she is surely right to return the focus to Egypt; to correct the inversion of the issue of colonisation. The claim that 'the supernaturally exaggerated representations of the barbaric, primitive Oriental found in *The Beetle* offer a rationale for xenophobia and for a continued British colonial presence within Egypt' may itself be an exaggeration, however.[36] The representations are, rather, a reflection of widely held attitudes that resulted from, and contributed towards, the rationale. Hurley seems not to note the racial ambiguity of the passage above. She does draw attention, quite rightly, to other kinds of lack of definition in Marsh's text, but does so in relation to the Beetle itself and to gender. She is correct to write of the follower of Isis that

> [s]he is able to cross the boundary between one gendered identity and another, she can cross the boundary separating the human and animal species, and even in her avatar of the Beetle she resists enclosure within the boundary of a definite species classification ... Whatever the Beetle was resists scientific analysis and classification: it can fit into no taxonomy of natural history.[37]

But this reading distracts from the socio-economic context that is responsible for such preoccupation with undefinability.

The stranger's appearance produces a struggle between old and new powers, between magic and the supernatural on the one hand and science and reason on the other. Although the Egypto-Arab looks like winning this when he is able to revive Woodville – the 'victim of modern science' – earning 'a feeling of quasi-respect' from Atherton (p.97), the latter is able to resist the Oriental's attempts to hypnotise him. Atherton believes his lack of imagination saves him from the mesmeric powers and in turn he deploys against the stranger scientific tricks that so impress him he pronounces himself Atherton's slave after disappearing and reappearing. Atherton counters the Oriental's attempt at hypnotism with a display of electrical power – his machine giving off an eighteen-inch spark. The effect on the stranger is immediate: 'He shook with terror. He salaamed down to the ground.' Atherton finds this alteration 'amusing' (p.102), as, no doubt, would Marsh's readers, for it reproduces the stereotype of the grovelling Arab. The foreigner may be a worshipper of Isis, but the 'salaaming' is meant to recall the Muslim, his prostration and entreaties acting as a reassurance to the nation still smarting from the death of General Gordon in the Sudan just a dozen years previously. Indeed, it would not be until the year after the publication of Marsh's novel that the Mahdi's successor, the Khalifa, Abdullah el Taashi, who had ruled the Sudan from the time of the Mahdi's death six months after the defeat of Gordon, would be defeated by Kitchener, who had his troops destroy the Mahdi's tomb. The reduction of the Oriental to a state of prone supplication offers, in fiction, a victory to compensate for Britain's humiliation in the Sudan. It performs a symbolic castration, as the threatening male figure falls to the ground. His cries – 'My lord! – my lord! – have mercy, oh my lord!' (p.102) – are an imposed recognition of Western superiority. It is not, however, as straightforward as that. Atherton is not a Lord. We are not meant to take the foreigner's address literally, but the very fact that Atherton is not an aristocrat – 'I am a plain man and I use plain speech' (p.106) – comically underlines the incongruity of the stranger calling him one. While this further emphasises the anachronistic nature of the worshipper of Isis, it also highlights the divisions within British society. Atherton's jealous opposition to Lessingham has covered these with the cloak of a love story, but they are all about class and the uneasy relationships between classes.

When Atherton reinforces his hold over the stranger through further shows of what he calls 'magic' – this time by sprinkling phosphorous bromide on the floor, creating flames and vapour – the creature seems to vanish and then reappear, 'prostrated on his knees … salaaming in a state of abject terror' and whining: 'I entreat you, my lord, to use me as your slave!' (p.103). There is something of Caliban's enslavement by Prospero here. Though the details differ, the enactment of colonial power has parallels with it.

The Egyptian (as we must assume him to be) explains that he wishes to gain revenge against Lessingham for having 'spilled the blood of her who has lain upon his breast'. Seeing that the man's 'words pointed to what it might be courteous to call an Eastern Romance' (p.103), Atherton concludes that: 'It was the old tale retold, that to the life of every man there is a background, – that it is precisely in the unlikeliest cases that the background's darkest' (p.104). In general terms, it may have been an old tale, but to Marsh's contemporaries at the end of the nineteenth century it was immediate and fresh, as a series of sexual scandals became scandalous because of their class components. It is because of this, no doubt, that Atherton assures the Egyptian – a little too urgently, one feels – that 'the Englishman's law is no respecter of persons. Show him to be guilty, and it would hang Paul Lessingham as indifferently, and as cheerfully, as it would hang Bill Brown' (p.104).

The Beetle, then, presents confusion in many realms. Its disturbance is simultaneously psychological, social, racial, and temporal. Towards the end of the novel, Lessingham recalls his captivity in Egypt and tells Champnell:

> do you know that I am on the verge of madness? Do you know that as I am sitting here by your side I am living in a dual world? I am going on and on to catch that – that fiend, and I am back again in that Egyptian den, upon that couch of rugs, with the Woman of the Songs beside me, and Marjorie is being torn and tortured, and burnt before my eyes! God help me! Her shrieks are ringing in my ears! (p.249)

We shall see a similar kind of dual vision at the end of H. G. Wells's *The War of the Worlds*, discussed in the next chapter. Whereas many of the narratives discussed in the previous chapter were designed to show a single picture – that of urban deprivation – *Dracula* and *The Beetle* accomplish their effects by having one world intrude upon another. We saw Holt – the unemployed clerk – tramping around the wasteland at the start of the novel. Alongside the realism of that scene, the appearance of the follower of Isis in London forces Lessingham to recall his fantastic experiences that belong to the supernatural, making his past invade the present. The trauma of this depends upon the racialised figure of the worshipper of the old ways and on the bestial manifestation.

As critics have recognised, the Egyptian antagonist stands as a foreign scapegoat. 'Marsh's beetle-human hybrid provides a powerfully exemplary grotesque embodiment of late Victorian anxieties in so many ways', writes Wolfreys,[38] who maintains that 'the beetle-creature is readable as a disruptive figure, one of prosopopoeia, that rhetorical figure for giving face or voice to what is unrepresentable. *The Beetle* "gives face" to everything that is unstable in late imperial culture.'[39] If Wolfreys is right to claim that '[t]he text confronts us with irresolvable contradictions',[40] then its genre plays its part in that. Roger Luckhurst rightly observes that 'genre is less a set of fixed narratives and images and more a constantly modulating mode – almost a way of thinking'. In the final decade of the nineteenth century – one that saw the publication of both *Dracula* and *The Beetle* – 'the Gothic careers off in numerous, sometimes contradictory directions, and it is important to have a generous rather than narrow definition of the genre at a time when it is undergoing rapid transition'. Noting that one of the icons of the Gothic is the entity that challenges absolute distinctions between the human and beast – another is that between life and death – Luckhurst remarks that: 'It is difficult sometimes to decide if a Gothic text is conservative or subversive for it is often both, simultaneously.'[41] The same can be said of many of the beasts that prowl these pages.

Notes

1 Bram Stoker, *Dracula* [1897], edited and with an introduction and notes by Roger Luckhurst (Oxford: Oxford World's Classics, 2011), p.128. Further page references will be given parenthetically in the text.
2 David Glover, *Vampires, Mummies, and Liberals: Bram Stoker and the Politics of Popular Fiction* (Durham, NC: Duke University Press, 1996), p.48. Glover has much to say about Stoker's ambivalence about Ireland and the function that Transylvania may perform as a kind of projection of Ireland.
3 David Punter, *The Literature of Terror: A History of Gothic Fictions from 1765 to the Present Day*, vol. 2, *The Modern Gothic* (London: Longman 1996), p.16.
4 Fred Botting, *Gothic* (London: Routledge, 1996), p.147.
5 Marina Warner, *Fantastic Metamorphoses, Other Worlds: Ways of Telling the Self* (Oxford: Oxford University Press, 2002), p.163.
6 Botting, *Gothic*, p.148.
7 Botting, *Gothic*, p.150.
8 Glover, *Vampires, Mummies, and Liberals*, p.137.
9 Glover, *Vampires, Mummies, and Liberals*, p.137.
10 Punter, *The Literature of Terror*, vol. 2, p.16.
11 See Chapter Six of my *Travellers in Africa: British Travelogues 1850–1900* (Manchester: Manchester University Press, 1994).
12 Cf. Franco Moretti, 'Dialectic of Fear', in *Signs Taken for Wonders: Essays in the Sociology of Literary Form* (London: Verso, 1988), pp.83–108.
13 As Fred Botting has noted: 'Van Helsing is more than a scientist: he is also a metaphysician who deals with "spiritual pathology" as well as physical disease, a psychic investigator or transcendental doctor … Van Helsing does not discount superstition and is the first to use sacred objects like the crucifix and the Host. Science involves mysteries and opens on to a more than rational plane in line with Victorian attitudes towards spiritualism and psychic investigation.' Botting further observes that the 'fusion of scientific knowledge and religious values is made possible by the demonic threat of Dracula'. See Botting, *Gothic*, p.149.
14 Stephen D. Arata, 'The Occidental Tourist: *Dracula* and the Anxiety of Reverse Colonization', *Victorian Studies* 33, 4 (Summer 1990), 634.
15 Arata, 'The Occidental Tourist', p.634.
16 Arata, 'The Occidental Tourist', p.635.
17 Alexandra Warwick, 'Vampires and the Empire: Fears and Fictions of the 1890s', in Sally Ledger and Scott McCracken, eds, *Cultural Politics at the Fin de Siècle* (Cambridge: Cambridge University Press, 1995), pp.204–205. See, also, the essays by Phyllis A. Roth and Christopher Craft in *Dracula: New Casebooks*, in Glennis Byron, ed. (Basingstoke: Macmillan, 1999).

18 Dracula tells Harker that 'the walls of my castle are broken; the shadows are many, and the wind breathes cold through the broken battlements and casements' (p.35).
19 Botting notes a feature of *Dracula* that is so obvious that we might otherwise overlook it: 'The place of a heroine … is taken by naive young lawyer Harker.' See Botting, *Gothic*, p.146.
20 Roger Luckhurst, 'Introduction', in Bram Stoker, *Dracula* (Oxford: Oxford University Press, 2011), p.xii.
21 Luckhurst, 'Introduction', p.vii.
22 Ken Gelder, *Reading the Vampire* (London: Routledge, 1994.), p.86.
23 Roger Luckhurst, 'Introduction', in Robert Louis Stevenson, *Strange Case of Dr. Jekyll and Mr. Hyde and Other Tales* (Oxford: Oxford University Press, 2006), p.vii.
24 Luckhurst, 'Introduction', *Dracula*, p.ix.
25 Luckhurst, 'Introduction', *Dracula*, p.ix.
26 Luckhurst, 'Introduction', *Dracula*, pp.xiv, xix.
27 Luckhurst, 'Introduction', *Dracula*, p.xiv.
28 William Baker, 'Introduction', in Richard Marsh, *The Beetle* [1897] (Stroud: Alan Sutton Publishing, 1994), p.vii. All further references will be to this edition and will be given parenthetically in the text. On the reception and popularity of *The Beetle* and for biographical information on Marsh, the pseudonym of Richard Bernard Heldmann (1857–1915), see Minna Vuohelainen, 'Richard Marsh's *The Beetle* (1897): A Late-Victorian Popular Novel', *Working With English: Medieval and Modern Language, Literature and Drama* 2, 1: Literary Fads and Fashions (2006), 89–100. The novel was first serialised over fifteen weeks from 13 March 1897 in *Answers* under the title *The Peril of Paul Lessingham: The Story of a Haunted Man*. See Vuohelainen, 'Richard Marsh's *The Beetle*', 91.
29 Roger Luckhurst, 'Introduction', in *Late Victorian Gothic Tales* (Oxford: Oxford University Press, 2005), p.xi.
30 Victoria Margree, '"Both in Men's Clothing": Gender, Sovereignty and Insecurity in Richard Marsh's *The Beetle*', *Critical Survey* 19, 2 (2007), 64.
31 Vuohelainen, 'Richard Marsh's *The Beetle*', 90.
32 Anonymous, *Teleny or The Reverse of the Medal* [1883] (Ware: Wordsworth Editions Limited, 1995), p.8.
33 E. A. Wallis Budge, *Egyptian Magic* [1901] (New York, NY: Dover Publications, Inc., 1971), p.222.
34 Richard Lehan, *The City in Literature: An Intellectual and Cultural History* (Berkeley, CA: University of California Press, 1998), pp.94–95.
35 Kelly Hurley, '"The Inner Chambers of All Nameless Sin": *The Beetle*, Gothic Female Sexuality, and Oriental Barbarism', in Lloyd Davis, ed., *Virginal Sexuality and Textuality in Victorian Literature* (Albany, NY: State University of New York Press, 1993), p.197.
36 Hurley, 'The Inner Chambers', p.198.
37 Hurley, 'The Inner Chambers', p.204.
38 Julian Wolfreys, 'Introduction', in Richard Marsh, *The Beetle* [1897] (Peterborough: Broadview Press, 2004), p.19.
39 Wolfreys, 'Introduction', *The Beetle*, p.19.
40 Wolfreys, 'Introduction', *The Beetle*, p.33.
41 Luckhurst, 'Introduction', *Late Victorian Gothic Tales*, p.xi.

CHAPTER THREE

Morlocks, Martians, and Beast-People

Probably the writer best known for populating his tales of the 1890s with beastly specimens is H. G. Wells. Often hailed as a prophetic figure, Wells is most firmly of his time, his texts born of attempts to come to terms with late nineteenth-century social and cultural anxieties. One can readily apply to Wells Rosemary Jackson's observation that:

> Like any other text, a literary fantasy is produced within, and determined by, its social context. Though it might struggle against the limits of this context, often being articulated upon that very struggle, it cannot be understood in isolation from it.[1]

The present chapter is concerned not only to identify the origins of the creatures that reside within Wells's writing, but to examine the form of the narrative vehicle in which they are transported. The focus is on three texts: *The Time Machine* (1895) and its metaphor of time travel; *The War of the Worlds* (1898) and its space travel (with Earth as the destination, rather than the departure point); and *The Island of Doctor Moreau* (1896) as a variant of the castaway voyage. I aim to show that the internal transformations that occur in Wells's tales (that is, the changes that are narrated within them) are complemented by the alterations that Wells effects to their external shape (that is, to the literary genres on which he draws for his scientific romances). Linda Dryden argues that Wells 'took the *fin de siècle* Gothic a stage further by subjecting it to a scientific scrutiny' and that '[i]n the modern Gothic, physical transformation from human to some bestial other is a central trope'.[2] Wells explicitly relates his metaphors of bodily alteration to social conditions. His linkage of them combines with his experiments in literary form to produce shifts in narrative perspective.

Feeling his way among his words

Like several of Wells's works, *The Time Machine* is usually hailed as an early science fiction tale.[3] In it, the Time Traveller remarks that: 'Time is only a kind of Space.'[4] The discussion that follows takes up this implied invitation to examine it as a travel narrative and will focus on its beastly imagery.[5] Like travel writing, science fiction tells us more about the society that produces it than about the world it ostensibly portrays, so Wells's story must be viewed in its fin de siècle context.

With its tale within a tale, the presentation of *The Time Machine* bears similarities to Joseph Conrad's later *Heart of Darkness* (1899, 1902). In the former, the framing narrator has an audience of professional gentlemen: a psychologist, medical man, provincial mayor, doctor, journalist, and an editor – all of whom try to make sense of what they are told, just as the narrator himself does. Wells has the Time Traveller speak about the problems of understanding and communicating what one has seen on one's journey:

> Conceive the tale of London which a negro, fresh from Central Africa, would take back to his tribe! … how much could he make his untravelled friend either apprehend or believe? Then, think how narrow the gap between a negro and a white man of our own times, and how wide the interval between myself and these of the Golden Age! (p.40)

Not only does the passage draw attention to the problems of cross-cultural translation and comprehension, as the Traveller pronounces himself unable to convey to his audience more than a little of the differences that he has found, but the image of a bemused African visiting a strange London reverses the direction of movement common in travel writing of the time. In so doing, it introduces the possibility of a different perspective, while the statement that there is little difference between an African and a modern white person defies dominant beliefs. Readers' values are thus questioned and their values destabilised.

The Time Traveller's difficulties in relating his experiences are apparent in his demeanour. The narrator speaks of him 'feeling his way among his words' (p.17) – a suitable image for the cautious linguistic exploration that occurs in *The Time Machine* and other contemporary works. A connection between spatial, verbal, and textual voyaging is thereby made. The early emphasis on finding one's way puts readers on their look-out, too. This is new and uncertain ground and it is in keeping with what Wells commented on in late 1895:

> the modern fanciful method takes the novelist to a new point of view. Stand aside but a little space from the ordinary line of observation, and the relative position of all things changes. There is a new proportion established. You have the world under a totally different aspect. There is profit as well as

novelty in the change of view. That is, in some small way, what I aim at in my books.[6]

Wells has the main character of *The Time Machine* tell his audience that the only difference between Time and Space is that '*our consciousness moves along it*' (p.8). His explanation assumes equivalence between cultural and temporal distance. He draws racial and beastly comparisons to make his point. Insisting that we can move about in Time, he comments:

> For instance, if I am recalling an incident very vividly I go back to the instant of its occurrence. I become absent-minded, as you say. I jump back for a moment. Of course we have no means of staying back for any length of Time, any more than a savage or an animal has of staying six feet above the ground. But a civilized man is better off than a savage in this respect. He can go up against gravitation in a balloon, and why should he not hope that ultimately he may be able to stop or accelerate his drift along the Time-Dimension, or even turn about and travel the other way? (p.10)

The Traveller's subsequent account interrogates the widely and confidently held idea that the 'savage' and the 'civilised' were separated, both physically and culturally, as he suggests above. Wells's use of narrative to demonstrate the problems of distinction and relativity has affinities with what, nearly a century later, the sociologist Norbert Elias writes of as the fifth dimension. Elias ascribes to this the standpoint of the observer, who not only looks on at the four dimensions, but is able to perceive

> the symbolic character of the four dimensions as means of orientation for human beings ... who are capable of synthesis and so are in a position to have present at the same time in their imagination what takes place successively and so never exists simultaneously.[7]

For Elias, this idea of synthesis also remedies the false distinction made between the natural and the social. Suggesting a model of 'people who can observe and investigate from different storeys and so from different perspectives' (i.e. who can appreciate the symbolic character of the four dimensions), he declares that:

> Time, which on the preceding step was recognizable only as a dimension of nature, becomes recognizable, now that society is included in the field of view as a subject of knowledge, as a human-made symbol and, moreover, a symbol with high object-adequacy.[8]

Although Elias makes little reference to literature, I shall wilfully misread 'storey' as a typographical error for 'story' and argue that the

Time Traveller's movement through the fourth dimension is observed and investigated by Wells, who uses his tale to inspect, from this fifth dimension, the symbolic construction of time in relation to physical, 'natural' time. Indeed, Wells shows this quite graphically, demonstrating the impossibility of achieving an easy synthesis. Much of the latter part of his text is taken up with a kind of dialectic between nature and society, and he deliberately avoids neat closure of the tale that would amount to an easy synthesis.

My approach will also draw on Bakhtin's idea of the 'chronotope':

> We will give the name *chronotope* (literally, 'time space') to the intrinsic connectedness of temporal and spatial relationships that are artistically expressed in literature …
>
> In the literary artistic chronotope, spatial and temporal indicators are fused into one carefully thought-out, concrete whole. Time, as it were, thickens, takes on flesh, becomes artistically visible; likewise, space becomes charged and responsive to the movements of time, plot and history. This intersection of axes and fusion of indicators characterizes the artistic chronotope.[9]

Using his Traveller's voyages through time, Wells takes existing conditions in the city and projects them forwards within Darwinist and quasi-Marxist terms, framed in fin de siècle mood and imagery. The time travel serves as a defamiliarising device, facilitating scrutiny of contemporary life. As with many 1890s texts, confidence about domestic society and imperial activity is undermined (in this case literally, as we shall see).

When the Traveller first arrives in the future, he wonders what changes may have happened to humanity, whether it might have 'lost its manliness' and

> developed into something inhuman, unsympathetic, and overwhelmingly powerful? I might seem some old-world savage animal, only the more dreadful and disgusting for our common likeness – a foul creature to be incontinently slain. (p.23)

The Traveller finds himself potentially in the position of the 'savage' – a post-Darwinian reversal, which would underline the fragile basis of any current boasts of superiority. But while assumptions of racial hierarchies are unsettled, gender values are not. 'Manliness' is associated with vigour and proposed as the vital quality of humankind. Further evidence of this comes with the appearance of the Eloi. The first one that the Traveller sees is a typical four feet tall, 'very beautiful and graceful creature, but indescribably frail'. It reminds him of 'the more beautiful kind of consumptive – that hectic beauty of which we used to hear so much' (p.24). The fragile, sickly type would be familiar to 1890s readers, given the plethora of commentaries on the aesthetes and decadence. The Elois' prettiness is soon equated with a lack of physical and mental strength – a connotation that preserves gender inequalities. Those 'pretty little people' with their 'child-like ease', their lack of facial hair, and their 'Dresden-china type of prettiness' may be superficially attractive (p.25), but when the Traveller realises that they think he came from the sun in a thunderstorm (thus betraying a level of ignorance and superstition commonly attributed to 'primitives'), then the situation becomes more disturbing, as they appear to be the intellectual equal of 'one of our five-year-old children' (p.26). The disjunction between linear time and progress is a shock; for the Traveller to be superior to the Eloi is as great an aberration as for the 'savage' to be superior to 'us'.

The Elois' lack of curiosity matches their unproductiveness (another fault widely attributed to 'savages', signifying at once their alleged lack of forethought and a justification for appropriating their land). The Traveller's 'general impression' of their world was of 'a long-neglected and yet weedless garden' (p.26). Their exclusively fruit diet (horses, cattle, sheep, and dogs are extinct) is also a sign of a loss of vigour; meat often being associated in Wells's time (and not only then) with manliness, though the association was not made uncritically: adherents of vegetarianism denounced meat-eating as degenerate and traced a line from it to cannibalism.[10]

The reification of the aesthetic in the Eloi points to an alarming decline in usefulness. Their limitations remind one of Darwin on the probability 'that disuse has been the main agent in rendering organs rudimentary'.[11] In the Traveller's attempts to account for this situation, Wells reflects on the problems of interpretation, and it is in this respect that the narrative is written from, so to speak, the fifth dimension.

When the Traveller begins to muse on the condition of the Eloi, his thoughts focus on the uniformity of their appearance. The apparent absence of 'the single house, and possibly even the household' leads him to deduce that he is witnessing a communistic society (p.29). He opines that 'the strength of a man and the softness of a woman, the institution of the family, and the differentiation of occupations are mere militant necessities of an age of physical force' and that the necessity for them will happily vanish in a more easeful, balanced, and secure society (p.30). We are already seeing the start of this process in our own time, he comments (and he may well have in mind such phenomena as the rise of the New Woman).

Immediately afterwards, the Traveller throws us off balance by admitting that he has since had to revise this speculation, because 'it fell short of the reality' (p.30). We infer that future revelations will force further revisions, making us cautious in our reception of the Traveller's theories. A kind of dialectic is thus set up. We absorb the Traveller's 'present' words, knowing they will be modified by subsequent events.

What the Traveller describes would indicate, to many readers, not progress but regression. Although he has hinted that he is uneasy at the Elois' mental state, he soon tries to console himself with the thought that he is witnessing the construction of a communistic utopia. However, it would have been widely known that to many social theorists, notably Herbert Spencer, the specialisation of function, which loss the Traveller celebrates, actually constituted the very fact of progress. 'Life in general has been more heterogeneously manifested as time has advanced',[12] wrote Spencer in an essay first published in the *Westminster Review* in April 1857: '[T]he transformation of the homogeneous into the heterogeneous, is that in which Progress essentially consists.'[13]

Where Spencer sees differentiation and hierarchy as vital conditions for civilisation, with the gap between the governing and the governed especially important, the Time Traveller wishes to reverse these markers, associating the desirable simplicity of the primitive with the communist. At this point there is bound to be confusion in most readers' minds, as there is in the Traveller's, as to whether society has moved backwards or forwards. Wells uses the Traveller's successive modifications of interpretation to add to his readers' uncertainty. Wells's chronotope, his narrative manipulation of time and space, positions the Traveller as a kind of floating interrogative. The question of the direction of change – advancement or degeneration – is fundamental and the Traveller's problems of comprehension are induced in part by the continuing debate over existing tendencies in fin de siècle society.

In a volume published thirteen years after *The Time Machine*, Wells dwelt on these concerns, but also included a passage that may be read as a coda on the method he adopted in the earlier story:

> The current syllogistic logic rests on the assumption that either A is B or it is not B. The practical reality is that nothing is permanent; A is always becoming more or less B. But it would seem the human mind cannot manage with that. It has to hold a thing still for a moment before it can think it … It cannot contemplate things continuously, and so it has to resort to a series of static snapshots. It has to kill motion in order to study it, as a naturalist kills and pins out a butterfly in order to study life.[14]

It would seem that Wells allows for this limitation while striving to overcome it. By having the Traveller stop off at a particular point in the future, go briefly further forward, return to tell his tale, then travel again, Wells provides the freeze frame, but does so within a larger picture of process. He supplies both a synchronic and diachronic perspective. He demands that we resist easy assumptions of finitude and of closed fact. For Wells, that which cannot be pinned down is as crucial as that which can:

> Every species is vague, every term goes cloudy at its edges ... Every species waggles about in its definition ...
> ... The finest type specimen you can find simply has the characteristic quality a little more rather than a little less.[15]

The waggle for Wells is Weena. The emotional affirmation she brings to the tale is clearly meant to transcend the material changes that occur to her and our worlds. Individual variation was the key to Darwin's theory of evolution, something which Wells himself reminds us of: 'it was only with the establishment of Darwin's great generalizations that the hard and fast classificatory system broke down and individuality came to its own'.[16] Wells's use of time travel, emphasising, as it does, indefinability and uncertainty, works against the then-predominant notions of type, essence, and wholeness.

The unreliability of interpretation, exemplified by the Traveller's theorising, makes it hard for readers to be certain about the truth of the Morlocks and the Eloi and of their relation to each other. 'We are "too blind" to understand Nature's meaning', wrote Darwin.[17] As well as the Traveller's reported attempts to understand what he witnesses, there is also the narrator's and his peers' uncertainty as to whether or not to accept the hero's account at all.

The old needs of the ape

Wells advises against the suppression of appetites (and he probably had little choice, given what was known of his indulgence of his own sexual ones): 'One has to accept these things in oneself ... even if one knows them to be dangerous things, even if one is sure they have an evil side.'[18] The Morlocks would not be the creatures they have become had it not been for the bourgeois Elois' suppression of their own baser selves and those they made serve them. Like Hyde in Stevenson's tale, the Morlocks represent the return of the psychologically and socially repressed. Wells was later to refer to the 'old needs of the ape but thinly overlaid by the acquisitions of the man'[19] – an idea which, although his reference in the context is principally to sexual urges, nevertheless clearly underlies the association of the Morlocks with humans' animal instincts. We can readily apply to the uninquiring Eloi the opening of the following comment by Wells on curiosity:

> I perceive hypertrophied in myself and many sympathetic human beings a passion that many animals certainly possess, the beautiful and fearless cousin of fear, Curiosity, that seeks keenly for knowing and feeling. Apart from appetites and bodily desires and blind impulses, I want most urgently to know and feel, for the sake of knowing and feeling. I want to go round corners and see what is there, to cross mountain ranges, to open boxes and parcels.[20]

Actual and intellectual adventure are conjoined here and they find rich expression in time travel.

In *First and Last Things* Wells would dismiss omniscience. *The Time Machine* dispenses with it. Neither the anonymous framing narrator nor Wells as author is able to supply the positive interpretation the Traveller cannot give. The Traveller, after his initial deductions, becomes a little more restrained in his judgements. He supposes that humanity had continued its fight against disease, discomfort, and danger and gradually attained the climax of the civilising process. But, he thinks, '[s]trength is the outcome of need; security sets a premium on feebleness' (p.31). The people are housed in splendid shelters and wear gorgeous costume, but seem to be engaged in no toil. He sees no signs of struggle, either social or economic: 'all that commerce which constitutes the body of our world, was gone' (p.32). From all this, he thinks it understandable that he should jump at the idea of a social paradise. Knowing, post-Darwin, however, that changes in conditions lead to adaptations to the change, he begins to worry that the frailties he encounters are an inevitable result of the triumph over Nature. He speculates that in the new environment of 'comfort and security, that restless energy, that with us is strength, would become weakness' (p.33). The passage would disturb the Traveller's audience, for it suggests that 'savage' survivals in civilised 'man' are necessary if one is not to sink into idleness and decay.

In an observation redolent of the 1890s, the Time Traveller muses on decadence. He comments that in conditions of security, energy 'takes to art and eroticism, and then come languor and decay' (p.33). The Traveller's Social Darwinist view equates lack of struggle with enervation. All that was left of the artistic impulse, he muses, was the Elois' dancing and singing and their decoration of themselves with flowers and even this would 'fade in the end into a contented inactivity', for '[w]e are kept keen on the grindstone of pain, and necessity' and, it seems to the Traveller, that 'hateful grindstone' had now been broken (p.33). Immediately afterwards, however, he comments that this theory and his idea that the Elois' efforts to control their population rates have succeeded too well, creating a decrease, are very plausible – like most wrong ones.

That the Eloi represent a regression is also apparent from their language, which to the Traveller seems 'excessively simple', with few 'abstract terms', 'little use of figurative language', and sentences usually of only two words (p.39). From this bare description it would be quite obvious, even to those who knew nothing of evolutionary theory, that such linguistic simplicity heralds no great advance in the development of the race. For those acquainted with evolutionary ideas, the connotations would be clearer still. We can again turn to Herbert Spencer for an identification of language with racial development. This is what he says on the matter:

> The lowest form of language is the exclamation, by which an entire idea is vaguely conveyed through a single sound; as among the lower animals ... [T]hat language can be traced down to a form in which nouns and verbs are its only elements, is an established fact. In the gradual multiplication of parts of speech out of these primary ones – in the differentiation of verbs into active and passive, of nouns into abstract and concrete – in the rise of distinctions of mood, tense, person, of number and case – in the formation of auxiliary verbs, of adjectives, adverbs, pronouns, prepositions, articles – in the divergence of those orders, genera, species, and varieties of parts of speech by which civilised races express minute modifications of meaning – we see a change from the homogeneous to the heterogeneous ... [I]t is more especially in virtue of having carried this subdivision of function to a greater extent and completeness, that the English language is superior to all others.[21]

Spencer's robust confidence in this route of progress is challenged by the condition of the Eloi as Wells forces us to confront the possibility of degeneration. (It may also be that by way of the Traveller's changes of mind and fallibility, Wells is questioning the credibility of those travellers whose observations were used as evidence by armchair anthropologists, as well as of those anthropologists who themselves travelled.) The Traveller's fluent relation of his narrative – his vacillation notwithstanding – encloses the alleged linguistic deficiencies of the Eloi just as other travellers' narratives contained the so-called primitive utterances of 'savages'. The cultural and temporal confusion in Wells's text is caused by the fact that rather than being our forebears, these inarticulate simpletons are our descendants. (It should not be forgotten though that pronominal identification works no less coercively in *The Time Machine*, pulling readers into the cultural position of the author.)

The theme of degeneration intensifies with the Traveller's nocturnal glimpse of the white ape-like figures that we come to know as the Morlocks. His sighting comes the night before another proof of the Elois' enervated state: their lack of effort to rescue Weena from drowning. The Traveller himself saves her and is rewarded with her affectionate gift of a garland of flowers. As he recalls this episode and its aftermath, he interrupts himself to declare that 'my story slips away from me as I speak of her' (p.43), a statement that interestingly, if unconsciously, attests to the destabilising effects of gender. Furthermore, when he later recounts another episode and remembers that Weena had placed some flowers in his pocket, not only does he break off his narrative, but the framing narrator re-emerges in the story for a rare moment:

> *The Time Traveller paused, put his hand into his pocket, and silently placed two withered flowers, not unlike very large white mallows, upon the little table. Then he resumed his narrative.* (p.56)

The female presence introduces an emotional quality which, though sought after by the narrator as a sign of humanity, is nonetheless dismissed at will as a disruption to rationality and purpose. The Traveller's intention of bringing Weena back to his present world is thwarted by her disappearance and probable death, though we must doubt whether his intention would have been realised in any case, and in this there are similarities with the unconsummated union of Good and Foulata in H. Rider Haggard's *King Solomon's Mines* (1885).

When, the night before Weena's rescue, the Traveller dreamily glimpses the Morlocks, they appear to him as 'white figures' and are variously described as 'greyish animal[s]' and 'white, ape-like creature[s] … carrying some dark body' (p.43). Encountering some later, on what he thinks is his fourth morning, the terms are repeated, but enlarged. He has an 'imperfect' impression of the creature he sees, but knows 'it was a dull white, and had strange large greyish-red eyes; [with] flaxen hair on its head and down its back'. The speed at which it moves means that he 'cannot even say whether it ran on all-fours, or only with its forearms held very low' (p.45). When he strikes a match to get a view of it scuttling down a shaft, it makes him shudder, as '[i]t was so like a human spider!' (p.45).

In *Children of the Ghetto*, published the same year as *The Time Machine*, Israel Zangwill has his narrator recall:

> a dull, squalid, narrow thoroughfare in the East End of London, connecting Spitalfields with Whitechapel, and branching off in blind alleys. In the days when little Esther Ansell trudged its unclean pavements, its extremities were within earshot of the blasphemies from some of the vilest quarters and filthiest rookeries in the capital of the civilized world. Some of these clotted spiders' webs have since been swept away by the besom of the social reformer, and the spiders have scurried off into darker corners.[22]

After his sighting of what looks like a human spider, the Time Traveller now has to modify his Social Darwinist reading to account for this new revelation. Doing so leads him in a different direction as he relays his gradual realisation that

> Man had ... differentiated into two distinct animals ... my graceful children of the Upper-world were not the sole descendants of our generation ... [T]his bleached, obscene, nocturnal Thing, which had flashed before me, was also heir to all the ages. (p.45)

His new interpretation has the Traveller thinking, too, of the economic environment that may have led to this development as he considers both the physical and social factors that may have resulted in the emergence of this second, subterranean species. He uses the concept of adaptation to the environment as a basis for a kind of Marxist explanation of what he sees, but prefaces this by warning of his theory that he soon felt it inadequate (p.46). The Morlocks' whiteness is seen as a natural reaction to their subterranean life, their pigmentation disappearing in response to the absence of light. The Traveller posits that the Morlocks toil underground for the benefit of the Eloi. He bases his interpretation on a projection from the current state of things, remarking that it seemed very clear to him 'that the gradual widening of the present merely temporary and social difference between the Capitalist and the Labourer was the key to the whole position' (pp.46–47). He has in mind the present 'tendency to utilize underground space for the less ornamental purposes of civilization'. He lists as examples the Metropolitan Railway in London, the increasing number of new electric railways, subways, and underground workrooms and restaurants. We might add (while we still have some memory of them) the miners who toiled underground to supply society's energy needs.

The Traveller speculates that Industry operated increasingly underground until the situation which he has found had been reached. Rhetorically, he asks his contemporaries: 'does not an East-End worker live in such artificial conditions as practically to be cut off from the natural surfaces of the earth?' (p.47). He also refers to the growing gulf between the rich and the poor, with the former seeking to distance themselves further physically and socially from the latter (including by endogamous marriages, which helps give the biological explanation for the development of two species). He deduces that above ground are the Haves, 'pursuing pleasure and comfort, and beauty, and below ground the Have-nots, the Workers getting continually adapted to the conditions of their labour' (p.47). The aristocracy are, literally, on top. Yet despite asserting of his explanation that he still believes it 'the most plausible one' (p.48), it is not long before he recants and feels it 'was all wrong' (p.54).

As befits a (soon-to-be) Fabian, the author seems to share the Traveller's lack of sympathy for, and identification with, the oppressed class. Besides the epithets already given them, the Morlocks are referred to as 'whitened Lemurs' and 'vermin', from whose 'half-bleached', 'pallid', and 'filthy cold' bodies the Traveller recoils (p.49). These reactions precede the Traveller's latest revision to his interpretation of the world in 802,701, which is to propose that the old relationship of dominance by the Eloi has long ended and that they have 'decayed to a mere beautiful futility' (p.54), possessing the earth only on sufferance, since the Morlocks are unable to endure the daylight and have maintained their old habits of service as an unconscious instinct 'because ancient and departed necessities had impressed it on the organism' (p.55). The Traveller senses that the Eloi are about to meet their Nemesis. Readers will pick up hints that they are the victims of cannibalism by the Morlocks, though the Traveller appears slow to grasp the implications of his own sightings:

> Even at the time, I remember wondering what large animal could have survived to furnish the red joint I saw. It was all very indistinct: the heavy smell, the big unmeaning shapes, the obscene figures lurking in the shadows, and only waiting for the darkness to come at me again! (p.52)

In the Traveller's greater feeling for the Eloi than for the Morlocks, an ambivalence is introduced, which parallels that of many middle-class Socialists' feelings towards the masses; feelings, if not of loathing, then certainly of distance and anxiety. As Bernard Bergonzi noted in the early 1960s: 'The Traveller's gradual identification with the beautiful and aristocratic – if decadent – Eloi against the brutish Morlocks is indicative of Wells's own attitudes.'[23] No matter how detached and scientific the Traveller tries to be about the dietary habits of the sons of labour – 'These Eloi were mere fatted cattle, which the ant-like Morlocks preserved and preyed upon – probably saw to the breeding of' – he is unable to maintain an aloofness as '[t]he Eloi had kept too much of the human form not to claim my sympathy' (p.59). Far from achieving objectivity, he feels himself stirred into action as he shares their degradation and fear. In a show of atavism, he finds himself longing 'very much to kill a Morlock or so', and it is only a desire not to endanger both Weena and his Time Machine that prevents him from seeking out and 'killing the brutes I heard' (p.63). That last phrase anticipates Kurtz's scrawled postscript in the report which Marlow finds in *Heart of Darkness*. The extent of this victory of passion over science is reinforced by the mention, almost immediately afterwards, of the Traveller's having authored seventeen scientific papers.

That night, when the Morlocks attack the Traveller and Weena (who vanishes and is presumed by the Traveller to have been killed), they are scared off by the fire that the Traveller has started. The art of fire-making was lost to this future world. In a confusion of self-defence and violent repugnance, the Traveller kills at least one of the 'human rats' (p.69) and cripples several more with an iron bar. Whether or not Wells intends the link, it recalls the descriptions of the urban poor as rats that we encountered in Chapter Two of the present study. The following morning the Traveller laughs bitterly at the memory of his innocent optimism at the apparently utopian surroundings. He now gives us his last view of the world of 802,701, but still concedes that it may be wrong. His final theory slightly modifies his previous one. He repeats his idea that humanity, having attained a balanced society with security, slumbered into a state with no social problems. A 'great quiet' had followed, which diminished and then eradicated intellectual activity: 'There is no intelligence where there is no change and no need of change.' The Eloi had 'drifted towards his feeble prettiness' and the Morlocks to 'mere mechanical industry', but this state of affairs lacked the absolute permanency required for stability. When food supplies to the Morlocks were disrupted, they 'turned to what old habit had hitherto forbidden', having retained more initiative than the Eloi (p.72). The Morlocks are the ones in control. They hunt the Eloi at will. Wells hints to us that the Morlocks are, literally, feeding off them. It is this, as critics have noted, that makes us shudder when, on his return, the fatigued Traveller is revived by the odour of 'good wholesome meat' (p.79). Such moments give rise to Lee's claim that *The*

Time Machine and *The Island of Doctor Moreau* 'ruthlessly dismantle the possibility of holding cannibalism as an "outside" against which we can define our culture'.[24] Lee makes the point that

> with the rise of Darwinism, cannibalism could no longer be strictly consigned to the 'outside' realm of the savage other. Now Victorian culture faced the idea that the line between humans and animals might not be one of division but of lineage. For many, this idea triggered the possibility that those animals consumed as meat were not essentially different from the 'we' who ate them.[25]

It is tempting to read the relationship between the classes psychoanalytically: the Morlocks as the id, living underground and adapted to darkness, the obscene nocturnal creatures; the Eloi afraid of the dark and subject to attack from the subterranean dwellers. Thus the appearance of the Morlocks above ground may be read as the return of the repressed. What interests me more about this image, though, is that, like Melville before him and Conrad afterwards, Wells questions, even reverses, the conventionally held moral attributes of whiteness.

After escaping the Morlocks' attempts to trap him inside the pedestal in which they have kept his machine, the Traveller inadvertently voyages even further into the remote future, finding scenes of 'abominable desolation' (p.76) as the earth 'had come to rest with one face to the sun' (p.75). Wanting to know more of the fate of the planet, he travels ever further into the future, stopping momentarily every thousand years or so, observing the dying of the sun. More than thirty million years on, it is bitterly cold and snowing. An eclipse of the sun is in progress. The Traveller is unnerved by the silence of the world. The only life he observes at first is some green slime on the rocks, but then, already feeling a horror of the darkness (a reminder of the fear felt by the Eloi), he is sickened by the sight of a solitary large jellyfish-like creature, hopping about on the shoal.

The Traveller then returns to the present. This brings us back full circle to the opening of the tale. The guests are all sceptical. Even the curious flowers and the time machine itself fail to convince. The only person who seems to have an open mind on what he has heard is the anonymous narrator. The next day he visits the Traveller to question him further. The Traveller, clutching a rucksack and a camera, tells the narrator to wait half an hour, and then he, the Traveller, will have specimens to prove that he does travel through time. The Traveller shuts his laboratory door, leaving the narrator to read a newspaper. Going into the laboratory to tell the Traveller that he has to leave because of an appointment, the narrator catches a glimpse of the phantasmic figure disappearing. Three years on, he is still waiting for the Traveller to come back, for '[a]s everybody knows … he has never returned' (p.83). The ending resolves nothing. The protagonist's journey is open-ended. His descriptions and interpretations of what he sees are clearly culture-bound and he is therefore limited in what he is able to apprehend of the objects themselves.

Monsters manufactured

The Island of Doctor Moreau has as one of its main themes the indeterminate relationship between the bestial and the human.[26] It also deliberately confuses the boundaries of realism and romance, producing an example of what Wells called his 'scientific romances', which have been said to 'define a new form'.[27] The effect of this generic compound is to have the narrative confusion destabilise the readers and so extend their vision of the world, in Wells's case through the 'cognitive shudder' that Darko Suvin has identified as a characteristic of science fiction.[28] It is an example of how the diffusion of Darwinian and post-Darwinian ideas of evolution contributed to the evolution of the novel.[29] Not only is it the case that in the late nineteenth century 'Darwinism mutated in a variety of ways',[30] but *The Island of Doctor Moreau* has itself been identified as a transitional text in Well's career, evidenced by his divided reactions to it.[31]

The radical implications of Wells's investigation of the problem of ascertaining the divide between the human and the bestial are lost in his focus on biological, rather than social conditions. Admittedly, he comes close to constructing a critical allegory of colonialism: not long after Prendick has arrived on the island, for example, he observes 'a man, going on all-fours like a beast!', but who 'had not been naked as a savage would have been' (p.41). Prendick's exploration of part of the island echoes the adventures of explorers: 'I began to realize the hardihood of my expedition among these unknown people' (p.42). The reader understands more readily than Prendick that the strange inhabitants cannot easily be classified as 'Other' in the way that explorers and scientific commentators were wont to label indigenous peoples of the territories they invaded. Three 'grotesque human figures' (one female, the others male) that Prendick finds squatting in 'a kind of glade' in a forest 'were naked, save for swathings of scarlet cloth about the middles, and their skins were of a dull pinkish drab colour, such as I had seen in no savages before' (p.43). Their hue makes them, of course, 'white', as is the case with the sloth-like creature he will meet later, which he describes as 'a dim pinkish thing' (p.61). The fact that Prendick has '[n]ever before ... seen such bestial-looking creatures' inverts the usual terms of colonialism in which animality is commonly ascribed to the dark-skinned (p.43). The gibbering and chanting of the pink creatures reinforces this impression.

Yet the possibilities of a sustained critique of colonialism are soon lost as Wells pursues instead the more general question, asked by Prendick about the man he had seen on all-fours, 'the Thing': 'What on earth was he – man or animal?' (p.45). As the story progresses, Wells directs this question to the state of humanity as a whole, losing sight of the possibilities for a subversive reading of colonialism.[32] For the moment, though, the interpretation holds. Prendick finds himself talking to the 'simian creature' with the 'black face' (p.58). This 'ape-like companion', with 'his hands hanging down and his jaw thrust forward' is not out of keeping with popular representations of black people (p.59). His powers of speech mark him as a man, but his English is broken. However, Prendick's remark on the Beast-People, that 'I did not know yet how far they had forgotten the human heritage I ascribed to them' (p.59), signals the broader allegory that is to emerge as he takes their condition to be the result of reversion to a former state. This conclusion will be challenged by Moreau's claim that they are improved animals – 'humanized animals – triumphs of vivisection' (p.77) – not deteriorated humans. Although Moreau's boast challenges Prendick's assumption of degeneration, the very terms of the question mean that the novel ends up allying itself with contemporary debates about the direction and shape of human development. This distracts from the more specific issue of colonialism and the questioning of innate superiority; it has the text ultimately transcend particular political problems and flatten out into a much more general comment on the duality of humanity.

When Moreau talks of operations that had already been carried out by others, such as the grafting of skin and bone, he uses the phrase 'monsters manufactured' (p.77) and goes on to tell Prendick that: 'These creatures you have seen are animals carven and wrought into new shapes. To that – to the study of the plasticity of living forms – my life has been devoted' (p.78). His study of the 'plasticity of living forms' is a frightening reminder of the mutability of species to which Darwin had called attention in *The Origin of Species*, where he declared, for example, that: 'Judging from the past, we may safely infer that not one living species will transmit its unaltered likeness to a distant futurity.'[33] Through the person of Moreau, Wells invites his readers to contemplate the identity of the power that can – or will – change us. Moreau's words also have added significance. It is not only living forms that are plastic, but social and cultural ones, too. These include literature.

Moreau brags that: 'It's not simply the outward form of an animal I can change. The physiology, the chemical rhythm of the creature, may also be made to undergo an enduring modification' (p.78). The link between outer and inner alteration has serious social and literary implications: social because it relates changes in outer to those in inner states, thereby calling into question moral absolutes; and literary because the relationship of the internal to the external has likely consequences for narration and characterisation (particularly once developments in psychology are considered).

When Prendick is back in London, he finds that his experiences on Moreau's island have left him with a vision that cuts through the mundane activities around him. As he brings his narrative up to date, he tells us that he has been troubled for many years by the fear that

> I could not persuade myself that the men and women I met were not also another, still passably human, Beast People, animals half-wrought into the outward image of human souls, and that they would presently begin to revert, to show first this bestial mark and then that. (p.149)

In the words of Chris Baldick, Prendick is 'clearly reinterpreting the struggle for existence in the capitalist metropolis as, only too literally, the law of the jungle'.[34] His perception of the animal truths behind the show of everyday reality calls into question, by throwing into relief, the substance of civilisation. But, as Suvin rightly observes of Wells's scientific romances of this period, the author's 'satisfaction at the destruction of the false bourgeois idyll is matched by his horror at the alien forces destroying it'.[35] This ambivalence is shown through, and is a result of, the recognition of the animal within the human and of the human within the animal.

Suitably for Wells the sexual libertine, the instinct which for authors of naturalistic novels perverts our humanity threatens to be perverted by civilised restraint. This is suggested by Prendick's misanthropy at the end of the book when he shuns 'cities and multitudes' and all but a few strangers. He ends his story in 'solitude', in hope of a celestial refuge for 'whatever is more than animal within us' (p.151). It is also suggested by a speech of Moreau's that hints at the threat posed by society in its manipulation and control of natural instinct:

> In our growing science of hypnotism we find the promise of a possibility of replacing old inherent instincts by new suggestions, grafting upon or replacing the inherited fixed ideas. Very much, indeed, of what we call moral education is such an artificial modification and perversion of instinct; pugnacity is trained into courageous self-sacrifice, and suppressed sexuality into religious emotion. (p.79)

Here Wells seems to be warning his readers about the social retraining of the human character away from its natural basis, perhaps reflecting contemporary fears of overcivilisation. We are all, Wells appears to be saying, at the mercy of redefinition. Moreau exclaims that '[a] pig may be educated' and that '[t]he mental structure is even less determinate than the bodily'. He maintains that 'the great difference between man and monkey is in the larynx ... in the incapacity to frame delicately different sound-symbols by which thought could be sustained' (p.79). Prendick disagrees and it is probable that Wells himself, while showing the impossibility of discerning where animality ends and humanity begins, hopes that his readers will awaken to the harm that could be done by allowing their instincts to be so modified.

Prendick observes that:

> A blind fate, a vast pitiless mechanism, seemed to cut and shape the fabric of existence, and I, Moreau (by his passion for research), Montgomery (by his passion for drink), the Beast People, with their instincts and mental restrictions, were torn and crushed, ruthlessly, inevitably, amid the infinite complexity of its incessant wheels. (p.108)

The beginning of this quotation is a classically naturalistic expression that might equally be at home in Dreiser's *Sister Carrie*, but Wells uses Prendick's dual vision to communicate the alienating effects of not being able to accept the incorporation of the animal and the human; of nature and society. Appropriately, if frustratingly, *The Island of Doctor Moreau*, 'while it may be Wells's most systematic study of the evolutionary dilemma, arrives at no conclusions', and Wells ends up in danger of transferring the conflicts in the book from society to biology.[36]

Prendick cannot come to terms with the social body. He describes himself thus: 'And even it seemed that I, too, was not a reasonable creature, but only an animal tormented with some strange disorder in its brain, that sent it to wander alone, like a sheep stricken with the gid' (p.150). Wells struggles to hold together the social and natural and to find a literary style that will demonstrate the plasticity of living forms.

'Seeing further': *The War of the Worlds*

Like *The Time Machine*, *The War of the Worlds* (1898) is partly about contemporary social conditions, but it is also, more overtly, about *writing* those conditions. Greater than the imagined war between humans and Martians is the actual conflict between ideas of realism and romance. This is quite apparent in the narrative, in which Wells's strategies clearly have to do with the problem of creating a fresh vision of the mundane. *The War of the Worlds* embodies a battle between forms of writing. On one side, we have realism – the local and everyday – and science; on the other, fantasy and romance. Wells's own description of his work as 'scientific romance' is probably a more accurate term for the outcome than the more popular designation of 'science fiction'. Another label has been supplied by Joseph Conrad, who in a letter to Wells called him 'a realist of the fantastic'.[37] Though interesting, this may be less helpful in that it could imply a straightforward transposition of method from one realm to another, whereas the process is more complicated than that.

Whatever name we choose to apply to Wells's method, it is more important to concentrate on its reflection of its present than to beam him up from his world and hail him as some kind of prophet. Stanislaw Lem is right to suggest that the impact of Wells's story was likely to be the stronger for its being published the year after Queen Victoria's Jubilee, though he greatly underestimates the nervousness already existing when he describes that time as

> the apogee of Victorianism, when the British Empire appeared to be the mightiest power on this planet at its very fulcrum of cocksureness, yet bearing within it the seeds of incipient stagnation, when nineteenth-century English bumptiousness had reached a peak of self-satisfaction.[38]

Fear of international competition, national and imperial decline, and racial and social degeneration was already tangible. Contemporary anxieties about decadence, degeneration, class unrest, and reverse colonisation are more significant than the Martians' function as a defamiliarising device by which these questions can be objectified.

As with *The Time Machine*, the narrative in *The War of the Worlds* seeks a position from which aspects of late nineteenth-century British society can be criticised. In the latter text, space performs the role that time plays in the former. True, the action of the later novel also occurs in the future, but it is a future so near to the readers that the only difference it seems to mark is that it allows for an event yet to occur (the landing of the Martians) to happen soon: 'early in the twentieth century', remarks the narrator, 'came the great disillusionment'.[39] That phrase is crucial to the story. Disillusionment is the subject of the text. The Martians are the means by which the narrator becomes disillusioned. It is a great indictment of his world that it should take the manifestation of such fantastic creatures – 'alien vampires', as Dryden calls them – to endow him with his new insight.[40] This is how the novel begins:

> No one would have believed, in the last years of the nineteenth century, that human affairs were being watched keenly and closely by intelligences greater than man's and yet as mortal as his own; that as men busied themselves about their affairs they were scrutinized and studied, perhaps almost as narrowly as a man with a microscope might scrutinize the transient creatures that swarm and multiply in a drop of water. With infinite complacency men went to and fro over this globe about their little affairs, serene in their assurance of their empire over matter … Yet, across the gulf of space, minds that are to our minds as ours are to those of the beasts that perish, intellects vast and cool and unsympathetic, regarded this earth with envious eyes, and slowly and surely drew their plans against us. And early in the twentieth century came the great disillusionment. (p.9)

Right at the beginning of the novel, then, the readers are offered a reverse perspective. The confidence of the imperialist is attacked. When the narrator undermines the complacency of 'empire over matter', his words refer to the scientific and technological capabilities of Western civilisation, on which the advance of capitalism depended, and to the imperial project. Wells's problem (it becomes his, though initially it is that of the society he is criticising) is that he must travel outside his society in order to find the position from which its stature can be diminished. Christianity cannot supply that vantage point, for 'God was a lie',[41] and Wells wondered:

> Why do people go on pretending about this Christianity? At the test of war, disease, social injustice and every real human distress, it fails – and leaves a cheated victim … Jesus was some fine sort of man perhaps, the Jewish Messiah was a promise of leadership, but our Saviour of the Trinity is a dressed-up inconsistent effigy of amiability, a monstrous hybrid of man and infinity, making vague promises of helpful miracles for the cheating of simple souls, an ever absent help in times of trouble.[42]

Nor can science readily offer the critical perspective, because if it did it would then be seen to be in the service of humanity, underlining the very dominance that Wells wishes to question. The answer is found in scientific romance, in the invasion of creatures to which the author gives scientific plausibility, but whose threat humanity's scientific knowledge is incapable of negating. The narrator does not travel to Mars. Nor in itself does the arrival of the Martians cause the readjustment of perspective in the novel. Civilised humanity is displaced by the Martians' superiority, which is such that conventional views of evolution as having brought Europeans almost to the ultimate point of progress are radically challenged. Wells corrals several bestial images to suggest this: 'we men, the creatures who inhabit this earth, must be to them at least as alien and lowly as are the monkeys and lemurs to us' (p.111); 'So some respectable dodo in the Mauritius might have lorded it in his nest, and discussed the arrival of that shipful of pitiless sailors in want of animal food. "We will peck them to death tomorrow, my dear"' (p.38); 'The bare idea of this [the Martians' injection of the fresh living blood of other creatures into their own veins] is no doubt horribly repulsive to us, but at the same time I think we should remember how repulsive our carnivorous habits would seem to an intelligent rabbit' (pp.133–134); '"It's just men and ants", says the artilleryman, "There's the ants build their cities, live their lives, have wars, revolutions, until the men want them out of the way, and then they go out of the way. That's what we are now – just ants. Only ... We're eatable ants"' (p.163); 'I felt as a rabbit might feel returning to his burrow, and suddenly confronted by the work of a dozen busy navvies digging the foundations of a house ... I was no longer a master, but an animal among the animals, under the Martian heel. With us it would be as with them, to lurk and watch, to run and hide; the fear and empire of man had passed away' (p.154); 'I began to compare the things to human machines, to ask myself for the first time in my life how an ironclad or a steam-engine would seem to an intelligent lower animal' (p.56). These comparisons of civilised humanity with monkeys, lemurs, scared rabbits, soon-to-be extinct dodos, and displaced ants emphasise humans' instability and compel readers to contemplate the effects of imposing their technology upon 'lower' beings. They suggest the vulnerability of humans, projecting globally the fears of decline in British authority that are present in many texts of the decade.

There is a moral, as well as a physical, dislocation to the narrative. In the first chapter, the narrator has this to say about the Martians:

> And before we judge of them too harshly, we must remember what ruthless and utter destruction our own species has wrought, not only upon animals, such as the vanished bison and the dodo, but upon its own inferior races. The Tasmanians, in spite of their human likeness, were entirely swept out of existence in a war of extermination waged by European immigrants, in

the space of fifty years. Are we such apostles of mercy as to complain if the Martians warred in the same spirit? (p.11)[43]

The invitation to think carefully about the actions we perform under the banner of progress could hardly be clearer, even if it is driven by fear of a like retribution, rather than by an altruistic sense of human equality and liberty. Just as Darwinian theories of race and progress had conflated physical and moral stature, so Wells (while drawing on them) had to do likewise in questioning his contemporaries' self-satisfaction. The critical tensions within the story have to do with Wells's desire specifically to critique 'our' (i.e. British) imperialism, while tracing natural laws applicable to all (and not only to humans). We might note, at this point, Conrad's description of the imperialism of 'our modern Conquistadores': 'Their achievement is monstrous enough in all conscience ... like that of a gigantic and obscene beast.'[44]

If one sees the whole of the human race as the hero one closes down questions that the text leaves open. Not only are we asked to reflect on the fate of the Tasmanians; there are direct references to rivalry and hostility between the European powers. The narrator recalls that soon after the first Martian vessel had landed, '[m]any people had heard of the cylinder, of course, and talked about it in their leisure, but it certainly did not make the sensation an ultimatum to Germany would have done' (p.39).

These tensions encourage one to review Catherine Belsey's reading of classic realism – not so much her definition, which 'permits the inclusion of all those fictional forms which create the illusion while we read that what is narrated is "really" and intelligibly happening: *The Hobbit* and *The Rainbow*, *The War of the Worlds* and *Middlemarch*'[45] – but her statement on closure:

> Classic realist narrative ... turns on the creation of enigma through the precipitation of disorder which throws into disarray the conventional cultural and signifying systems. Among the commonest sources of disorder at the level of plot in classic realism are murder, war, a journey or love. But the story moves inevitably towards *closure* which is also disclosure, the dissolution of enigma through the re-establishment of order, recognizable as a reinstatement or a development of the order which is understood to have preceded the events of the story itself.[46]

One can hardly quarrel with the first half of that passage, but the ending of *The War of the Worlds* seems not to conform to the rules observed in the second part. It preserves a dual vision that makes the readers doubt that either cognitive or social order has been satisfactorily re-established.

The social and moral questioning is achieved by a narrative juxtaposition of the everyday and the fantastic. Critics have frequently commented on this. It has been intelligently elaborated by Rosemary Jackson in her discussion of the paraxial area which 'could be taken to represent the spectral region of the fantastic, whose imaginary world is neither entirely "real" (object), nor entirely "unreal" (image), but is located somewhere indeterminately between the two'.[47] Wells's narrator himself draws our attention to the arrangement, saying: 'The most extraordinary thing to my mind, of all the strange and wonderful things that happened upon that Friday, was the dovetailing of the commonplace habits of our social order with the first beginnings of the series of events that was to topple that social order headlong' (p.39). From this and other utterances it is clear that the focus of the narrative will not be on the Martians (the source of disorder) but on the capacity of the social order to respond to their threat. The narrator must be able to observe both the order and the challenge to it. To do this he must be positioned within that order, but also be able to observe it from without. It is important therefore that we have an idea of the unnamed narrator as both representative and unique. He moves inside and outside society. This is what he writes of himself:

> Perhaps I am a man of exceptional moods. I do not know how far my experience is common. At times I suffer from the strangest sense of detachment from myself and the world about me; I seem to watch it all from the outside, from somewhere inconceivably remote, out of time, out of space, out of the stress and tragedy of it all. This feeling was very strong upon me that night. Here was another side to my dream. (p.36)

Ostensibly these words are provoked by his flight from the Martians' Heat-Ray, yet one may infer that they are true of his constitution more generally; that they identify him as precisely the sort of individual who will be able to give a reading of the situation that is at once involved and detached. As readers, we have to guard against an easy acceptance of his self-diagnosis. After all, he can no sooner remove himself from his time and space than can we or the author. He might wish, like many writers, to live by the illusion that he possesses a depth of vision others lack because he has the unusual ability to step outside his everyday surroundings, but wherever one treads one carries the imprint of one's milieu.

Against such activity, however, is set the force of nature, which appears ultimately irresistible. On the face of it, *The War of the Worlds* treats this theme in a similar way to *The Strange Case of Dr. Jekyll and Mr. Hyde* and *Heart of Darkness* in that nature is seen as operating internally as well as externally. So in Wells's text one concern is the danger of the conquest of civilisation by pre- (or anti-)social urges. This threat arises not from the Martians, but from the responses of 'civilised' people to them. The narrator indicates as much when he relates the details of his flight from the Martians and their 'pitiless sword of heat'. After falling with the exhaustion caused by 'the violence of my emotion and of my flight', he

> sat up, strangely perplexed. For a moment, perhaps, I could not clearly understand how I came there. My terror had fallen from me like a garment. My hat had gone, and my collar had burst away from its stud. A few minutes before there had only been three real things before me – the immensity of the night and space and nature, my own feebleness and anguish, and the near approach of death. Now it was as if something turned over, and the point of view altered abruptly. There was no sensible transition from one state of mind to the other. I was immediately the self of every day again, a decent ordinary citizen. The silent common, the impulse of my flight, the starting flames, were as if it were a dream. I asked myself had these latter things indeed happened. I could not credit it. (p.35)

Like Marlow in *Heart of Darkness*, the narrator experiences a vision of the wilderness invading the civilised world. The signs of everyday existence are lost in a moment of metaphysical revelation, and are then suddenly recovered, leaving the narrator with the altered consciousness that affords him a view of his ordinary self and of the eternity of nature that will obliterate him. His altered point of view gives him a dual perspective, which remains with him throughout and beyond the rest of his story. It is in this sense that the text avoids the act of closure that Belsey contends is a feature of classic realist narratives. The narrator witnesses the re-emergence of animal behaviour as panic sets into the multitude and he hears of the 'savage struggle' (p.66) for places in the special evacuation trains and of people 'fight[ing] savagely' (p.99) for standing room in the carriages. The reappearance of these bestial characteristics, also marked by the failure to observe property rights – 'As they [the scattered multitudes] grew hungry the rights of property ceased to be regarded' (p.114) – shakes any lingering certainty that civilised humanity has reached a secure position at the top of the evolutionary ladder.

At the end of the story, the narrator feels 'an abiding sense of doubt and insecurity in my mind' (p.192). He tells of how he still witnesses two worlds:

> I sit in my study writing by lamplight, and suddenly I see again the healing valley below set with writhing flames, and feel the house behind and about me empty and desolate. I go out into the Byfleet Road, and vehicles pass

MORLOCKS, MARTIANS, AND BEAST-PEOPLE   131

> me, a butcher-boy in a cart, a cabful of visitors, a workman on a bicycle, children going to school, and suddenly they become vague and unreal, and I hurry again with the artilleryman through the hot, brooding silence ...
>
> I go to London and see the busy multitudes in Fleet Street and the Strand, and it comes across my mind that they are but the ghosts of the past, haunting the streets that I have seen silent and wretched, going to and fro, phantasms in a dead city, the mockery of life in a galvanized body. (p.192)

This is not the recovery of the established order, but a continuing revision of one's view of reality. The narrator sees through the superficial signs of mundane existence to place these alongside historical and biological truths (if one accepts the Martian invasion as constituting part of the history of his surroundings). He manages to gain a diachronic perspective alongside the synchronic: he can see ordinary everyday activities and how they fit into a larger timescale. This allows him to question the solidity of modern urban life. He has already told us, at the height of the panicked evacuation of the capital, that '[b]y ten o'clock the police organization, and by mid-day even the railway organizations, were losing coherency, losing shape and efficiency, guttering, softening, running at last in that *swift liquefaction of the social body*' (p.99, my emphasis). And he has shown us the metaphysical depth underlying the quotidian in the city, what he calls the 'mockery of life in a galvanized body' (p.192) – a phrase that critics have noted recalls the Martians themselves, perhaps as a kind of objective correlative for the imperialist urban dwellers. The railway that kills or injures the Egyptian invader in Marsh's *The Beetle*, as we saw in Chapter Two, is no threat to the Martians, but the collapse of infrastructure forces a shift in perception. It also illustrates the quality that leads one critic to claim that: 'Of *fin-de-siècle* authors, H.G. Wells best understood historical contingency and the relationship between order and chaos.'[48]

Both author and narrator intend their tale to enlarge if not transform their readers' vision. Near the end of the book the narrator exclaims:

> The broadening of men's views that has resulted can scarcely be exaggerated. Before the cylinder fell there was a general persuasion that through all the deep of space no life existed beyond the petty surface of our minute sphere. Now we see further. (p.191)

Wells has had to combine elements of realism and romance so that each may be seen more clearly through its estrangement by the intrusion of the other. The narrator's declaration that now we see further might be said to satisfy Lukács's criterion of realism:

> If literature is a particular form by means of which objective reality is reflected, then it becomes of crucial importance for it to grasp that reality as it truly is, and not merely to confine itself to reproducing whatever manifests itself immediately and on the surface. If a writer strives to represent reality as it truly is, i.e. if he is an authentic realist, then the question of totality plays a decisive role ...
>
> ...
>
> ... So the crux of the matter is to understand the correct dialectical unity of appearance and essence. What matters is that the slice of life shaped and depicted by the artist and re-experienced by the reader should reveal the relations between appearance and essence without the need for any external commentary.[49]

In *The War of the Worlds* Wells goes some way to showing the surface of life; he provides in his geographical and domestic settings the kind of detail which Henry James called 'solidity of specification' and which, for James, constituted the 'air of reality [which] ... seems to me to be the supreme virtue of a novel – the merit on which all its other merits ... helplessly and submissively depend'.[50] But for Wells, this sort of solidity is plainly insufficient.[51] Indeed, his phantasmical imagery makes that supposed solidity insubstantial. In doing this, he opposes appearance and essence quite deliberately and is finally unable to decide between them. His method illustrates the truth of Jackson's observation that:

> Fantasy is not to do with inventing another non-human world: it is not transcendental. It has to do with inverting elements of this world, re-combining its constitutive features in new relations to produce something strange, unfamiliar and *apparently* 'new', absolutely 'other' and different.[52]

Wells achieves this through the tropes of space travel and the monstrous Martians. Dryden describes the latter as 'a new type of Gothic monster, but one whose inspiration comes from earlier Gothic forms'.[53] As with physical entity, so with literary form. Through his dissolution of generic borders, Wells's narrative innovations call into question the solidity of his readers' social world. His metaphors of travel and animality play an essential part in this.

'Monkey on a gridiron!'

Wells's treatment of transformation and travel is not confined to his science fiction and gothic tales. His comic romance, *The Wheels of Chance* (1896), tells of the critical adventure that befalls draper's assistant

Mr Hoopdriver during a cycling holiday along the southern coast of England. Hoopdriver finds himself rescuing Jessie Milton, a naïve seventeen- to eighteen-year-old with aspirations to be a New Woman, from Mr Bechamel, a family friend in his early thirties who (unbeknown to her) is already married. Somewhat uncertainly, she has run away with Bechamel from her stepmother. Bechamel 'came into my life, and talked to me of art and literature, and set my brain on fire'.[54] He promised to help her earn a living by writing (p.98). The transformation Jessie had sought was from sheltered captivity to a life of freedom: 'I wanted to come out into the world, to be a human being – not a thing in a hutch' (p.154). She wants to 'write Books and alter things. To do Good ... to lead a Free Life and Own myself ... to obtain a position as a Journalist' (p.180); to leave conventional Surbiton and to be unconventional.

Although humorously handled, transformation is dealt with no less seriously in this tale than in the others of Wells's discussed in this chapter. Similar connections between money, class, and beastliness are made. Moreover, the ending leaves open the question of whether or not the transformation will ultimately be accomplished. Jessie's rather reluctant restoration to her stereotypically unpleasant stepmother leaves Hoopdriver with only her urging his self-improvement – for which she will send him books – to leave in his mind the possibility of a social advancement that might, in six years' time, make him a suitable match.

Two factors make possible Hoopdriver's (would-be) transformation: his vacation and the encounters with Jessie. Early on in his holiday, the narrator tells us that:

> Only those who toil six long days out of the seven, and all the year round, save for one brief glorious fortnight or ten days in the summer time, know the exquisite sensations of the First Holiday Morning. All the dreary, uninteresting routine drops from you suddenly, your chains fall about your feet. (p.20)

There is a comic tone to the passage, but it is far from flippant: wage labour is a threat to independence, and its gradation can further limit one's freedom. Also, in common with other texts we have examined, self-definition is gendered and identified with masculinity. Thus:

> No more Manchester Department for ten days! Out of Manchester, a Man. The draper Hoopdriver, the Hand, had vanished from existence. Instead was a gentleman, a man of pleasure, with a five-pound note, two sovereigns, and some silver at various convenient points of his person. At any rate as good as a dook, if not precisely in the peerage. (p.29)

But Wells, who had himself been apprenticed to a draper, brings Hoopdriver down to earth again as, reaching involuntarily for his money, he takes his right hand off the handlebar and his bicycle violently swerves towards the cemetery. It is a striking symbol of the social precariousness that Hoopdriver faces should he climb off his saddle. Even so, his temporary climb sees him differentiate himself from people he regards as beneath him. Of those who have positioned in the road a half-brick which he just misses, he thinks: 'Mischievous brutes there were in the world to put such a thing in the road ... Ought to prosecute a few of these roughs, and the rest would know better' (p.30).

Another sign of his in-between status comes later when a young boy calls him '[m]onkey on a gridiron!' (p.40). This occurs as Hoopdriver is pursuing Jessie and just after the narrator has observed:

> The situation was primordial. The Man beneath prevailed for a moment over the civilised superstructure, the Draper. He pushed at the pedals with archaic violence. So Palæolithic man may have ridden his simple bicycle of chipped flint in pursuit of his exogamous affinity. (p.39)

This is but a comic treatment of a theme evident in others of Wells's works and those of many of his contemporaries: the extent to which the primitive remains intact under the civilised veneer.

Further evidence of class distinction comes when Hoopdriver mentally compares Jessie with his female co-workers: 'She was a real Young Lady. No mistake about that! None of your blooming shop girls' (p.40). But he reminds himself of his own standing: 'What's the good of thinking such things ... I'm only a blessed draper's assistant' (p.41). He notes that she is from a wealthy family: 'Her machine couldn't have cost much under twenty pounds.' Class embarrassment is reinforced by a gender one. Hoopdriver speculates that Jessie is 'one of these here New Women' (p.42), but it is as likely that his awkwardness has as much to do with her being a woman at all as with her being a new one.

With a new-found confidence born of Jessie's trust, Hoopdriver plans to get Jessie's and Bechamel's bicycles, so that he can escape with her. His 'intelligence now was a soaring eagle; he swooped on the situation at once' (p.141). Then, cycling away with Jessie, Hoopdriver 'was in the world of Romance' (p.150). Under the benediction of the magical moonlight, 'rode our two wanderers side by side through the transfigured and transfiguring night' (p.152). Hoopdriver presents an altered self by giving his name to her as Chris Carrington and later as Benson and entertaining her wrong guess that he comes from South Africa (pp.188–189). His escape from his mundane existence is temporary, but dramatic:

in illegal possession of a stolen bicycle, a stolen young lady, and two stolen names, established with them in an hotel that is quite beyond his means, and immensely proud of himself in a somnolent way for these incomparable follies. (p.161)

Reflecting on his inadequacy, Hoopdriver

> ... wonder[s] what Adam'd think of me – as a specimen. Civilisation, eigh? Heir of the ages! I'm nothing. I can't do anything. – Sketch a bit. Why wasn't I made an artist?
> 'Beastly cheap, after all, this suit does look in the sunshine.' (p.174)

It may seem light-hearted, but the phrase 'heir of the ages' echoes the Traveller's dread inference when he catches sight of a Morlock and wonders about the destiny of the human race.

When Hoopdriver feels the weight of his lies become too much, he admits to Jessie that he is not a wealthy South African, but a humble draper's assistant. He is ashamed of having to be 'just another man's hand' and had lied to her because 'I wanted somehow to seem more than I was' (p.248). The previous night he had lain awake, 'thinking what a got-up imitation of a man I was' (p.249). He complains about the draper's lot:

> It's not a particularly honest nor a particularly useful trade; it's not very high up; there's no freedom and no leisure – seven to eight-thirty every day in the week; don't leave much edge to live on, does it? – real workmen laugh at us, and educated chaps like bank clerks and solicitors' clerks look down on us ... Without capital there's no prospects; one draper in a hundred don't even earn enough to marry on. (pp.253–254)

Hoopdriver thinks about 'what I really am, and what I might have been. Suppose it was all different–'. Jessie tells him to '*[m]ake* it different', and her remedy is that classic Victorian prescription: '*Work*' (p.258). Self-effacing as ever, Hoopdriver, believes it is too late for him to begin afresh. When they part with the understanding that he will work to improve himself and Jessie has asked him: 'What will you be – what can a man make of himself in six years' time?' (p.290), he trips over a rabbit hole.

John Batchelor's dismissal of *The Wheels of Chance* as 'facetious and superficial' is too harsh, especially as he earlier remarks (while discussing the Time Traveller's machine as based on a bicycle) that Wells 'saw the bicycle as a revolutionary, democratic form of transport which would initiate social change; it was one of the very few activities in which men and women could enjoy each other's company without chaperones'.[55]

Wells himself has pointed to the seriousness of his book, grouping *The Wheels of Chance* with one of a number of works dealing with the 'theme of the floating *persona*, the dramatized self [that] recurs at various levels of complexity and self-deception'. The 'endeavour to anchor *personas* to a common conception of reality' has, he writes, been a main strand of interest throughout his life.[56] He identifies Hoopdriver as one of these personas. He may have in mind Hoopdriver's propensity to fantasise about roles for himself that he plays out in his mind, but the idea of the floating persona can apply equally, whether intentionally or not, to Hoopdriver's social situation.

It could be argued that the lack of fixity applies to genre also: much of the novel has a dramatic feel, with many more passages of dialogue than one finds in several other of Wells's writings from the 1890s. In fact, Wells later wrote (from 1903 to 1904) a play, *Hoopdriver's Holiday*, based on the novel.[57] Furthermore, in the novel, Wells includes several references to other writers – Conan Doyle, Gissing, Kipling, Ibsen, Schreiner, Besant, Rider Haggard, Marie Corelli, Ouida, Shakespeare, and Christina Rossetti – and to ideas about what novels should represent and how. Hoopdriver's imaginative flights – 'His entire life, you must understand, was … a series of short stories linked only by the general resemblance of their hero' (pp.67–68) – constitute transformations of his everyday existence.

That the novel should be taken seriously is also indicated by the fact that Wells wrote it during a year-and-a-half's residence in Woking, where he also composed *The War of the Worlds* and *The Invisible Man*. He learned to ride his bicycle – 'a description of [the] state of my legs … became the opening chapter of the *Wheels of Chance*' – and '[I] wheeled about the district marking down suitable places and people for destruction by my Martians'.[58] Indeed, we might remember that the Time Traveller's machine was an 'adapted bicycle – one of the most common symbols of social liberation in the 1890s'.[59] It is the perfect image of the ordinary and extraordinary that informs his writing, which in turn alters generic boundaries as it aims to transform our vision.

Notes

1 Rosemary Jackson, *Fantasy: The Literature of Subversion* (London: Routledge, 1981), p.3.
2 Linda Dryden, *The Modern Gothic and Literary Doubles: Stevenson, Wilde and Wells* (Basingstoke: Palgrave Macmillan, 2003), pp.147, 164.

3 The story was first serialised in *The New Review* in five instalments between January and May 1895 and was published in book form by Heinemann in May of that year. Page references in this chapter are to H. G. Wells, 'The Time Machine', in *Selected Short Stories* (Harmondsworth: Penguin, 1958) and will be given parenthetically in the text. On the tale's origins in Wells's earlier three-part story, 'The Chronic Argonauts' (1888), see, for example, Lovat Dickson, *H. G. Wells: His Turbulent Life and Times* (London: Readers Union, Macmillan, 1971), pp.62–63.
4 Wells, 'The Time Machine', p.9.
5 In doing so I draw upon and develop my essay, 'Wells's Fifth Dimension: *The Time Machine* at the Fin de Siècle', in Tracey Hill and Alan Marshall, eds, *Decadence and Danger: Writing, History and the Fin de Siècle* (Bath: Sulis Press, 1997), pp.64–74.
6 Interview with Wells in the *Weekly Sun Literary Supplement*, 1 December 1895, quoted in Dryden, *The Modern Gothic and Literary Doubles*, p.148. Dryden observes that the interview appeared as Wells was about to publish *The Island of Doctor Moreau*. It was also, of course, the year that *The Time Machine* was published.
7 Norbert Elias, *Time: An Essay*, Edmund Jephcott, trans. (Oxford: Blackwell, 1993), p.36.
8 Elias, *Time*, p.36.
9 M. M. Bakhtin, 'Forms of Time and of the Chronotope in the Novel', in *The Dialogic Imagination: Four Essays by M. M. Bakhtin*, Michael Holquist, ed., and Caryl Emerson and Michael Holquist, trans. (Austin, TX: University of Texas Press, 1981), p.84.
10 One critic has argued that in Wells's work: 'meat becomes both something capable of shaping narrative structure and the visceral evidence of an imperial culture in which social interest is inseparable from appetite and illumination is bound to carnage. In both *The Time Machine* (1895) and *The Island of Doctor Moreau* (1896), the seeker of information … is figured as a sublimated hunter of human meat.' Michael Parrish Lee, 'Reading Meat in H. G. Wells', *Studies in the Novel* 42, 3 (Fall 2010), 250. On contemporary attacks on meat-eating, see Lee, 'Reading Meat', p.251.
11 Charles Darwin, *The Origin of Species by Means of Natural Selection*, last (sixth) edition [1872] (London: Watts & Co., n.d.), p.381.
12 Herbert Spencer, 'Progress: Its Law and Cause', in *Essays on Education and Kindred Subjects* (London: J. M. Dent & Sons, 1911), p.158.
13 Spencer, 'On Progress', p.154.
14 H. G. Wells, *First and Last Things: A Confession of Faith and Rule of Life* [1908] (London: Watts & Co., 1929), p.21.
15 Wells, *First and Last Things*, p.16.
16 Wells, *First and Last Things*, pp.27–28.
17 Darwin, *The Origin of Species*, p.400.
18 Wells, *First and Last Things*, p.51.
19 Wells, *First and Last Things*, p.123.
20 Wells, *First and Last Things*, p.53.
21 Spencer, 'On Progress', pp.164–165.
22 Israel Zangwill, *Children of the Ghetto: A Study of a Peculiar People* [1895] (Cambridge: Black Apollo Press, 2004), p.24.
23 Bernard Bergonzi, *The Early H. G. Wells: A Study of the Scientific Romances* (Manchester: Manchester University Press, 1961), p.56.
24 Lee, 'Reading Meat', p.250.

25 Lee, 'Reading Meat', p.251.
26 H. G. Wells, *The Island of Doctor Moreau* [1896] (Harmondsworth: Penguin Books, 1946), p.148. Further page references to this edition will be given parenthetically.
27 John Huntington, *H. G. Wells and Science Fiction* (New York, NY: Columbia University Press, 1982), p.xi.
28 Darko Suvin, 'Wells as the Turning Point of the SF Tradition', in Bernard Waites et al., eds, *Popular Culture: Past and Present* (London: Croom Helm, 1982), p.132.
29 For more on this influence, see Gillian Beer, *Darwin's Plots: Evolutionary Narrative in Darwin, George Eliot and Nineteenth-Century Fiction* (London: Ark, 1985), though Beer makes no reference either to American naturalism or to Wells.
30 John Glendening, *The Evolutionary Imagination in Late-Victorian Novels: An Entangled Bank* (Aldershot: Ashgate, 2007), p.46.
31 Glendening, *The Evolutionary Imagination in Late-Victorian Novels*, p.51. Glendening argues this on thematic and stylistic lines. In the former case, he maintains that *Moreau* 'appears to announce its author's efforts to extricate himself from the snarls of evolutionary theory' and that '[i]n later works he was free to transmute Lamarckian optimism and Darwinian pessimism into a cautionary vision of a possible ideal future always in doubt'. As regards style and Wells's changing responses to the text, Glendening observes that although '[l]ater in his life Wells characterized the story as a satirical fantasy or romance with a story line not to be taken seriously … [,] in the immediate wake of its publication [he] argued against critics who had questioned the efficacy of Doctor Moreau's methods of altering animals, contending that they are not unrealistic at all'. Glendening identifies it as situated 'somewhere between realism and satirical fantasy' (p.51).
32 David Punter also identifies the elements of colonial criticism, pointing out that Moreau is 'the white "aristocrat" who presides over a colonial society in which … fears of reversion … are ever-present'. David Punter, *The Literature of Terror: A History of Gothic Fictions from 1765 to the Present Day*, vol. 2, *The Modern Gothic* (London: Longman, 1996), p.13.
33 Darwin, *The Origin of Species*, p.407.
34 Chris Baldick, *In Frankenstein's Shadow: Myth, Monstrosity, and Nineteenth-Century Writing* (Oxford: Clarendon Press, 1987), p.156.
35 Suvin, 'Wells as the Turning Point', p.129.
36 Huntington, *H. G. Wells*, p.68. Suvin judges this to be the case in all but the 'maturest moments' in Wells's science fiction. Suvin, 'Wells as the Turning Point', p.129.
37 Quoted in John Batchelor, *H. G. Wells* (Cambridge: Cambridge University Press, 1985), p.22.
38 Stanislaw Lem, 'H. G. Wells's *The War of the Worlds*', in Rhys Garnett and R. J. Ellis, eds, *Science Fiction Roots and Branches: Contemporary Critical Approaches* (Basingstoke: Palgrave Macmillan, 1990), p.26.
39 H. G. Wells, *The War of the Worlds* [1898] (London: Pan Books Ltd., 1975), p.9. Further references will be given parenthetically and are to this edition.
40 Dryden, *The Modern Gothic and Literary Doubles*, p.179.
41 H. G. Wells, *Experiment in Autobiography: Discoveries and Conclusions of a Very Ordinary Person (Since 1866)* (New York, NY: The Macmillan Company, 1934), p.45.
42 Wells, *Experiment in Autobiography*, p.46.
43 Tasmanians were not, in fact, wiped out to extinction, but survived through

intermixing with whalers and others, though the consequences continue to provoke difficult questions about racial and cultural purity.
44 Joseph Conrad, letter to R. B. Cunninghame Graham, quoted in Baldick, *In Frankenstein's Shadow*, pp.171–172.
45 Catherine Belsey, *Critical Practice* (London: Methuen, 1980), p.51.
46 Belsey, *Critical Practice*, p.70.
47 Jackson, *Fantasy*, p.19.
48 Glendening, *The Evolutionary Imagination in Late-Victorian Novels*, p.28.
49 Georg Lukács, 'Realism in the Balance', in *Aesthetics and Politics: Ernst Bloch, Georg Lukács, Bertolt Brecht, Walter Benjamin, Theodor Adorno* (London: Verso, 1980), pp.33–34.
50 Henry James, 'The Art of Fiction', in Roger Gard, ed., *Henry James: The Critical Muse. Selected Literary Criticism* (London: Penguin, 1987), p.195. This essay was first published in *Longman's Magazine* in 1884. For the details and accuracy of Wells's geographical setting of the story, see Iain Wakeford, 'Wells, Woking and *The War of the Worlds*', *The Wellsian* 14 (Summer 1991), pp.18–29.
51 As he explains in *Experiment in Autobiography*. See p.410 et seq.
52 Jackson, *Fantasy*, p.8.
53 Dryden, *The Modern Gothic and Literary Doubles*, p.180.
54 H. G. Wells, *The Wheels of Chance* [1896] (London: J. M. Dent & Sons Ltd., n.d.), p.154. Further page references will be given parenthetically in the body of the chapter.
55 Batchelor, *H. G. Wells*, pp.44, 10.
56 Wells, *Experiment in Autobiography*, p.532. The rest of the group he gives as *Research Magnificent*, *Christina Alberta's Father*, and *The Bulpington of Blup*.
57 Batchelor, *H. G. Wells*, p.53.
58 Wells, *Experiment in Autobiography*, p.458.
59 Peter Keating, *The Haunted Study: A Social History of the English Novel 1875–1914* [1989] (London: Fontana Press, 1991), p.357.

CHAPTER FOUR

'Beast and man so mixty': The Fairy Tales of George MacDonald[1]

Fairies might seem to have little in common with the unattractive Beast-People of the preceding chapters, but no matter how different their appearance, they perform something of a similar role. 'I[f] fairy tales, are about anything, they are about transformation',[2] writes a biographer of George MacDonald (1824–1905), the subject of the present chapter. According to one study of the genre, fairy tales not only symbolise 'transformation and its borders' and take a myriad forms, but they 'can represent cultural as well as personal transitions'.[3]

MacDonald transformed the fairy tale, taking the traditional form and restructuring it, 'giving it a moral vision, without killing it'.[4] Even the very existence of his fairy tales constitutes a type of transformation since he turned to them after writing verse, and 'the themes which throbbed through its lines were to take other forms, notably in fairy tales and romances'. There were further transformations, moreover, for MacDonald 'never seemed happy with his books in any form and they changed radically from edition to edition'.[5]

Money was a determinant in MacDonald's writing, also, for he 'turned from writing verse to prose through economic necessity'.[6] William Raeper quotes him saying in 1893 that: 'I had to write for money, and prose pays the best; and I have had to write hard, too. I have always two novels on the stocks at once – I used to manage three.'[7] At MacDonald's peak, Raeper records, he was paid between 800 and 1,000 pounds per novel.[8] Creative imagination and money – the latter 'the great corrupter' in his writings[9] – rub together productively, but also in tension. 'Riches indubitably favour stupidity ... poverty, mental and moral development', MacDonald wrote.[10] Like a number of his contemporaries (including the pre-Raphaelites), MacDonald turned to a former age for values he thought wanting in his own:

MacDonald was a vigorous adherent of the nineteenth-century cult of medievalism, a protest against the materialism of his day. He saw enshrined in medievalism all the virtues which he felt necessary to build a Christian society ... It is easy to see how repulsed MacDonald had been by the *laissez-faire* ethics of selfishness and material gain.[11]

Although Raeper distinguishes between MacDonald's fairy tales and fantasies, I shall treat both forms alike in this chapter because Raeper sees them both as 'deal[ing] with transformation and plumb[ing] the workings of inner reality', thinks the 'leap from fairy-tale to fantasy a short one, moving from a traditional to a personal structure, but retaining the deeper purpose', and believes MacDonald to be wishing, through his fantasy, 'to transform his readers' relationship with the world'.[12]

Raeper describes MacDonald as 'an explorer of the unconscious'[13] and observes that '[o]ne of [his] struggles ... was to bring unconscious material to consciousness',[14] an attempt Raeper sees as especially evident in the 1895 work, *Lilith*, which will form the focus of this chapter. This observation, together with the fact that for MacDonald books were 'portals to other worlds',[15] allows us to read MacDonald's writing as constituting another kind of travel. On the face of it, *Lilith* operates as an example of what Mendlesohn labels the 'portal-quest fantasy', in which 'a fantastic world is entered through a portal' and is 'about entry, transition, and negotiation', but Mendlesohn shows that MacDonald's tale is more complicated than this and that it moves between the other four categories of fantasy that she outlines.[16]

Like science fiction, fairy tales and fantasy writing are not an escape from social realities, but a projection of them. As Kath Filmer puts it:

> What fantasy does ... is to confront readers with inescapable, perhaps unpalatable, truths about the human condition – cultural, social, psychological and spiritual – and then to posit alternatives which address the particular injustices, inequalities and oppressions with which the writer takes issue ... Far from being escapist, fantasy literature may be at the very least morally discomfiting, its demands uncompromising, its ideals attainable only at great cost – involving self-sacrifice and self-denial, and finally the development and maintenance of an acute social conscience.[17]

Sometimes, as in *Lilith*, the protagonists journey between the everyday and the fairy worlds. Even when stories are set entirely in the realm of the fairies, traces of the real are apparent. Far from being a conservative retreat from the mundane, fairy tales possess the potential for radical questioning of it. In the words of U. C. Knoepflmacher:

Addressed to both children and adults, MacDonald's fairy tales enlist paradox, play, and nonsense in a relentless process of destabilizing priorities he wants his readers to question and rethink. The possibilities offered by an elusive yet meaningful alternative order thus replace the dubious certitudes of everyday life.[18]

Describing MacDonald's 'life-long distrust of ready-made systems and conventional assumptions', Knoepflmacher compares the author's intent to 're-tailorize' these 'adventitious wrappings' with that of his 'fellow-Scot and mentor', Thomas Carlyle.[19] It is tempting to make something of their shared nationality; to suggest that their marginal position is partly responsible for their unconventional views. Indeed, the present volume implicitly pursues such a line by following this chapter on MacDonald (which includes discussion of Welsh writer Arthur Machen) with one on the Irish writer Oscar Wilde. However, MacDonald and Wilde were very different from each other in their backgrounds, beliefs, and practices, while an Englishman who (in that sense) wrote from the centre, William Morris, wrote radical tales. National and cultural marginality are important, but political views are more so and neither should be automatically equated. In the case of MacDonald, it is true that his 'childhood in the north of Scotland, together with his Scottish ancestry, go far in helping one to understand the man',[20] and that, in particular, the rural landscape and, above all, the influence of his religious upbringing are reflected in his writing, but most of his adult life was spent in England. As one of his most thorough biographers warns, 'it is a mistake to read the novels with too keen a biographical eye'.[21]

To MacDonald, multiple shapes are intrinsic to the telling: 'A genuine work of art must mean many things; the truer its art, the more things it will mean', he stated in an 1893 essay,[22] and his wife wrote to a correspondent who admired *Phantastes* that 'he has always told his friends to take any meaning they themselves see in it'.[23] Fixed meanings do not apply:

> A fairytale is not an allegory. There may be allegory in it, but it is not an allegory. He must be an artist indeed who can, in any mode, produce a strict allegory that is not a weariness to the spirit. An allegory must be Mastery or Moorditch.[24]

This is one reason why MacDonald could exclaim: 'I do not write for children, but for the childlike, whether of five, or fifty, or seventy-five',[25] a practice that Knoeplfmacher believes led him to hope that he 'might help grownup readers shed their acquired dependence on linear time and dissolve their sense of spatial constraints'.[26] Imagination is key. It is imagination that discovers the laws of history: 'the cycles in which events return, with the reasons of their return, recognizing them notwithstanding metamorphosis'. Without the influence of the imagination, 'no process of recording events can develop into a history'.[27] It is superior to intellect.

Oddly mingled

It is worth comparing MacDonald's remarks on the imagination with Arthur Machen's similar comments in his introduction to the 1916 edition of his 1894 story *The Great God Pan*:

> The logical understanding is the prison-house of Wordsworth's supreme and magistral ode; it is the house of prudent artifice, of the calculations of means to the end; it is the region where things can be done by recipe, where effects are all foreseen and intended. It is the house of matter and the house of the mechanism. And when youth does anything well or pretty well, it is because youth has not wholly been overcast by the shadows of the prison-walls; it is because it does not understand.[28]

Machen says of his tale of a shape-shifting woman with satyric proclivities that

> since the story was conceived and written in solitude, and came from far off lonely days spent in a land [in Wales] remote from London, and from literary societies and sodalities ... it stands, not for the ferment of the 'nineties, but for the visions that a little boy saw in the late 'sixties and early 'seventies. (p.17)

Like MacDonald's, this tale also deals with two worlds. Machen's Dr Raymond, who operates on seventeen-year-old Mary, whom he rescued from the gutter and whose life is, he thinks, therefore his to use as he sees fit, believes in the existence of a real world beyond the illusory everyday one; a world that the ancients, who 'knew what lifting the veil means', called 'seeing the God Pan' (p.32). A brief operation on Mary will allow her to see the God Pan. Almost immediately after the operation, '[t]he muscles of her face were hideously convulsed, she shook from head to foot, the soul seemed struggling and shuddering within the house of flesh'. It is described as 'a horrible sight' that has 'Mr. Clarke, the gentleman chosen by Dr Raymond to witness the strange experiment of the God Pan' (p.43) rush forward as Mary falls 'shrieking to the floor' (p.41). Again we have a text in which respectability and dissolution are conjoined. Clarke is 'a person in whose character caution and curiosity were oddly mingled; in his sober moments he thought of the unusual and the eccentric with undisguised aversion … yet he secretly hugged a belief in fantasy' (p.43). His 'sole pleasure was in the reading, compiling, and rearranging of what he called his "Memoirs to Prove the Existence of the Devil"' (p.44). In this disjunction between his public and private faces, he resembles many of those secret seekers of sin that we have seen in similar stories, just as Dr Raymond is part of the brotherhood of mad, bad, or misguided scientists that includes Dr Moreau and, at the other end of the century, Dr Frankenstein.

The irruption of nature is at the heart of social panic. (The God Pan gave rise to the word panic.) This is proved again when, one evening in London, Villiers, a graduate of Wadham College and 'eminently well-to-do' (p.55), bumps into his old college friend Charles Herbert, 'his face altered and disfigured by poverty and disgrace' and now a beggar (p.56). Herbert tells Villiers of how his fall followed his marriage to Helen. She is apparently the orphaned child of an English father and an Italian mother, and a

> woman, if I can call her a 'woman', [who] corrupted my soul. The night of the wedding I found myself sitting in her bedroom in the hotel, listening to her talk. She was sitting up in bed, and I listened to her as she spoke in her beautiful voice, spoke of things which even now I would not dare whisper in blackest night, though I stood in the midst of wilderness … In a year … I was a ruined man, in body and soul. (p.58)

Herbert sold all his property and Helen took all his money before leaving him. Once more the ideas of the unspeakable and namelessness occur. Herbert will not tell Villiers of all that happened; otherwise, '[y]ou would pass the rest of your life, as I pass mine, a haunted man, a man who has seen Hell' – and he thinks his wife did not have a real name, because '[o]nly human beings have names' (p.59). Like other figures that we have looked at, she combines beauty and repulsiveness (p.64). Not long after this meeting with Villiers, Herbert is found dead from, it is presumed, starvation. Four gentlemen also die, apparently by hanging themselves. The narrator makes an explicit comparison with the Ripper murders: 'The police had been forced to confess themselves powerless to arrest or to explain the sordid murders of Whitechapel; but before the horrible suicides of Piccadilly and Mayfair they were dumbfounded' (p.90). A fifth suicide provides a second link with a Mrs Beaumont, whose unique appearance inspires in Austin a 'kind of dim far-off memory, vague but persistent' (p.93), and whom at least the first and fifth suicides visited shortly before their deaths. The last of these, Crawshaw, had been seen by Villiers just before his death and is described by him as a 'lost soul'. Villiers

> could never have supposed that such an infernal medley of passions could have glared out of any human eyes ... the man's outward form remained, but all hell was within it ... when I passed down Ashley Street and heard the closing door, that man no longer belonged to this world; it was a devil's face I looked upon. (p.97)

During the next three weeks, Villiers discovers that Mrs Beaumont, the former Mrs Herbert, and the former Helen Vaughan are one and the same. His inquiries have seen him descend to the social depths. Once more we have another example of a gentleman adventuring into the underworld:

> assuming, as I do assume, that her record was not of the cleanest, it would be pretty certain that at some previous time she must have moved in circles not quite so refined as her present ones. If you see mud on the top of a stream, you may be sure that it was once at the bottom. I went to the bottom. I have always been fond of diving into Queer Street for my amusement, and I found my knowledge of that locality and its inhabitants very useful. (p.103)

In fact, Villiers learns that Mrs Herbert/Beaumont had first been known there as a seventeen- or eighteen-year-old five or six years previously and had stayed a year, gathering sickening and 'nameless infamies' to her name that make even the 'worst den in London too good for her' (p.104). After the Paul Street case, she returned for eight months, then disappeared, and returned again some months before, making regular visits. When Villiers shows Austin a manuscript that details the entertainment Mrs Beaumont provided for her 'choicer guests' (p.106), Austin is horrified. Villiers remarks that: '"Yes; it is horrible enough; but after all, it is an old story, an old mystery played in our day, and in dim London streets instead of amidst the vineyards and the olive gardens."' He refers to the Great God Pan as

> an exquisite symbol beneath which men long ago veiled their knowledge of the most awful, most secret forces which lie at the heart of all things; forces before which the souls of men must wither and die and blacken ... Such forces cannot be named, cannot be spoken, cannot be imagined except under a veil and a symbol, a symbol to the most of us appearing a quaint, poetic fancy, to some a foolish tale. (p.107)

Again there is the meeting of respectability and sin, a conjunction that renders unstable the existing shape of things: 'But you and I, at all events, have known something of the terror that may dwell in the secret place of life, manifested under human flesh; that which is without form taking to itself a form' (p.107). (Granted, Villiers's speech might mean only that he and Austin have observed this condition in others and that their knowledge of the terror is thus second-hand, but I think that Villiers's earlier speech about diving into Queer Street makes it much more likely that first-hand knowledge is meant.) Villiers determines to offer Mrs Beaumont a choice between hanging herself and being exposed to the police. A note at the end of the book informs the reader that she died in her house on 25 July 1888, suggesting that she took the former option. In the final chapter, appropriately titled 'Fragments', we are presented with the translation of a Latin manuscript found among the papers of the well-known physician Dr Robert Matheson, of Ashley Street, after his death in 1892. The document, dated the day of Mrs Beaumont's death, records Matheson's 'horror and revolting nausea' at what he sees on the bed,

> lying there black like ink, transformed before my eyes. The skin, and the flesh, and the muscles, and the bones, and the firm structure of the human body that I had thought to be unchangeable, and permanent as adamant, began to melt and dissolve ...
>
> ... here there was some internal force, of which I knew nothing, that caused dissolution and change.
>
> Here too was all the work by which man had been made repeated before my eyes. I saw the form waver from sex to sex, dividing itself from itself, and then again reunited. Then I saw the body descend to the beasts whence it ascended, and that which was on the heights go down to the depths, even to the abyss of all being. The principle of life, which makes organism, always remained, while the outward form changed. (p.114)

At last:

> I saw nothing but a substance as jelly. Then the ladder was ascended again ... [here the MS. is illegible] ... [sic] for one instant I saw a Form, shaped in dimness before me, which I will not farther describe. But the symbol of this form may be seen in ancient sculptures, and in paintings which survived beneath the lava, too foul to be spoken of ... [sic] as a horrible and unspeakable shape, neither man nor beast, was changed into human form, there came finally death. (p.115)

The illegibility of part of the manuscript conveys the sense of the ineffable. A few pages later in a fragment, Dr Raymond informs Clarke that Helen, whose death Clarke witnessed, is the daughter of the Mary on whom he had experimented. Mary had given birth to her nine months after that night, never regaining her reason and dying shortly after the birth. Raymond knows that he was wrong to have 'ruined the reason of a human being by a foolish experiment, based on an absurd theory' (pp.119–120). He had forgotten that 'when the house of life is thus thrown open, there may enter in that for which we have no name, and human flesh may become the veil of a horror one dare may not express. I played with energies which I did not understand' (p.120). Clarke witnessed the end of it when he saw the death of Mrs Beaumont/ Helen Vaughan:

> The blackened face, the hideous form upon the bed, changing and melting before your eyes from woman to man, from man to beast, and from beast to worse than beast, all the strange horror that you witnessed, surprises me but little. (p.120)

Raymond knew what he had done as soon as Helen was born. When the child was five years old, he surprised it several times 'with a playmate, you may guess of what kind'. He had sent Helen away; the rest of her story is now known to him; and now 'she is with her companions' (p.120).

Through its employment of various journeys, *The Great God Pan* dissolves several boundaries, including those between past and present; science and myth; reason and the supernatural; moral constraint and sexual indulgence; self-control and abandonment.

Growing up

In MacDonald's work, too, physical form changes. Creatures are alternatively – or at once – human and animal. Gender is unstable. These instabilities press readers to look anew at the confused shapes; at the collapsed meanings. There is an element of the divine in the process. Rather than feeling defeated by Darwinian evolution, MacDonald appropriates science to poetry and poetry to God. There is no science without hypothesis, he writes, and 'the construction of any hypothesis whatever is the work of the imagination'.[29] In his works of the 1860s, MacDonald emphasised the childlikeness of God and condemned in contemporary Evangelicalism the 'tyranny of stupid logic over childlike intuitions'.[30] Certain of his writings (such as *Lilith*) reflect his belief that the spiritual and physical worlds are not completely separate.[31]

Lack of fixity in MacDonald's work is not a direct response to social confusion, but rather an expression of religious conviction. In Hein's words, MacDonald 'had little esteem for attempts to achieve doctrinal preciseness in areas in which Scripture itself is vague'.[32] Hein quotes from a sermon in which MacDonald

> affirmed that Christians in general were 'far too anxious to be definite, and have finished, well-polished systems, forgetting that the more perfect a theory about the infinite the surer it is to be wrong – the more impossible it is to be right.' The evident reason why no system of thought could be 'right,' in any exclusive sectarian sense, was simply that the mind was capable of containing it.[33]

Fairy tales provide MacDonald with a form that allows for openness. As Raeper puts it: 'MacDonald happily invited an imaginative participation in the meaning of his stories. Such openness is a marked difference from the intrusive adult voices intent on laying down the law in the Victorian nursery.'[34] In *Lilith*, Vane is transported to a fantastic world, into and from which he journeys several times. But the absence of definition to shapes conveys MacDonald's moral concerns. His desire to avoid a closed way of viewing God and nature leads to an openness that extends beyond a religious conception to an intellectual one that has implications for ways of reading his narratives and seeing the world. Knoepflmacher claims that MacDonald 'resembles those modern symbolists for whom the very instability of interpretation provided a fertile source of meaning' and that '[h]is very best stories operate within a new space, a borderland in which old certitudes must be dismantled before they can be reinvigorated'. Knoepflmacher goes on to state that: 'MacDonald's fairy tales dramatize a struggle for endurance, a permanence that can only be achieved through full immersion into uncertainty and flux.'[35]

But just as the real and the fantastic rub against and enter each other in MacDonald's tales, so the physical world is present in his theological speculations. Hein notes that MacDonald hated the phrase 'getting on', which summarised the materialism of the Evangelicals, who 'had come to feel that economic gain was the just reward for righteous living'.[36] He never approved of the 'perennial desire of the middle class to rise in the world of trade and affluence'.[37] Like Wilde, his tales often moralise against the worship of money. MacDonald was attracted to Christian Socialism and lived for some years in poverty. He met Charles Kingsley, admired his work, and was friends with both Octavia Hill and John Ruskin. He was himself involved with efforts to alleviate the lot of the poor.[38] It would be quite wrong, then, to dismiss MacDonald's tales as simply other-worldly. McGillis is right to notice the element of subversion in his writing (which feature he shares with his friend Lewis Carroll):

> MacDonald's work, especially *The Princess and Curdie*, recognizes the need to examine and question the myths with which Victorian society orders itself. The separation of rich and poor and the Victorian view of female dependence and fragility are two social myths with which MacDonald is concerned. He does not provide his young readers with an easy escape into fantasy; rather, he encourages them to think about social and spiritual matters. MacDonald's children's books are as much about growing up in this world as they are about preparing ourselves for heaven.[39]

MacDonald's tales are more directly reflective of society than Carroll's Wonderland.

The fantastic jostles with the everyday in MacDonald, and his readers are meant not only to learn from this relationship, but to do so by thinking for themselves about it. The relative absence of a didactic voice means that readers are invited actively to engage with the narrative. Whether this means that the process is any less manipulative is debatable – it is, after all, another strategy aimed at the same end: the moral improvement of the reader. However, it probably is true to claim, as McGillis does, that in MacDonald's work '[t]he most sought-after change is change in people'; and, as Raeper does, that it 'transforms the minds of those who read him'.[40] His writings are designed so that transformation should apply to those outside the tale as much as to those within it: indeed, the physical alterations witnessed in many of his characters symbolise the consequences of moral improvement or degeneration. Religious conviction can, as McGillis suggests in the above quotation, directly affect one's dealings with society. Raeper draws out the wider appeal of change: 'The longing for transformation that many of his readers feel finds fulfilment in the movement from unbelief to belief, in peasants becoming noblemen, in women becoming corpses, witches, angels or saints.'[41]

MacDonald's eschewal of single interpretations imbues his writing with a quality that has been seen both as modernist in its symbolic richness and as an anticipation of postmodernism in its open-endedness.[42] McGillis sees the latter in MacDonald's avoidance of closure in his stories.

Beast-selves

One of MacDonald's best-known works is *Lilith* (1895). It explores the relationship of the fantastic to the real; of the divine to the secular; of beauty (moral and physical) to ugliness; of children to parents; and of man to woman. In an oft-quoted remark from his introduction to the novel, C. S. Lewis proclaims that what MacDonald 'does best is fantasy – fantasy that hovers between the allegorical and the mythopoeic'.[43] But despite Lewis's explanation that the 'quality which had enchanted me in his imaginative works turned out to be the quality of the real universe, the divine, magical, terrifying and ecstatic reality in which we all live' (p.xii), such a statement might distract from the material detail of that reality.

The novel begins: 'I had just finished my studies at Oxford, and was taking a brief holiday from work before assuming definitely the management of the estate' (p.5). Education, work, property, and class are signalled from the start as significant. The next sentence informs us that the narrator was an orphan: 'My father died when I was yet a child; my mother followed him within a year, and I was nearly as much alone in the world as a man might find himself' (p.5). One might be tempted to launch from here into Freudian readings – as some critics have been: MacDonald was eight-years-old when his own mother died, and Hein records, a touch superfluously one suspects, that he was 'deeply affected by his mother's death'.[44] MacDonald's father lived on well into his son's adulthood, however, and in any case MacDonald is using the narrator's parentless upbringing for two main purposes: first, to set up a movement that is completed at the end of the book when he meets with everyone's true parents, Adam and Eve; second, to place him as a man who has no place. I mean by this latter comment that the narrator, whom we shall know as Vane, lacks (apart from his time at Oxford) the usual marks of social status, an absence that allows MacDonald to judge the man positively by his own (moral) qualities.

In a scene-setting which in its air of the Gothic and its evocation of a house and family 'of some antiquity' recalls Poe and Hawthorne (p.5), MacDonald further loosens the narrator's ties. Rather than providing stability, the lineage confirms one's own impermanence:

> Nothing surely can more impress upon a man the transitory nature of possession than his succeeding to an ancient property! Like a moving panorama mine has passed from before many eyes, and is now slowly flitting from before my own. (pp.5–6)

It is a curious passage, because this kind of possession can only be transitory if seen from the viewpoint of the individual. In fact, the condition described by Vane here is that of family ownership; of inheritance. In that sense, ownership can only be seen as temporary if there is a threat to unearned wealth. That the narrator is an orphan allows MacDonald to show him looking at 'his' property anew. The fresh perspective introduces an impression of impermanence that reflects the larger insecurity of the aristocracy. Of course, MacDonald intends a Christian homily contrasting earthly riches with spiritual wealth. At the same time, a potentially radical message about the fragility and ultimate irrelevance of material goods is delivered. The commentary is soon made more explicit. When he finds himself in another world – that which lies through the mirror in the garret – Vane wonders: 'how was life to be lived in a world of which I had all the laws to learn?' He has the following thought:

> I had never yet done anything to justify my existence; my former world was nothing the better for my sojourn in it: here, however, I must earn, or in some way find, my bread! But I reasoned that, as I was not to blame in being here, I might expect to be taken care of here as well as there! I had had nothing to do with getting into the world I had just left, and in it I had found myself heir to a large property! If that world, as I now saw, had a claim upon me because I had eaten, and could eat again, upon this world I had a claim because I must eat – when it would in return have a claim on me! (pp.23–24)

Entry into this other world affords Vane the reflection that he owes his original world a debt. He has done nothing to deserve the property that he has inherited. He is the undeserving rich. MacDonald's moral seems to go beyond the Victorian creed of self-help and radically to criticise those who feed off society without paying anything back. The spongers and scroungers, he rightly suggests, are those whose considerable wealth is made at everyone else's expense. Vane's continued hope that he can be given unearned food in his new world blatantly contradicts his new realisation that things are best worked for.

The narrator knows little more of his ancestors than that several of them were given to study, as he himself is. He is constantly seeing and looking for

> strange analogies, not only between the facts of different sciences of the same order, or between physical and metaphysical facts, but between physical hypotheses and suggestions glimmering out of the metaphysical dreams into which I was in the habit of falling. (p.5)

The house, which he has not seen from the time his guardian took him away as a child until he returned to take possession of it around a month before, has a large library. The latter contains a portrait of one of his ancestors and is, he hears tell and sees for himself, haunted by a Mr Raven – librarian to Sir Upward – who passes through the closed door from the library to a closet. Vane learns the identity of the ghostly old man from his (Vane's) butler, who also informs him that an ancient woman of the village had said that Upward was 'a great reader ... not of such books only as were wholesome for men to read, but of strange, forbidden, and evil books; and in so doing, Mr. Raven, who was probably the devil himself, encouraged him'. Upward and Raven, the woman had said, had suddenly disappeared and Upward was never seen again, but Raven 'continued to show himself at uncertain intervals in the library' (p.9).

One day the narrator follows the old librarian through passages, up a winding stair, and into the main garret where he faces a tall old-fashioned mirror that 'reflected neither the chamber nor my own person'. In it he sees a strange and wild landscape and a 'large and ancient raven' with which, stepping closer to observe it, he finds himself 'nose to beak ... in the open air, on a houseless heath' (p.11). He has entered

> a world, or call it a state of things, an economy of conditions, an idea of existence, so little correspondent with the ways and modes of this world – which we are apt to think the only world, that the best choice I can make of word or phrase is but an adumbration of what I would convey. I begin to fear that I have undertaken an impossibility, undertaken to tell what I cannot tell because no speech at my command will fit the forms in my mind. Already I have set down statements I would gladly change did I know how to substitute a truer utterance; but as often as I try to fit the reality with nearer words, I find myself in danger of losing the things themselves, and feel like one in process of awaking from a dream, with the thing that seemed familiar gradually yet swiftly changing through a succession of forms until its very nature is no longer recognisable. (pp.12–13)

The suggestion that there exists beyond Vane's everyday world a realm that is more real – or more true at least – risks making our material world less important than it is. At worst, and in some other nineteenth-century writers, this way of thinking forces an acceptance of worldly hardship in exchange for the consolation of spiritual reward. Such a view is pernicious when the hardship is caused by social conditions that could be ameliorated with effort, but is less so when held of incurable sickness. One often witnesses the latter attitude in MacDonald's reactions to his own frequent illnesses and the deaths of his children and friends; and, as has been remarked earlier, MacDonald did show an active interest in assisting the poor and was himself helped from poverty many times by gifts and loans from friends. There is thus some reason to free him from the charge that his belief in another, higher world is as socially conservative as that of some. A virtue of his ideas as communicated in the quotation above is that they invite us to consider the adequacy and appropriateness of language to describe one's environment and one's experiences in it. The fitness of narrative itself is thus called into question. It is not just a matter of word games however. MacDonald is making a serious point about social position. Vane's journey into the other world enacts a kind of rebirth. When asked by the raven who he is,

> I understood that I did not know myself, did not know what I was, had no grounds on which to determine that I was one and not another. As for the name I went by in my own world, I had forgotten it, and did not care to recall it, for it meant nothing, and what it might be was plainly of no consequence here. I had indeed almost forgotten that there it was a custom for everybody to have a name! (p.14)

Name in nineteenth-century society, as we have seen in *The Strange Case of Dr. Jekyll and Mr. Hyde*, for example, means more than a forename and surname. Rather, it is one's social status and moral reputation. The narrator's efforts to remember his name are in vain, because in his new place one's character will define one's shape afresh. This revisionary impulse of MacDonald's is hardly confined to *Lilith*. Hein notes that MacDonald often railed against the hierarchy of the British class system:

> His indignation was prompted not by a desire to do away with it – he was not especially democratic in his thinking – but by the perception that it seemed persistently to invert an hierarchy of true being. In a more ideal society people would be arranged on a social scale according to their moral and spiritual qualities, so that power and influence would be in the hands of truly worthy people. So it will be in the kingdom of God.[45]

Such an outlook clearly has radical potential.

As does Wells in *The Time Machine*, MacDonald uses the new world in which Vane finds himself as a defamiliarising device. Raven tells the visitor: 'if you understood any world besides your own, you would understand your own much better' (p.25). The suggestion is that a larger vision is necessary in order to comprehend one's ordinary environment. Travel, in both the actual and metaphorical sense, is meant here.

Another defamiliarising device employed is that of beastliness. More explicitly than in many of the other texts examined in the present volume, *Lilith* utilises animality for obvious symbolic purposes. 'Every one ... has a beast-self', Vane is told by Raven,

> and a bird-self, and a stupid fish-self, ay, and a creeping serpent-self too – which it takes a deal of crushing to kill! In truth, he has also a tree-self and a crystal-self, and I don't know how many selves more – all to get into harmony. You can tell what sort a man is by his creature that comes oftenest to the front. (p.30)

Vane's journey will see him encountering many kinds of beasts in his new symbolic landscape, which represents (among other things) the 'burial-ground of the universe', presided over by the raven, who 'was sexton of all he surveyed!' (p.27). It is a place, we shall see more clearly later, that seems to hold those who are dead and awaiting resurrection. When Vane flees and finds himself back in his library, he asks: 'Which was the real – what I now saw, or what I had just ceased to see? Could both be real, interpenetrating yet unmingling?' (p.37). His question invites us to speculate on the relationship between the material and spiritual worlds and encourages us to look for the divine in the mundane. Significantly, the library is one of the ways into and out of the other world; and when he had been walking with the sexton in a cold place, Vane had observed aisle upon aisle of couches on which sleeping things lay. He had wondered: 'Was this the sexton's library? were these his books? Truly it was no half-way house, this chamber of the dead!' (p.33). The idea of books as a passage between worlds is reinforced when Vane reads a manuscript of his father's that someone has left out. In it his father recorded a visitation, soon after his own father's (Vane's grandfather's) death, from Mr Raven, his great grandfather's (Sir Upward's) librarian. Raven talks of the other world, his home, to which he has now established a right of way through the house. 'A book', Raven remarks, 'is a door in, and therefore a door out.' That world is not a better one throughout, but is 'so much another that most of its physical, and many of its mental laws are different from those of this world. As for moral laws, they must everywhere be fundamentally the same' (p.40). MacDonald's message here would appear to be that we must practise or aspire to moral goodness consistently: that there is a universal morality, a continuum. Books, with their imagination and their poetry (which we must remember includes science), provide a bridge to this other world; the one that connects with our own. Raeper notes that libraries figure large in the writings of MacDonald, who referred in *There and Back* to a 'bookscape'. They are places 'filled with knowledge and mystery'.[46]

Lilith embodies this principle, and it exhibits a transformation of genres. Raeper points out that MacDonald 'adapted the Gothic conventions to his own ends'.[47] Its use of the manuscript is just one element of the Gothic (another being the old house with its mysterious garret and the ghostly comings and goings through the library). Additionally, Raeper notes that

> many of the preoccupations of the Gothic novel are MacDonald's own – its horror of and fascination with sex, the obsession with the supernatural and immortality, the exploration of the divine and demonic potentials of the human spirit, and the whiff of charnel-houses and graveyards.[48]

Fantasy, writes Raeper, 'is supremely the literature of transition, for one thing actually changes into another, though the fear was that one could become either an angel or a beast'. While '[o]ne of Darwin's legacies was a fear of the bestial nature within' and obvious figures for these were the vampire and werewolf, '[i]n MacDonald the constant association of women with predatory cat-like creatures reaches its purest expression in *Lilith*, who actually possesses the ability to change herself into a leopardess'. Raeper continues: 'MacDonald's symbols for women – corpse, ghost and cat – expose his own inner anxieties, but, according to a Jungian model, they can be applied to the human psyche at large.'[49]

The religious overtones are clear, if symbolic. And there are traces of science fiction, such as when Vane's father reports Raven speaking 'much about *dimensions*, telling me that there were many more than three, some of them concerned with powers which were indeed in us, but of which as yet we knew absolutely nothing' (p.41).[50] This seems distinctly Wellsian. As with other texts examined in the present book, the narrative structure of *Lilith* displays, as well as describes, transformations. MacDonald develops a generic admixture that brings changes to conventional styles and forms. The composition reflects this: 'No fewer than eight pre-publication drafts of *Lilith* exist, and the story underwent many mutations between the first drafts and the published book.'[51] MacDonald's purpose seems to be to direct attention to the interrelationship of the two (or more) worlds. This aim becomes apparent, also, during a conversation that Raven has with Vane about the meaning of home. When Vane asks Raven to tell him the nearest way home, Raven replies:

> 'I cannot … you and I use the same words with different meanings. We are often unable to tell people what they *need* to know, because they *want*

to know something else, and would therefore only misunderstand what we said.' (p.45)

If this is read as a speech against multiple meanings, it would be at odds with MacDonald's stress on the imagination and on the coexistence of the two worlds. And so it should be taken rather as a desire for harmony, the importance and desirability of which MacDonald underlines elsewhere in his writings.

Like Wells's Time Traveller, Vane breaks off from his narrative to comment on it and on his situation. MacDonald has his narrator explain the problems of communicating the experiences of one world to another. Vane's remarks anticipate by a century scholarly observations on the pitfalls of cross-cultural communication. Studies of travel and translation have shown how travellers who journey from one culture to another can only describe the unfamiliar through terms that are familiar. Concepts, people, creatures, plants, and so on, that are encountered for the first time must either remain alien or be rendered less strange by being translated into a known language and taxonomy. MacDonald's mind may be on the spiritual or metaphysical here, but his adventures in fantasy mean that his use of travel and shape-shifting motifs helps make the point for him. Thus, Vane states, for example:

> Here I interrupt my narrative to remark that it involves a constant struggle to say what cannot be said with even an approach to precision, the things recorded being, in their nature and in that of the creatures concerned in them, so inexpressibly different from any possible events of this economy, that I can present them only by giving, in the forms and language of life in this world, the modes in which they affected me – not the things in themselves, but the feelings they woke in me. (p.46)

Even this, Vane confesses, he does 'with a continuous and abiding sense of failure'. He finds it impossible

> to present more than one phase of a multitudinously complicated significance, or one concentric sphere of a graduated embodiment. A single thing would sometimes seem to be and mean many things, with an uncertain identity at the heart of them, which kept constantly altering their look. (p.46)

He is unsure of the ability of himself or of any of the 'communicating media of this world' to convey even to 'one who knew the region better than myself' the 'reality of my experience' in the other, strange world (pp.46–47). While Vane is in no doubt that he 'was actually regarding a scene of activity, I might be, at the same moment, in my consciousness aware that I was perusing a metaphysical argument' (p.47). Like the appearance and significance of the world that Vane has visited, the implications of this passage are manifold. MacDonald applies to the motifs of shape-shifting and transformation a reflection on the problems faced by travellers who wish to report back on the things they have seen. He employs this commentary to suggest the impossibility of passing on accurate knowledge of the spiritual world. Two issues besides the lack of a single fixed meaning are involved here: what can be known and what can be communicated to others. These matters are taken up in MacDonald's next chapter (number 10, 'The Bad Barrow'), in which Vane finds himself with an 'attendant shadow', a 'bird-butterfly' which 'flew with a certain swallow double' and whose 'wings were very large, nearly square, and flashed all the colours of the rainbow'. Vane is so entranced by their splendour and beauty that he stumbles over a rock and lies stunned. When he comes to, 'the creature was hovering over my head, radiating the whole chord of light, with multitudinous gradations and some kinds of colour I had never before seen'. He continues, but hits another stone as he cannot take his eyes off the being:

> Fearing then another fall, I sat down to watch the little glory, and a great longing awoke in me to have it in my hand. To my unspeakable delight, it began to sink toward me. Slowly at first, then swiftly it sank, growing larger as it came nearer. I felt as if the treasure of the universe were giving itself to me – put out my hand, and had it. But the instant I took it, its light went out; all was dark as pitch, a dead book with boards outspread lay cold and heavy in my hand. I threw it in the air – only to hear it fall among the heather. Burying my face in my hands, I sat in motionless misery. (p.47)

Vane's words are an expression of the huge gulf between superficial and real knowledge; between books and experience; between the mundane and the spiritual worlds. An attempt to capture the latter in the former is bound to fail. It is no wonder that Vane is left in sad stillness; his progress halted. Of course, there is an irony in MacDonald's using a book, *Lilith*, to make his point about the inadequacy and comparative sterility of books compared with deep knowledge, but it may be countered in his defence that the world of which he writes is infinitely more meaningful.

As he walks on, Vane is confronted by several monsters, 'hideous creatures, no two alike', that threaten him, but from which he is saved by the light of the moon that paralyses them (p.49). They include an animal like a tiger and another like a worm. 'In some of them, beauty of colour enhanced loathliness of shape: one large serpent was covered from head to distant tail with feathers of glorious hues' (p.49). Heading for the hills as the moon descends, Vane sees a woman with a white mist floating about her, which she tries to grasp and wrap around herself. She is beautiful, but her face exhibits such pride and misery that Vane can scarcely believe what he sees. Her eyes are dead. Suddenly she falls and writhes in pain:

> A moment more and her legs, hurrying from her body, sped away serpents. From her shoulders fled her arms as in terror, serpents also. Then something flew up from her like a bat, and when I looked again, she was gone. (p.50)

Fleeing in terror, Vane is pursued by many dark objects, the leading one of which 'threw himself upon me with a snarl of greedy hate' (p.50), but they fall in the angry light of the moon. In the next chapter, 'The Evil Wood', Vane resumes his journey in the strange world. His passage through it is reminiscent of Pilgrim's ordeals in the book by Bunyan that influenced Macdonald and of which he was 'passionately fond'.[52] MacDonald's writing however is more textured, combining spiritual elements with intellectual and artistic modes, including the Gothic, Romanticism, and psychological reflection, unavailable to the seventeenth-century author. These ingredients are present, for example, in Vane's description of looking at a forest at twilight:

> Presently, to my listless roving gaze, the varied outlines of the clumpy foliage began to assume or imitate – say rather *suggest* other shapes than their own. A light wind began to blow, it set the boughs of a neighbour tree rocking, and all their branches aswing, every twig and every leaf blending its individual motion with the sway of its branch and the rock of its bough. Among its leafy shapes was a pack of wolves that struggled to break from a wizard's leash: greyhounds would not have strained so savagely! I watched them with an interest that grew as the wind gathered force, and their motions life. (p.52)

In his fancy he sees in the shape of another mass of foliage a group of horses' heads and forequarters, their necks moving with the wind. The Gothic takes over as we read of the heads:

> how gaunt, how strange! – several of them bare skulls – one with the skin tight on its bones! One had lost the under jaw and hung low, looking unutterably weary – but now and then hove high as if to ease the bit. (p.53)

Above these floats the 'form of a woman, waving her arms in imperious gesture'. Vane is unsettled by these shapes and at the thought that they might 'overpower my brain with seeming reality' (p.53), but darkness then descends and he falls asleep once more. He hears and in the moonlight discerns a furious battle between skeletons and phantoms: 'Bones of men and horses lay scattered and heaped; grinding and crunching them under foot fought the skeletons.' In this 'battle of the dead' (p.53), a ghastly parody of worldly conflicts, presided over by the woman he had seen before and who urges its participants to slay one another,

> skeleton jaws and phantom-throats swelled the deafening tumult with the war-cry of every opinion, bad or good, that had bred strife, injustice, cruelty in any world. The holiest words went with the most hating blow. Lie-distorted truths flew hurtling in the wind of javelins and bones. Every moment some one would turn against his comrades, and fight more wildly than before, *The Truth! The Truth!* still his cry. (pp.53–54)

The suggestion is that those who fight proclaiming to have right on their side may not, in fact, possess such legitimacy. As we shall see, this is only one of many instances of MacDonald's use of the dream or fantasy world to cast critical light on our everyday one. As Filmer notes, 'for MacDonald, the spiritual is inseparable from the psychological and the social'.[53] In a way, the world into which Vane has travelled seems more real for its stripping away of superfluities so that we see the essence of things and the contrast between what is professed and actuality. The text's criticisms, in which travel and animality play a central role, assume more direct commentary on social and economic arrangements as Vane's journey continues. When he is befriended and fed by children who call themselves the Little Ones and Vane a good giant, he is told that some grow up to be bad giants (though rather like Wells's Eloi they show little curiosity, understanding of causality, or desire to change). His response to hearing that '[t]he bad giants are very proud of being fat' is: 'So they are in my world … only they do not say *fat* there, they say *rich*' (p.66). The exchange occurs after the children had watched Vane picking and enjoying an apple or two and then freed him after he had been taken captive and set to labour by two giants, one of whom 'growled like a beast' (p.57). Vane is tempted to stay with his small friends, but concludes that: 'I must rise and continue my travels, in the hope of coming upon some elucidation of the fortunes and destiny of the bewitching little creatures' (p.68). His resolve to leave is strengthened – for his sake and that of the children – after a beating by one of the giants. One of the children warns him to beware of the Cat-woman, the giant woman who lives in the desert, but Lona, who has assumed the role of protector of him and of her fellow children, whispers that the Cat-woman will not hurt him.

MacDonald has Vane learn about himself and about the society he has left behind. The lessons that *Lilith* offers have the tale conform to Farah Mendlesohn's model of the portal-quest narrative: i.e. that more than other categories of fantasy, it embodies the genre's reliance on a moral universe; 'that it is less an argument with the universe than a sermon on the way things should be, a belief that the universe should yield to moral precepts'.[54] The narrative's suggestions for improvement in *Lilith* operate on personal, social, and spiritual levels. All are linked. One of the conclusions Vane draws from his experiences in the other world is that he should spend less time by himself. Hungering after 'the voice and face of my kind – after any live soul, indeed, human or not, which I might in some measure understand', Vane recoils from the 'hell of horror' of wandering alone, 'a bare existence never going out of itself, never widening its life in another life, but, bound with the cords of its peculiarities, lying an eternal prisoner in the dungeon of its own being!' He regards

> with wonder my past self, which preferred the company of book or pen to that of man or woman, which, if the author of a tale I was enjoying appeared, would wish him away that I might return to his story. I had chosen the dead rather than the living, the thing thought rather than the thing thinking! 'Any man,' I said now, 'is more than the greatest of books!' I had not cared for my live brothers and sisters, and now I was left without even the dead to comfort me! (pp.83–84)

One of the sights that Vane sees is a 'mouldering carriage of ancient form' (p.88), with the skeletons of a horse, coachman, and, inside, of two people who awaken as Vane looks in on them. They are a promiscuous Lord and his former wife. Raven tells Vane:

> The male was never a gentleman ... and in the bony stage of retrogression, with his skeleton through his skin, and his character outside his manners, does not look like one. The female is less vulgar, and has a little heart. But, the restraints of society removed, you see them now just as they are and always were! (pp.93–94)

Raven goes on to inform Vane that they had been the handsomest couple at court and still seem to regard themselves as such. 'They felt themselves rich too while they had pockets, but they have already begun to feel rather pinched!' Now that they cannot escape each other and there is no one else of their kind, 'they must at last grow weary of their mutual repugnance, and begin to love one another! for love, not hate, is deepest in what Love "loved into being"'. They will 'by and by develop faces, for every grain of truthfulness adds a fibre to the show of their humanity' (p.94).

Vane, whose experiences have made him 'like a child, constantly wondering, and surprised at nothing' (p.94), is not put out by the appearance of Raven, even when the latter's coat-lapels fly out, and 'I thought the metamorphosis of *homo* to *corvus* was about to take place before my eyes' (as it soon does) (p.95).

The incident described above illustrates MacDonald's combination of spiritual inquiry, moral examination, and social criticism. His use of the fantastic supplies him with a landscape in which these elements commingle in ways that seem at once as strange and familiar to us as they do to Vane. The beasts that the protagonist encounters on his journey enable MacDonald's reflections on religion, society, and ethics. Often these are at the expense of the wealthy. For example, when Vane speaks with a woman of Bulika who is sheltering from the Princess's leopardess, he asks her many questions, as an inquiring traveller would. She tells him that the people of Bulika 'never did anything except dig for precious stones in their cellars. They were rich, and had everything made for them in other towns.' It is, she says, a disgrace to work. In reply to Vane's asking her how they were rich if none of them earned money, she replies that 'their ancestors had saved for them, and they never spent. When they wanted money they sold a few of their gems.' Asked about the poor, she responds: 'I suppose there must be [some], but we never think of such people. When one goes poor, we forget him. That is how we keep rich. We mean to be rich always' (p.120). The object of MacDonald's satire is the British aristocracy.

Near the end of his journey, Vane finds (in a chapter titled 'The Journey Home') that harmony has been achieved: 'The world and my being, its life and mine, were one. The microcosm and macrocosm were at length atoned' (p.243). After his meetings with all of the creatures listed above and many others, including a great white leech ('a pale savage' [p.111]), and often finding himself dangerously close to being a meal for them, Vane is at the head of the army of the Little Ones and animals that invades the giants' city and subsequently effects Lilith's repentance through Mara, the Lady of Sorrows. Lilith is then laid to peace with Lona, the daughter whom she had earlier killed, and with other children. In the final chapter, 'The Endless Ending', Vane, who has Mara much with him, occupies a dream-like state, waiting to wake into the life beyond. He has not sought the mirror again, but sometimes when he looks at his books, 'they seem to waver as if a wind rippled their solid mass, and another world were about to break through' (p.251). He has glimpses, sensations, or memories of that other world and now he waits, asleep or awake, for that final awakening.

Lilith herself embodies transformations: 'the persona of Lilith herself has … a long and complex history, changing and reappearing in various works of literature throughout the nineteenth century, and forming and reforming throughout MacDonald's own work as well'. She was '[o]riginally a character in Jewish mythology, probably based on an earlier Babylonian figure'.[55] She was Adam's first and insubordinate wife. She has been figured as Lamia, vampire, demon, and succubus; as sin in *Paradise Lost*; and as siren. In Raeper's words: 'Lilith had a changeable identity therefore and writers, finding little basis for her existence, found it possible to clothe her in many different guises.' She provides, argues Raeper, 'a hermetic key to the understanding of all [MacDonald's] work, for he was always dogged by this sinister figure'.[56]

In many ways MacDonald's works seem very different from those considered elsewhere in this volume. His tales purport to take his readers into another world, a fantastic realm with spiritual richness at a time when many of his contemporaries doubted. Similar themes and impulses to those present in the works discussed in previous chapters are apparent, however, and he offers sharp social and moral observations. No less than in those other texts, metaphors of travel and beasts propel the meaning: even if that is that there is no single meaning. The fascination with shape-changing and with the relationship between different worlds (the spiritual and the everyday; life and death) reflects an uneasy mixture of insecurity, desire, and uncertainty. Carole Silver argues that '[t]he Victorian study of fairy lore acts as an excellent reflector of both the dominant ideas and the concealed anxieties of the era'.[57] We might extend the observation to Victorian fairy tales themselves.

Notes

1. The quotation is from George MacDonald, *The Princess and the Goblin* (1872). See George MacDonald, *The Princess and the Goblin* and *The Princess and Curdie*, edited and with an introduction by Roderick McGillis (Oxford: Oxford University Press, 1990), p.97.
2. William Raeper, *George MacDonald* (Tring: Lion, 1987), p.308. Raeper adds that: 'It is the failure of the Victorian moralists to see this that caused their tales to be so dull and constricting' (p.308).
3. Diane Purkiss, *Troublesome Things: A History of Fairies and Fairy Stories* (London: Penguin Books, 2001), p.4.
4. Raeper, *George MacDonald*, p.315.
5. Raeper, *George MacDonald*, p.195.
6. Raeper, *George MacDonald*, p.125.

7 Raeper, *George MacDonald*, p.182.
8 Raeper, *George MacDonald*, p.194.
9 Raeper, *George MacDonald*, p.210.
10 Quoted in Raeper, *George MacDonald*, p.86.
11 Raeper, *George MacDonald*, p.329.
12 Raeper, *George MacDonald*, p.321.
13 Raeper, *George MacDonald*, p.11.
14 Raeper, *George MacDonald*, p.368.
15 Raeper, *George MacDonald*, p.372.
16 Farah Mendlesohn, *Rhetorics of Fantasy* (Middletown, CT: Wesleyan University Press, 2008), p.xix. The other categories identified by Mendlesohn are the Immersive Fantasy, Intrusion Fantasy, and the Liminal Fantasy.
17 Kath Filmer, 'Introduction', Kath Filmer, ed., *The Victorian Fantasists: Essays on Culture, Society and Belief in the Mythopoeic Fiction of the Victorian Age* (Houndmills: Macmillan, 1991), pp.1–12 (p.3).
18 U. C. Knoepflmacher, 'Introduction', in George MacDonald, *The Complete Fairy Tales*, edited and with an introduction and notes by U. C. Knoepflmacher (London: Penguin Books, 1999), p.vii.
19 Knoepflmacher, 'Introduction', p.vii.
20 Rolland Hein, *George MacDonald: Victorian Mythmaker* [1993] (Whitethorn, CA: Johannesen, 1999), p.27.
21 Hein, *George MacDonald*, pp.35–36. Hein is remarking here specifically on MacDonald's imaginative reworking in his Scottish stories of 'materials from his own past', but the point applies more generally.
22 MacDonald, 'The Fantastic Imagination', in *The Complete Fairy Tales*, p.7.
23 Raeper, *George MacDonald*, pp.145–146.
24 MacDonald, 'The Fantastic Imagination', pp.7–8.
25 MacDonald, 'The Fantastic Imagination', p.7.
26 Knoepflmacher, 'Introduction', p.xii.
27 George MacDonald, 'The Imagination: Its Functions and Its Culture' (1867), in *A Dish of Orts* [1893] (Whitethorn, CA: Johannesen, 1996), p.16.
28 Arthur Machen, 'Introduction', in *The Great God Pan* [1894] (London: Creation Books, 1996), pp.17–18. Further page references will be given parenthetically.
29 MacDonald, 'The Imagination: Its Functions and Its Culture', p.13.
30 George MacDonald, *Malcolm* [1875], quoted in Hein, *George MacDonald*, p.57.
31 See Hein, *George MacDonald*, pp.256, 268–269, 271, 281–283.
32 Hein, *George MacDonald*, p.130.
33 Hein, *George MacDonald*, p.129.
34 Raeper, *George MacDonald*, p.313.
35 Knoepflmacher, 'Introduction', p.xix.
36 Hein, *George MacDonald*, p.58.
37 Hein, *George MacDonald*, p.125.
38 Raeper, on the other hand, suggests that MacDonald was 'probably at heart the kind of aristocratic old Tory that Ruskin was' and that while '[h]e certainly believed in bettering the lot of ordinary people, and hoped that the quality of their lives would be transformed ... he did not link this into any political transformation such as the Webbs or Karl Marx sought'. Raeper, *George MacDonald*, p.262.
39 McGillis, 'Introduction', p.xv.

40 McGillis, 'Introduction', p.xvi; Raeper, *George MacDonald*, p.202.
41 Raeper, *George MacDonald*, p.202.
42 McGillis identifies what he calls MacDonald's 'prescience for what we think of as the postmodern spirit' (p.xvi).
43 C. S. Lewis, 'Introduction', in George MacDonald, *Lilith: A Romance* [1895] (Grand Rapids, MI: Wm. B. Eerdmans, 1981), p.ix. All further page references to *Lilith* are to this edition and will be given parenthetically. Lewis's preface first appeared, in slightly longer form, in 1946.
44 Hein, *George MacDonald*, p.32.
45 Hein, *George MacDonald*, p.445.
46 Raeper, *George MacDonald*, p.186.
47 Raeper, *George MacDonald*, pp.199, 201.
48 Raeper, *George MacDonald*, p.199.
49 Raeper, *George MacDonald*, p.201.
50 The words of the manuscript are italicised by MacDonald; 'dimensions' is not, thus giving it an emphasis that I have indicated here through italics.
51 Raeper, *George MacDonald*, p.367. For more on the variants, see Raeper, pp.420–422 and David L. Griffith, 'George MacDonald's Lilith A: A Transcription' (MA Thesis, Virginia Polytechnic Institute and State University, 2001).
52 C. N. Manlove, *Modern Fantasy: Five Studies* (Cambridge: Cambridge University Press, 1975), p.60.
53 Kath Filmer, 'La Belle Dame Sans Merci: Cultural Criticism and Mythopoeic Vision in *Lilith*', in Kath Filmer, ed., *The Victorian Fantasists*, pp.90–103 (p.98).
54 Mendlesohn, *Rhetorics of Fantasy*, p.5.
55 Raeper, *George MacDonald*, p.365.
56 Raeper, *George MacDonald*, p.366. Raeper further notes that 'MacDonald sometimes … describ[ed] women as demons or vampires' (p.367).
57 Carole G. Silver, *Strange and Secret Peoples: Fairies and Victorian Consciousness* (Oxford: Oxford University Press, 1999), p.57. Silver lists among these ideas and anxieties '[c]oncerns about change and growth in children, about the status of women in marriage and divorce, about the discovery of new and alien racial groups, and about the sources of evil, occult and natural' (p.57).

CHAPTER FIVE

Oscar Wilde: 'an unclean beast'[1]

Butterfly and ape

Appropriately, given his propensity for role-playing, Oscar Wilde attracted a variety of animal comparisons. These may have been largely forgotten now, replaced by the baser images of his three trials, which supplied another infamous conjunction of sex and animality.[2] In 1895 Wilde sued the Marquis of Queensberry for libel. Queensberry was the father of Wilde's lover Lord Alfred Douglas and had accused Wilde of 'posing as a somdomite [sic]'.[3] Wilde was himself then prosecuted for, and convicted of, committing acts of indecency in private with members of his own sex, an offence which, under section 11 of the Criminal Law Amendment Act 1885, carried a sentence of two years' imprisonment with hard labour. After the jury failed to agree on most counts, Wilde faced a retrial. Part of what was felt to be at stake is clear from a review of Max Nordau's *Degeneration* (which was published in an English translation in 1895) that appeared in the *Weekly Sun*, three weeks after Wilde's conviction and sentencing. As Ed Cohen observes, the notice drew an implicit contrast between Wilde's behaviour and Nordau's book, which it described as 'a manly, healthy, and badly-needed protest against some of the inanities and – the word is not too strong – bestialities which raise their barren and brutal heads in the literature of our time'. The reviewer declared Nordau's work to be 'entitled, therefore, to the admiration of every honest, pure, and manly man'.[4] Cohen affirms that while the review made no direct mention of Wilde it had him in its sights: the condemnation of inanities and bestiality makes this clear.

The review reads like a desperate attempt to salvage some sense of masculinity in the face of Wilde's effeminacy. Its tautology of 'manly man' reeks of nervous desperation and insecurity. But alongside this concern to protect the boundaries of gender and sexuality is the horror of a breakdown in class positions. Cohen shows that the press coverage of the trials reported defence counsel Edward Carson's questioning of

Wilde about inappropriate liaisons with socially inferior men. These men were younger than Wilde, less well educated, and 'out of employment':

> of their antecedents Wilde professed to know nothing ... in the manner of their introduction to Wilde and his subsequent treatment of them all were in the same category, leading to the same conclusion that there was something unnatural and what might not ordinarily be expected in the relations between them.[5]

Cohen deduces from this that Wilde's social crime was to flout the distinctions between the classes that those in 'polite' society thought it necessary to maintain. Carson's intention in questioning Wilde was meant, Cohen believes, 'to suggest that the very fact of these relationships was improper'.[6]

Wilde's disturbance of class positions is further discussed by Joseph Bristow. Drawing on the work of Regenia Gagnier, Bristow notes of Lord Henry Wotton in *The Picture of Dorian Gray* that he and most of Wilde's dandies are

> men who were born into the landed classes, and yet who have the prerogative to mock the idleness of the rich.
> ... Everywhere Wilde's dandies are at once aristocratic in their bearing, and yet in jeopardy of losing their reputations.[7]

That last sentence suggests the precariousness of the upper classes and the disparity between self-perception and actual status. Wilde's wit, with its irony and parody, is born of, and exploits, this disjunction. His life and writing act as a vehicle from which one can observe the changing class landscape of Britain, and this is no less pronounced than the shifts in gender that are more commonly surveyed in examinations of Wilde and his work. Had the relationships between the classes not already been permeable in some respects, the outrage at Wilde's conduct might have been more contained.

The public perception of Wilde reveals, if obliquely, the confusion of class. In his classic study of the 1890s, Holbrook Jackson, considering Wilde's position in early 1895 'at the height of his fame and power', writes that despite the flattery, amused attention, and luxury of success, Wilde never won public respect. Jackson quotes from a contemporary article that voices 'popular suspicion' of Wilde:

> Where he does excel is in affectation. His mode of life, his manner of speech, his dress, his views, his work, are all masses of affectation. Affectation has become a second nature to him, and it would probably now be utterly impossible for him to revert to the original Oscar that lies beneath it all. In

fact, probably none of his friends have ever had an opportunity of finding out what manner of man the real Oscar is ... For the present ... we may content ourselves with the reflection that there is no serious danger to be apprehended to the State from the vagaries of a butterfly.[8]

The light, flighty, colourful creature is rather different from the 'sedulous ape' Wilde played to Balzac earlier[9] and from Arthur Symons' later description of Lautrec's portrait of Wilde: 'The face is bestial.' Symons' vituperative comments are aroused by disgust with Wilde's 'vices' and 'perversions'. Symons judges Wilde to be suffering from

> one of those sexual inversions which turned him into a kind of Hermaphroditus ... As he grew older the womanish side of him grew more and more evident. Lautrec saw him in Paris, and in the appalling portrait of him he shows Wilde, swollen, puffed out, bloated and sinister. The form of the mouth which he gave him is more than any thing exceptional; no such mouth ought ever to have existed: it is a woman's that no man who is normal could ever have had.[10]

Symons's revulsion at the prospect of androgyny testifies to a deep discomfort with the unsettling of boundaries; the commingling of elements that convention prefers kept separate. In a fascinating re-evaluation, Bristow has argued that the image of the effeminate homosexual man to which Wilde contributed, if not himself formed, was 'firmly established in the public imagination' only after Wilde was sent to Reading Gaol.[11] Through Wilde one can see that gender and sexuality exhibit changes in shape and identity akin to the larger social changes outlined above and within previous chapters of the present study.

The unthreatening image of the butterfly and the condemnation of the beastly ape as abnormal and corrupt indicate the polarity of responses to Wilde and the uncertainty about where to place him. As Jackson shows, Wilde cultivated artificiality and valued it above nature; but that society should be so bothered by this is surely a sign of its own confusion about the real and the false, nature and the unnatural. To a large extent, this must be due to social structures and conventions having themselves been increasingly exposed as artificial. Class movements, as well as gender and sexuality, contributed to this. Symons' attribution of bestiality seems quite opposed to the comparison with a butterfly. Where the latter denotes a light prettiness, suggesting effeminacy,[12] the former indicates a heavy masculinity. The choice of such very different creatures to describe Wilde signals ambivalence about him and his audience. These diverse perceptions are rooted in the economic environment. Wilde's enduring wit has made him seem transcendent, while his status as iconic persecuted homosexual has focused attention on the sexual body. The material elements of the world that Wilde inhabited are often overlooked, even though they are intertwined with those more celebrated aspects. 'Neither to myself nor others', wrote Wilde to his publisher Leonard Smithers in 1897 after being freed from jail,

> am I any longer a joy. I am now simply an ordinary pauper of a rather low order: the fact that I am also a pathological problem in the eyes of German scientists is only interesting to German scientists: and even in their works I am tabulated, and come under the laws of *averages*! *Quantum mutatus*![13]

Bristow starkly summarises Wilde's predicament: 'his drastic transformation from a dandified art critic whose plays entertained thousands of theatre-goers to a debased pervert gathered such momentum in the late 1890s that there seemed no way of reversing the process'.[14] As if to demonstrate how unstable the connection was between circumstance and personal image, Jackson follows Robert H. Sherard's view of Wilde, in late 1894, as declining in spiritual beauty and 'oozing with material prosperity'. He writes that Wilde's friends observed, alongside his successes as a playwright, 'a coarsening of his appearance and character'.[15] Sherard and Jackson's is the more romantic view in that it perpetuates the idea of wealth causing corruption. Whether what helped destroy Wilde was his becoming ostentatiously prosperous or a pauper, the importance of the economic situation is unarguable.

Bristow underlines Wilde's 'acute awareness that the dandified man of letters is likely to be defeated by the puritanical attitudes of late Victorian England that sought to transmogrify many a forbidden pleasure into a form of monstrosity'.[16] He sees Wilde as compromised with those forces and warns against assuming that Wilde was, by virtue of his socialist politics, his Irish nationality, and his homosexuality, an entirely oppositional figure.[17] He believes Wilde's stance to be tactical and labels him an 'insider dissident: a figure who provoked the commonsensical mentality of bourgeois England by entertaining it from within its ranks'.[18] The tussle over position, meaning, and value will form the focus of the discussion of Wilde's selected writings in various genres that takes up the remainder of this chapter.

Two tales

i) Bulls, bears, and the butterfly

Many of Wilde's short tales are characterised by a morality that often involves images of animals and insects and turns upon episodes of transformation. They may be aimed at children, but that ought not to blind us to their economic references. Several of the tales are relevant to our discussion. One of them reveals this in its very title. In 'The Model Millionaire', a young man, Hughie Erskine, visits the studio of his painter friend, Alan Trevor. Erskine had every accomplishment except that of making money and lives on

> two hundred a year that an old aunt allowed him. He had tried everything. He had gone on the Stock Exchange for six months; but what was a butterfly to do among bulls and bears?[19]

This butterfly has no vocation. It possesses looks, but no substance. In addition to these six months on the Stock Exchange, Erskine had spent a little longer as a tea-merchant before getting bored, as he did subsequently with selling dry sherry: 'Ultimately he became nothing, a delightful, ineffectual young man with a perfect profile and no profession' (*MM*, p.77).

Wilde's portrait of Erskine finely draws the predicament of the young man whose demeanour is out of step with his material circumstances. The picture is emblematic of a type that belongs to the period: the man who experiences a disparity between his accustomed or anticipated social status and his actual financial standing. Erskine has been left little by his father apart from his 'cavalry sword and a *History of the Peninsular War* in fifteen volumes'. He is in love with Laura Merton, the daughter of a retired Colonel who had served in India: 'They were the handsomest couple in London, and had not a penny-piece between them' (*MM*, p.77). Erskine's prospective father-in-law has ruled out any talk of engagement until Hughie has 10,000 pounds of his own. Erskine's worth is in his looks – a showy but insubstantial wealth.

When Erskine visits Trevor he discovers him painting the portrait of a wizened old beggar, whose apparel and piteous appearance excite his sympathy. His feelings towards the itinerant are heightened when he is told that the artist will earn 2000 guineas for the painting while his model is paid only a shilling an hour. Erskine is moved by this injustice to present a sovereign to the old man while Trevor is absent from the room. Apart from a few coppers, the money is all that he has on him. The gesture means that Erskine will be unable to afford to ride in hansoms for a fortnight, but he feels that the 'forlorn and wretched' old man needs the money more than he himself does (*MM*, p.79).

Through Erskine's generosity, Wilde criticises the exploitation of the poor by the rich and asks awkward questions about their treatment in art. Later that night, Trevor tells Erskine in the Palette Club that: 'What you call rags I call romance. What seems poverty to you is picturesqueness to me' (*MM*, p.80). This is a discomfiting remark from which one may infer that even in politically sympathetic representations of poverty an aesthetic response is what matters. At this point the tale seems to be self-conscious: it, too, appears to include the poor in its larger frame. But the story at once grows more difficult. When accused by Hughie of heartlessness, Trevor insists that '[a]n artist's heart is his head ... and besides, our business is to realize the world as we see it, not to reform it as we know it' (*MM*, p.80). A serious point is thus made about the role of the artist. Before this can be pondered, however, Wilde makes ostentatious play with the plot, having Trevor reveal to the now-embarrassed Erskine that the beggar was in fact his (Trevor's) great friend Baron Hausberg, who

> is one of the richest men in Europe. He could buy all London tomorrow without overdrawing his account. He has a house in every capital, dines off gold plate, and can prevent Russia going to war when he chooses. (*MM*, p.80)

Hausberg had commissioned Trevor to paint him as a beggar and seemed greatly amused by Hughie's present. When told of this gift by Hughie, Trevor bursts into laughter and predicts: 'you'll never see it again. *Son affaire c'est l'argent des autres.*' At best, he thinks, '[h]e'll invest your sovereign for you ... pay you the interest every six months, and have a capital story to tell after dinner' (*MM*, p.81). But Trevor (though not, I think, the reader, for the twist seems quite predictable) is to be surprised. He had told the Baron about Erskine's frustrated love and the Baron sends Hughie a cheque for 10,000 pounds allowing the wedding, at which the Baron makes a speech and Trevor is best man, to take place. Trevor concludes that '[m]illionaire models ... are rare enough; but, by Jove, model millionaires are rarer still' (*MM*, p.82).

The ending seems an evasion: the serious glance at poverty that the tale offered is averted by the humorous failure of recognition. Indeed, it might be deduced from the twist that the moral of the story is that charity should not be given, because it can so easily be misdirected. Even a more sympathetic interpretation might be that charitable gestures are worth making, because they may benefit the donor. More than this, the tale provokes questions that it leaves unanswered: we do not really know why the Baron wants to dress as a beggar; we are ignorant of his nationality and where he lives. We are aware that he is an aristocrat who is still very rich, though both the scale and the preservation of his wealth are unusual.

Ultimately, the tale is like the butterfly itself: decorous and flighty. All the same, through its protagonist's momentary anger and discomfort it encourages in its readers a consciousness of poverty and reflection on the relationship between art and its subject. If the moral seems confused, the archness of the ending supplies an uneasy closure which, in its contrivance, draws attention to the tale's unresolved problems.

ii) The swallow

A tale similar to 'The Model Millionaire' is 'The Happy Prince' (1888). Here, instead of the butterfly, the narrative is piloted by a bird. In an unnamed city stands a statue of the Happy Prince, covered in fine gold leaf, with two sapphires for eyes, and a ruby on his sword-hilt. The Prince is encountered by a swallow whose migration to Egypt has been delayed by a now-broken courtship of a Reed. The swallow discovers the Prince weeping and is told by the statue that: 'When I was alive and had a human heart ... I did not know what tears were, for I lived in the Palace of Sans-Souci, where sorrow is not allowed to enter.' The Prince never bothered to inquire what lay beyond the walled garden in which he played since 'everything about me was so beautiful'. But after he died he was 'set up here so high that I can see all the ugliness and all the misery of the city, and though my heart is made of lead yet I cannot choose but weep'.[20] Once again this tale rests on the discovery of poverty and gains its effects from the juxtaposition of wealth and deprivation. The Prince detains the swallow by persuading him to perform a series of charitable deeds on his behalf, distributing his jewels to the poor. One of his sapphires is bestowed on a little match-girl whose matches are spoiled through having fallen into the gutter and who faces a beating from her father. (The year of the story's first publication, 1888, was the year of the match-girls' strike.) Giving away his sapphire eyes has left the Prince blind. The swallow, feeling a warm glow from his charitable missions, tells the Prince he will stay with him always, though the Prince's moral detention of him has meant that winter has now set in. Pronouncing that '[t]here is no Mystery so great as Misery', the blind Prince asks the swallow to fly over the city and to tell him what he sees.

> So the swallow flew over the great city, and saw the rich making merry in their beautiful houses, while the beggars were sitting at the gates. He flew into dark lanes, and saw the white faces of starving children looking out listlessly at the black streets. (*HP*, p.143)

The swallow's journey enacts what nineteenth-century writers and campaigners from the late 1840s onwards, and with renewed determination in the 1880s and 1890s, saw and showed to others: the unequal ownership and distribution of wealth.

The swallow tells the Prince of two little boys lying in each other's arms under a bridge for warmth. They have been told by a watchman that they cannot lie there and have had to move out into the rain. In a move that symbolises what might happen if the monarchy were divested of its wealth, the Prince instructs the bird to take off, 'leaf by leaf', the fine gold with which he is covered and to 'give it to my poor; the living always think that gold can make them happy' (*HP*, p.144). When the swallow brings the gold to the children, they become happy and cry that they now have bread. But as the snow and then the frost bite, the swallow dies. As he does so, the Prince's leaden heart breaks in two, an event that the narrator flatly and unconvincingly attributes to the 'dreadfully hard frost' (*HP*, p.144). The next morning the Mayor sees the now-unadorned statue of the Prince and decides, as do the Town Councillors, who always follow his lead, that it should be pulled down because it looks so shabby. The sight of the dead swallow at the statue's feet causes the officials to issue a proclamation forbidding birds to die there (meaning, one assumes, in the city, rather than just around the statue). The Mayor and all the Town Councillors then quarrel among themselves over the wish of each to have a statue of himself erected to replace the one of the Prince. That has now been melted down in the furnace – except for the leaden heart, which will not melt and is discarded on the dust-heap where the swallow's body also lies. The tale ends with God ordering one of his angels: 'Bring me the two most precious things in the city.' The angel returns with the leaden heart and the dead bird:

> 'You have rightly chosen,' said God, 'for in my garden of Paradise this little bird shall sing for evermore, and in my city of gold the Happy Prince shall praise me.' (*HP*, p.145)

It is a complex ending. God's words subvert worldly notions of wealth. The golden city over which He rules is one in which the gold is transmuted: it is not at all the same substance that is worshipped in the mundane world, but instead constitutes a kind of spiritual richness. It offers an alternative set of values to the life that the Prince and his subjects previously lived. Characteristically, Wilde realises this other world by keeping to the theme word 'gold' but changing its meaning. However, two complications emerge from the construction of this divine alterity. The first has to do with its separation from the material world and the second concerns its ambivalent moralism.

First, from the beginning of the tale, Wilde has already clearly introduced the question of the relationship between aesthetics and materialism. The second paragraph of the tale (all of whose paragraphs are short), further describing the statue of the Happy Prince, reads thus:

> He was very much admired indeed. 'He is as beautiful as a weather-cock,' remarked one of the Town Councillors who wished to gain a reputation for having artistic tastes; 'only not quite so useful,' he added, fearing lest people should think him unpractical, which he really was not. (*HP*, p.137)

The implied narrative disdain of those who confuse art with usefulness is reinforced near the end of the tale, when the denuded statue is pulled down and the University's Professor of Art remarks: '"As he is no longer beautiful he is no longer useful ..."' (*HP*, p.145). By this stage the narrator has had the Prince exhibit a quite different kind and standard of beauty, one that exposes the superficiality of views such as the Professor's. In showing the poverty of those, Wilde risks succumbing to a conventional morality, one that he confuses with a more radical challenge to the social order. Again, though, as with 'The Model Millionaire', the conclusion seems ambiguous. On the one hand, the moral might be that those who give selflessly to people in need will find an eternal reward. On the other hand, if we do take this to be the moral, then such acts of charity cease to be altruistic because they are motivated by the promise of a spiritually richer life. From a socialist perspective, these acts achieve nothing: they do not affect the structure of social arrangements and they lead to the self-destruction of the do-gooder, who is survived by the uncompassionate pragmatist. In John Stokes's words: 'Wilde's parabolic fantasies [are] simultaneously liberating and repressive.'[21]

Stokes outlines the transformation and progression that take place in Wilde's fairy tales. Mentioning 'The Young King' and 'The Happy Prince', after a short consideration of 'The Portrait of Mr. W. H.', he notes that in these stories, 'Wilde outlines two realms of beauty: the transient and the permanent, the meretricious and the meritorious'. Stokes observes that Wilde gives no sign that charitable (or 'noble') acts will gather any reward other than the *de facto* achievement of a higher aesthetic ideal:

> The progression is rather from an innate capacity to appreciate beautiful things to an awareness of what the creation of that beauty involves in human terms, to a final point, reached only after suffering and sacrifice, when a transcendent beauty is attained. The fairy-tales tell of the refinement of the Aesthetic principle; the beauties of the moral life, which in themselves compensate for nothing, are only discovered when Aesthetic indulgence has been transformed.[22]

According to Stokes, Wilde's '[a]esthete-martyrs achieve their transcendence only after partial confrontation with repressed knowledge – the knowledge of "cost"'.[23] This process is exemplified by the Happy Prince's discovery of the poverty and misery in his city. Stokes neatly traces a dialectic in the tales:

> If satisfaction is at first unwittingly at the expense of others – their labour and their suffering – in its later moral phase it is at the expense of the Aesthete himself – the renunciation of beauty; finally, in the dream of art and sympathy reconciled, transcendence becomes collaborative, since the Aesthete's charity is rewarded by admiring love, and the quality of beauty is attributed to his personality.[24]

That, of course, is what happens at the end of 'The Happy Prince' and also at the end of 'The Young King'. But I am not sure that the synthesis or even the thesis and antithesis are quite as ordered as Stokes would have it. The journey of the swallow is very complicated – its migration to the land of sensuality and riches in Egypt is interrupted by its shorter but more revealing journeys within the city, which repeat the Prince's own intellectual and perceptual journey outside his walled garden. The resolution Stokes detects is highly plausible: the Prince and the bird are rewarded with God's love for their sacrificial charity, endowing them with beautiful personalities. Yet if this is Wilde's conclusion, it is hardly sufficient to tie up the loose threads that remain. For those readers who are not ready to accept God's love (or who do not accept that there is a God to love), the collaboration looks a party too short. For those who do believe in God's love, the matter of worldly reform may still call for something more structural than individual charity. If Stokes is implying that Wilde has found an answer to his own continuing exploration of the relationship between

Art and Life, aesthetics and materialism, it can only be a balance that fits Wilde's personal interests and views.

Essaying beasts

It is not only in his short fiction that Wilde expresses his meaning through or against animals. The bestial is evident in his critical writing also and contributes to a similar oscillation between radicalism and conservatism. In 'The Soul of Man under Socialism' (1891), Wilde espouses an individualism that is to be arrived at through Socialism. His argument manages to combine an urge to help the working classes with a loathing of their uncultured lives. Wilde was not alone in this. Among other writers, his contemporaries H. G. Wells, George Bernard Shaw, and George Gissing conjoined a radical politics with a personal distaste for the objects of their political cause. Although Wilde's theories of art and society seem more idiosyncratic, some of his beastly images belong to a familiar menagerie. For example, he writes of the mob as a monster, hardly a novel description, but one that communicates a particular anxiety throughout the 1880s and 1890s as a result of the growing unease about the unemployed and striking workers, whose presence was noted in the introduction to the present book.[25] However, apart from that image, Wilde strikes an individual note. True, when he writes about those 'great many people' who 'do the work of beasts of burden' and amongst whom 'there is no grace of manner, or charm of speech, or civilization, or culture, or refinement in pleasures, or joy of life' (*SM*, p.3), he sounds as if he is voicing the disdain felt by any number of the middle and upper classes, but he departs from this point to make two statements that are more radical. The first is that the work that the poor are '*compelled* to do ... is quite uncongenial to them', and the second is that they are '*forced*' to it 'by the peremptory, unreasonable, degrading Tyranny of want' (*SM*, p.3, my emphasis). Wilde insists that the poor *are* exploited – they *have* to perform these brute labours, because they have 'no private property of their own' (*SM*, p.3). It is not that these people are suited only to the performance of such deadening tasks; it is that they are given no choice by those who do possess private property. They are brutes not by nature, but by social organisation:

> From their collective force Humanity gains much in material prosperity. But it is only the material result that it gains, and the man who is poor is in himself absolutely of no importance. He is merely the infinitesimal atom

of a force that, so far from regarding him, crushes him: indeed, prefers him crushed, as in that case he is far more obedient. (*SM*, p.3)

Unlike many of his contemporaries, Wilde distinguishes between the character and situation of the poor: he does not assume that the poor are inherently or innately degraded because they live lives of degradation. Nor does he have any truck with the idea of the deserving poor as conventionally laid down by Henry Mayhew and subsequent commentators. Although his comments look predictable at first, they take a subversive turn:

> the best amongst the poor are never grateful. They are ungrateful, discontented, disobedient, and rebellious. They are quite right to be so. Charity they feel to be a ridiculously inadequate mode of partial restitution, or a sentimental dole, usually accompanied by some impertinent attempt on the part of the sentimentalist to tyrannize over their private lives. Why should they be grateful for the crumbs that fall from the rich man's table? They should be seated at the board, and are beginning to know it. (*SM*, p.4)

Wilde goes beyond criticising acts of charity: he recommends that the poor take exactly the kind of action that their social superiors so dreaded. Claiming that it 'is both grotesque and insulting' to say that the poor should practise thrift, he declares:

> Man should not be ready to show that he can live like a badly fed animal. He should decline to live like that, and should either steal or go on the rates, which is considered by many to be a form of stealing. As for begging, it is safer to beg than to take, but it is finer to take than to beg. No: a poor man who is ungrateful, unthrifty, discontented, and rebellious, is probably a real personality, and has much in him. He is at any rate a healthy protest. As for the virtuous poor, one can pity them, of course, but one cannot possibly admire them. They have made private terms with the enemy, and sold their birthright for very bad pottage. (*SM*, pp.4–5)

In Wilde's view, if the poor are bestial it is not because they are essentially animal-like or because their environment makes them unavoidably so; rather, they should fight to assert their humanity. For Wilde, in 'The Soul of Man', animality does not signify the working classes and the unemployed so much as it signifies a rotten social order. It is *that* which is beastly. Of course, it may be argued that Wilde is simply posturing; that his argument is typically designed both to cause moral shock and display his wit. Some of his carefully structured phrases (for example, the chiasmus of 'it is safer to beg than to take, but it is finer to take than to beg') resemble the kind of aphorism to be found in his plays.

Yet even if his sincerity is doubted, it is better to adopt the posture than not. Such is Wilde's conviction (or posture) that he declares 'agitators are so absolutely necessary' *because* they 'are a set of interfering, meddling people, who come down to some perfectly contented class of the community, and sow the seeds of discontent amongst them' (*SM*, p.5).

Wilde argues that 'Individualism ... is what through Socialism we are to attain to. As a result the State must give up all idea of government.' It must, he says, leave people alone. He disparages democracy as 'simply the bludgeoning of the people by the people for the people'. His justification for his corruption of Lincoln's dictum is that 'all authority is quite degrading. It degrades those who exercise it, and degrades those over whom it is exercised.' Abuses of authority create a 'good effect', because they induce the 'spirit of revolt and Individualism that is to kill it', but

> [w]hen it [authority] is used with a certain amount of kindness, and accompanied by prizes and rewards, it is dreadfully demoralizing. People, in that case, are less conscious of the horrible pressure that is being put on them, and so go through their lives in a sort of coarse comfort, like *petted animals*, without ever realizing that they are probably thinking other people's thoughts, living by other people's standards, wearing practically what one may call other people's second-hand clothes, and never being themselves for a single moment. (*SM*, p.13, my emphasis)

Wilde's criticism of democracy for pampering its subjects into unoriginality marks his own originality. There may be a suspicion that in much of his writing this is bound up with a kind of intellectual posturing; a cerebral dandyism; but in his prison and post-prison writings, one cannot doubt that his experience has given his imagery a deep sincerity. When, in 'The Ballad of Reading Gaol', he describes the prisoners as apes, he is one of them: 'Like ape or clown, in monstrous garb/With crooked arrows starred,/Silently we went round and round,/The slippery asphalte yard ...'[26] This is by no means the privileged labelling of the Other by the more fortunate that we see in naturalistic writing or sociological commentaries. And when the subject and dedicatee of the poem, Charles Thomas Wooldridge, who had premeditatedly killed his wife, meets his punishment, '[t]hey hanged him as a beast is hanged'.[27] Wilde's remarks earlier in the poem force a sympathetic identification of himself with Wooldridge:

A prison wall was round us both,
   Two outcast men we were:
The world had thrust us from its heart,
   And God from out His care:

And the iron gin that waits for Sin
   Had caught us in its snare.[28]

John Stokes points to a troubling aspect of this identification: 'In his efforts to place himself in some appropriate relationship to a condemned man Wilde suppresses the knowledge that the man's crime – murder – is of a radically different kind from his own alleged offences.'[29] Yet Wilde's purpose is surely to expose conditions that are hidden both from human and divine eye:

> This too I know – and wise it were
> If each could know the same –
> That every prison that men build
> Is built with bricks of shame,
> And bound with bars lest Christ should see
>   How men their brothers maim.[30]

There, where 'lean Hunger and green Thirst/Like asp with adder fight',[31] the 'vilest deeds' flourish and the good wastes away.[32]

It is evident from Wilde's letters to the press after his release from prison that he has seen and felt jail to be a brutalising, bestial place. And it is clear from his having already written in 'The Soul of Man' that 'a community is infinitely more brutalized by the habitual employment of punishment, than it is by the occasional occurrence of crime' (*SM*, p.13), that his critical eye is on the society that makes victims of its criminals.

In his post-prison letters, Wilde again subverts the usual animal imagery. Instead of regarding the inmates as essentially brutish, as many observers and commentators of the time would have done, he believed them dehumanised by their treatment:

> Deprived of books, of all human intercourse, isolated from every humane and humanising influence, condemned to eternal silence, robbed of all intercourse with the external world, treated like an unintelligent animal, brutalised below the level of any of the brute-creation, the wretched man who is confined in an English prison can hardly escape becoming insane.[33]

In his first post-prison letter, Wilde narrated the case of a man who had indeed been driven to lunacy by the conditions of his punishment. Wilde writes that a few days previously he (Wilde) had been

> startled by the prison silence being broken by the most horrible and revolting shrieks, or rather howls, for at first I thought some animal like a bull or a cow was being unskilfully slaughtered outside the prison walls. I soon realised, however, that the howls proceeded from the basement of the prison, and I

knew that some wretched man was being flogged. I need not say how hideous and terrible it was for me ...

The next day, Wilde's last Sunday in prison, he sees the victim of the flogging 'at exercise, his weak, ugly, wretched face bloated by tears and hysteria almost beyond recognition'. Wilde observes the man 'grinning like an ape, and making with his hands the most fantastic gestures'.[34] The man 'was a living grotesque'.[35] This is neither the patronising classification of the middle-class observer nor the shocked self-disgust of the discoverer of the ape within. It is instead and emphatically the political protest against society of one who has witnessed and suffered its operations.[36] Degeneration is externally forced on people by the society that has marginalised them. Wilde's animal imagery, like his aphorisms, employs commonly used terms, but undermines their usual meanings. This can be illustrated with another simian simile. In his second post-prison letter, Wilde complains that prisoners are allowed to see their friends only four times a year for twenty minutes each visit:

> Under the present system the prisoner is either locked up in a large iron cage or in a large wooden box, with a small aperture, covered with wire netting, through which he is allowed to peer. His friends are placed in a similar cage, some three or four feet distant, and two warders stand between, to listen to, and, if they wish, stop or interrupt the conversation such as it may be ... To be exhibited, like an ape in a cage, to people who are fond of one, and of whom one is fond, is a needless and horrible degradation.[37]

In a departure from the way that contemporary criminologists, social commentators, and novelists wrote of such people, Wilde is saying that it is society that makes apes of its outcasts. 'And outcasts always mourn', he wrote in the 'Ballad of Reading Gaol'.[38] After this realisation his lighter wit may have been displaced, but his radical overturning of beastly referents as they were normally employed shows greater continuity of method than has sometimes been supposed. What links his pre- and post-prison writings, besides the manner of his wit, is his gaze at the backcloth of society against which people stand. His focus is on the social context of his characters, not on their behaviour and attitudes separate from it. 'Authority is as destructive to those who exercise it as it is to those on whom it is exercised', he writes.[39]

Each bestial sense

Since Wilde acted his own life as though it were an artistic production, it is appropriate that the beastly epithets used by and about him correspond to the changes in his situation. On 24 April 1882, Wilde visited the Lincoln penitentiary in Nebraska. Viewing photographs of the inmates, he said of one prisoner: 'here's a beast, an animal ... nothing of the man left'. Reinforcing this conventional view of criminal appearance, Wilde wrote to Helena Sickert: 'They were all mean looking, which consoled me, for I should hate to see a criminal with a noble face' (*E*, p.191). It would not be until his incarceration that such straightforward acceptances of criminal physiognomy and conduct would be complicated. Henry James, who met Wilde in North America early in 1882, described him as 'an unclean beast' (*E*, p.171).[40] On its front page, the *Washington Post*, again during Wilde's North American tour, juxtaposed a drawing of Wilde holding a sunflower with one of a 'citizen of Borneo' holding a coconut (*E*, p.168). Whistler drew a caricature of Wilde as a pig.[41] Wilde's homosexuality was, of course, at the heart of the transformation in his circumstances, but it would be quite wrong to overlook the role played by material (economic and political) conditions. After all, it was society that criminalised him. Again, his own usage reflects his moral ambivalence. Ellmann quotes Wilde as telling Robert Sherard the day after he, Wilde, picked up a (female) prostitute: '"What animals we all are, Robert"'. It is a highly conventional utterance of the commonplace view that the excitement and gratification by women of males' sexual urges brings out the beast in men. The impression is reinforced when Ellmann quotes, straight afterwards, from Wilde's poem 'The Sphinx': 'You wake in me each bestial sense, you make me what I would not be' (*E*, p.206). Yet if we compare this with Ellmann's summary of Wilde's view – 'Wilde had always held that the true "beasts" were not those who expressed their desires, but those who tried to suppress other people's' (*E*, p.406) – we get back to the idea of Wilde taking conventional imagery and overturning it. When Wilde was ill during the last few months of his life and suffering from '[t]he mussel poisoning – as he persisted in calling it – which had begun in the summer of 1899 [and which] had brought great red splotches on is arms, chest, and back', causing irresistible itchiness, he said to Robert Ross, 'I am more like a great ape than ever' (*E*, p.544). Of course, the self-applied label is generated by the humorous image of Wilde scratching himself as an ape does, but the humour is uncomfortable and describes a wholly different creature from the butterfly of Wilde's younger days.

Wilde's antagonist, the Marquis of Queensberry, wrote to his son, Lord Alfred Douglas, calling him, Douglas, a 'reptile' (*E*, p.423); he sent to his daughter-in-law (the wife of his son Percy) an illustration from a popular weekly of an iguanodon, commenting: '[p]erhaps an ancestor of Oscar Wilde' (*E*, p.446); and he threatened to shoot Wilde like a dog (*E*, p.428). None of this is to suggest for a moment that Wilde is unique in being compared to an animal or in comparing others to animals. But the variety of animal similes and metaphors employed by and about him is unusual and indicates the difficulty of pinning him down. Ellmann writes that 'Wilde prided himself on living a life not double but multiple'. Ellmann elaborates thus: 'He could be with Parnell and Gladstone one night, with Wilson Barrett and Ellen Terry the next, with young men the next. And Constance, with his children, was always there to neglect or not' (*E*, p.267). The brief list concisely indicates the range of Wilde's social movement, and this is important. It would work against him in court during his suit against Queensberry for libel when cross-examined by Queensberry's barrister, Edward Carson, who questioned Wilde about his liaisons with

> Charley Parker and his brother, one a valet, the other a groom, whom Wilde had met through Taylor. Asked if he knew their occupations, Wilde replied, 'I did not know it, but if I had I should not have cared. I didn't care twopence what they were. I liked them. I have a passion to civilise the community.' This was the opposite of his condemnation of the general reading public, and Carson was quick to fasten upon 'the valet and the groom' as strange companions for an artist ...
>
> ...
> ... He vividly contrasted Wilde's artistic élitism with his democratic taste for common boys. (*E*, pp.424–425)

It is possible that had Wilde restricted his choice of sexual partners to members of his own class he would have caused less of a scandal and escaped punishment, though Queensberry's rabid behaviour makes that unlikely. What does seem true is that Wilde's cross-class relationships aroused greater disapproval than would otherwise have been the case. In addition to Wilde's multiple sex lives, however, were the multiple aspects of his social position and character. Transformation is central to these, and in many of them money is crucial.

Ignoring for present purposes Wilde's move from Dublin to Oxford and his relationship to Catholicism, his first major transformation came with his marriage and becoming homosexually active, and the second with his imprisonment. In both, money played a part: in the first, because his own and his brother's relative impoverishment led their mother to encourage them to find marriage partners of means; in the second, because the laws of the time encouraged blackmail.

Ellmann writes that after Wilde's seduction in 1886 by Robert Ross, which both men represented as Wilde's first homosexual encounter, Wilde was changed:

> For Wilde homosexual love roused him from pasteboard conformity to the expression of latent desires. After 1886 he was able to think of himself as a criminal, moving guiltily among the innocent ... Up to that time Wilde could think of himself as misunderstood; now he had to promote misunderstanding. (*E*, pp.261–262)

According to Ellmann, '[h]omosexuality fired his [Wilde's] mind. It was the major stage in his discovery of himself' and it gave him a 'changed outlook' (*E*, p.265). His journalistic writings of these years (Ellmann speaks of '1886 on, but especially in 1887 and 1888') constituted

> a way of organizing his attitudes towards literature, art, nature, and life; they exhibit a freshness not often present in his earlier work, as if to suggest that running foul of the law in his sexual life was a stimulus to thought on every subject. At last he knew where he stood. His new sexual direction liberated his art. It also liberated his critical faculty. (*E*, p.270)

The second major transformation of Wilde's life came with his imprisonment. Ellmann reports many of his visitors commenting on the drastic change in his appearance and quotes his sister-in-law Lily, who visited him on 22 October 1895, as writing: 'He is very altered in *every* way' (*E*, p.462). Wilde's wife, Constance, wrote to her brother that her husband 'is an absolute wreck compared with what he was' and told Edward Burne-Jones, who recorded her remark in his diary entry for 22 February 1896, that 'he was changed beyond recognition' (*E*, p.468). The physical signs of these changes were observed by Wilde's few visitors: he grew thinner, his graying hair had been cut shorter (a particular cause of his low morale), and he would often cry. Robert Ross wrote to Oscar Browning on 12 November 1895, after seeing Wilde for the first time since his arrest, and describes the prisoner thus:

> Mentally his condition is much better than I had dared to hope though his mind is considerably impaired. Physically he was much worse than anyone had led me to believe. Indeed I really should not have known him at all. This I know is an ordinary figure of speech, but it exactly described what I

experienced. His clothes hung about him in loose folds and his hands are like those of a skeleton. The colour of his face is completely changed, but this cannot be altogether attributed to his slight beard. The latter only hides the appalling sunken cheeks. A friend who was in court would not believe it was Oscar when he first came in.[42]

The occasion of Ross's visit was the proceedings against Wilde for bankruptcy, the second and final stage of the hearing for which occurred on 12 November 1895. Then, Wilde's friends having failed to raise the sum required to pay off his debts, 'he was officially declared bankrupt and his affairs put in the hands of a receiver' (*E*, p.462). There can be no doubt that the possession or lack of money both accompanied and helped bring about the changes in Wilde's fortunes. In an essay on Wilde, Regenia Gagnier quotes Karl Marx's dictum that 'capital [was] not a thing, but a social relation between persons'.[43] Money was an important currency in Wilde's relationships with people. This was especially so after his release from prison when he was constantly having to borrow from friends (and to beg from strangers). It is also a theme of Ellmann's biography that, prior to Wilde's imprisonment, Douglas drained Wilde, both emotionally and financially.

Additionally and crucially, Wilde feared greatly for his sanity.[44] Later, Wilde himself would say that '[p]rison has completely changed me' (*E*, p.508). And on another occasion he is reported to have declared: 'I died in prison' (*E*, p.474).

A changed Wilde would lead to a changed art. He affirmed after his prison sentence the attitude he had displayed in the years before it, that '[m]y life is like a work of art' (*E*, p.508). Appropriately, for one who was so completely altered by his incarceration, his post-prison writing would also be drastically affected. In his last year in jail he wrote (from January to March 1897) *De Profundis*. In July 1897, two months after his release, he began 'The Ballad of Reading Gaol', which he completed in October. It was published in February the following year. Apart from these, his post-prison letters to *The Daily Chronicle* in May 1897 and March 1898 are his only significant prison and post-prison works. All are characterised by an explicit concern with the experience and effects of prison life. The frivolous side of his wit had been killed off.

De Profundis, Wilde's extraordinary autobiographical letter to Lord Alfred Douglas, is a critical document in Wilde's life and thought. In it he advises Douglas to 'let the reading of this terrible letter – for such I know it is – prove to you as important a crisis and turning-point of your life as the writing of it is to me'.[45] Near the beginning of this long communication, Wilde writes: 'You did not realise that an artist, and especially such an artist as I am ...' (p.40). But in his manuscript Wilde had originally written 'was' instead (p.206). This switch of tense attests to his struggle to cling to his primary identity. Part of the fascination of *De Profundis* is that it shows Wilde coming to terms with the changes in his life. Transformation becomes a major theme of the letter; transformation in both life and art, a linkage that is unsurprising given Wilde's long-standing connection of the two. Moreover, Wilde roots change in its material context: a sad refrain throughout the document is his having been brought to bankruptcy by Douglas's bleeding of his money. He calculates that 'between the autumn of 1892 and the date of my imprisonment I spent with you and on you more than £5000 in actual money, irrespective of the bills I incurred' (p.43).[46]

In *De Profundis* Wilde insists on the transformative powers of art. He does so to such an extent that the work performs what it observes: the alteration, through art, of one's environment. In the progress of the letter, Wilde makes of his immediate surroundings a base for a new beginning in his life. In place of the ostentatious display of wealth and aesthetic objects is an almost austere attention to the soul. The letter, then, contains the elements that are the focus of the present book: the journey (at least as metaphor), transformation, and images of bestiality. Wilde refers to Queensberry's 'bestial and half-witted grin' and his 'apelike face' (p.131) and calls him an 'ape' (p.81). In that first description, class is also involved since he writes of Queensberry thus: 'the stableman's gait and dress, the bowed legs, the twitching hands, and the hanging lower lip' (p.131). The latter image has racial connotations, too: Africans and other 'savages' were often labelled as possessing the same feature. Wilde's class-based sneer at Queensberry is unpleasantly difficult to reconcile with his own cross-class liaisons, which he himself described as 'feasting with panthers'. Mixing the metaphor, he represented himself as a 'snake-charmer', luring the 'brightest of gilded snakes' whose 'poison was part of their perfection' (p.132). But his intention seems to be to open a gap between the Marquis' and society's sense of his (Queensberry's) status and his actual level. The designation of Queensberry as an ape is meant similarly to undermine society's view of itself. 'I who appealed to all the ages', writes Wilde, 'have had to accept my verdict from one who is an ape and a buffoon' (p.81). Thus Wilde reverses the charges: he indicts society for allowing the genius of his art to be crushed by the ape Queensberry. The simian epithet scorns society for permitting degeneration to occur: instead of having evolved from the ape, Wilde's contemporaries are in thrall to it. Because of the close identification of his life with his art, Wilde was able to present an attack on one as an attack on the other.

In a much-quoted passage, Wilde announces: 'I was a man who stood in symbolic relations to the art and culture of my age.' There follows what might appear an immodest, but is probably an accurate account of his genius and accomplishments, including his statement that: 'I altered the minds of men and the colours of things: there was nothing I said or did that did not make people wonder' (p.95). He therefore claims to effect change in others. Wilde's near two years in prison have led him to 'find hidden away in my nature' humility – 'the ultimate discovery at which I have arrived; the starting point for a fresh development' (p.96). His new-found humility 'is the one thing that has in it the elements of life, of a new life, a *Vita Nuova* for me' (p.97). If this new birth sounds like a resurrection, the affinity with Christ does not stop there. The sense of humility supplies another link, but so, too, do the emphases on spiritual richness within material poverty and on the poetry of suffering. Although Wilde insists that he has found religion of no consolation, his self-identification with Christ grows stronger as the letter goes on. 'Sorrow … and all that it teaches one, is my new world', he keens, as he reminds us: 'I used to live entirely for pleasure' (p.104). Part of Wilde's transformation is an emotional one, but it affects his understanding of art, also: 'sorrow, being the supreme emotion of which man is capable, is at once the type and test of all great Art'. There might appear to be continuity with Wilde's former views. He writes that: 'What the artist is always looking for is that mode of existence in which soul and body are one and indivisible: in which the outward is expressive of the inward: in which Form reveals' (p.105). In fact, there has been a fundamental alteration in Wilde's thinking on art. Where before he had delighted in disjunction, masks, and lying, he now insists on wholeness:

> behind Sorrow there is always Sorrow. Pain, unlike Pleasure, wears no mask … Truth in Art is the unity of a thing with itself: the outward rendered expressive of the inward: the soul made incarnate: the body instinct with spirit. For this reason there is no truth comparable to Sorrow. (pp.105–106)

No more can there be for Wilde a joyful, teasing display of difference between what is said, how it is said, and what is meant. If he is adopting a mask, he wears it consistently.

Invoking Pater and Wordsworth, Wilde announces: 'I see a far more intimate and immediate connection between the true life of Christ and the true life of the artist.' He goes on to confess his pleasure that 'long before Sorrow had made my days her own and bound me to her wheel', he had written in *The Soul of Man* that

> he who would lead a Christ-like life must be entirely and absolutely himself, and had taken as my types not merely the shepherd on the hillside and the prisoner in his cell but also the painter to whom the world is a pageant and the poet for whom the world is a song. (p.109)

Mention of his earlier essay underlines what Wilde would have us believe: that his present situation is a development rather than a recasting of his life. Wilde proceeds with his ever closer identification of Christ with art. He writes both of Christ's humility and his own. When he remarks that '[a]bove all, Christ is the most supreme of Individualists' (p.113), the reader cannot but be reminded of his earlier pronouncements on individualism (for example, and especially, in *The Soul of Man*), and his offering himself as an embodiment of it. But when he goes into more detail we can appreciate how the comparison with Christ is made through Wilde's changed circumstances:

> It is man's soul that Christ is always looking for. He calls it 'God's Kingdom' … and finds it in everyone. He compares it to little things, to a tiny seed, to a handful of leaven, to a pearl. That is because one only realises one's soul by getting rid of all alien passions, *all acquired culture,* and *all external possessions* be they good or evil. (p.113, my emphases)

It is not easy to imagine the pre-prison Wilde recommending that we eschew all acquired culture and certainly not all possessions. Wilde's life and work before he was jailed depended on a choosy but conspicuous consumption. There *is* a transformation here, and it coincides – probably consequentially – with destitution. Wilde absorbs his new criminal status into a long-standing preoccupation of his by proffering himself as a kind of martyr.[47]

Just as Wilde's life underwent a transformation, so too did his views on art and his own artistic practice. In 'The Decay of Lying' (published in 1891), he had written of the restrictions of the 'prison-house of realism'.[48] Now that he had first-hand experience of an actual jail his attitude changed. His few prison and post-prison writings show – even in their lack – the difficulty he now faced in avoiding realism. Suddenly, the 'monstrous worship of facts' seemed not so grotesque.[49]

A monster without a myth

Continuing this examination of beastly imagery, travel metaphor, and transformation we now turn to a brief discussion of Wilde's plays. Their radical edge has been softened by their enduring popularity with theatre audiences. In fact, Wilde's dramas provide a cutting vision of the role of money in society. His subject is largely the effect of wealth on conduct. He wittily exposes the discrepancy between conventional morality and upper- and upper-middle class behaviour. In *The Importance of Being Earnest* the incongruities do not stop there. Wilde takes the familiar form of the comedy of misunderstanding and invests it with complexities so that it operates on a deep economic level, too. Some of the characters lack the money to go with their social standing. Others, who do possess wealth, lack the moral precepts that warrant their position in the social hierarchy. None of them has any moral consistency. When they fall in love they do so playing at romance or following fortunes. Early in the play Algernon announces to Jack: 'I happen to be more than usually hard up.'[50] But Jack himself is in debt, owing the Savoy nearly 700 pounds. Ironically (one of many ironies), he can afford to pay the bill – he has, in the words of Jack, 'heaps of money' (*I*, p.362) left to him by 'Old Mr. Thomas Cardew' (*I*, p.361) who adopted Jack as a young boy. The reason Jack will not pay the bill (until a solicitor arrives demanding it) is that he has invented a dissolute younger brother in London, whom he has to visit to keep in order. This brother he calls Ernest, and it as Ernest that Algernon has known him: 'my name is Ernest in town and Jack in the country' (*I*, p.361). Ernest does not have heaps of money, but 'is one of those chaps who never pays a bill. He gets writted about once a week' (*I*, p.362). The charade is matched by Algernon, who has a fictitious friend in the country, Bunbury. Light-hearted these imagined characters may seem to be, but they testify to a serious question about identity. Algernon remarks to Jack: 'it isn't easy to be anything nowadays. There's such a lot of beastly competition about' (*I*, p.363). Algernon's apparently flippant observation underlines Wilde's own views on the importance of individualism and suggests the difficulty of achieving this. Another beastly image emphasises the point. Of Lady Bracknell, Jack declares: 'Never met such a Gorgon ... [sic] I don't really know what a Gorgon is like, but I am quite sure that Lady Bracknell is one. In any case, she is a monster, without being a myth, which is rather unfair' (*I*, p.370). In other words, Lady Bracknell is a hideous creature without the status of one. Whether because of her character or the age in which she lives, or both, she does not excite. She is a mundane monster, and this, Wilde seems to imply, is what her flat society has produced.

If Wilde mocks the superficiality of love in modern society through Gwendolen and Cecily – the women suggest they can love Jack and Algernon respectively only so long as they believe each is called Ernest – he exposes through Lady Bracknell the empty materialism of her world. She gives her consent to the marriage between Cecily and Algernon only when she learns from Jack that Cecily has '[a]bout a hundred and thirty thousand pounds in the Funds' (*IV*, p.409). Jack says this with studied casualness, the better to reveal Lady Bracknell's motives. She soon denies that she approves of mercenary marriages, but her words almost immediately on being told of Cecily's fortune are: 'Miss Cardew seems to me a most attractive young lady, now that I look at her' (*IV*, p.409). Similarly, her assessment of Jack's suitability as Gwendolen's husband depends both on his wealth and his family. On the former count she is satisfied, but on the latter she is not. His disclosure that he was brought up by the late Mr Thomas Cardew, who had found him in a handbag he had mistakenly been given in the cloak-room at Victoria Station, prompts her to forbid any further intercourse between Jack and Gwendolen. As Wilde has her put it: 'You can hardly imagine that I and Lord Bracknell would dream of allowing our only daughter … to marry into a cloak-room, and form an alliance with a parcel' (*I*, p.370). Wilde makes Lady Bracknell gloriously pompous, but the laughs he extracts at her expense should not mask the play's seriousness about class. Lady Bracknell exclaims a little earlier in the same speech:

> To be born, or at any rate bred, in a hand-bag, whether it had handles or not, seems to me to display a contempt for the ordinary deficiencies of family life that reminds one of the worst excesses of the French Revolution. And I presume you know what that unfortunate movement led to? (*I*, pp.369–370)

Wilde may be poking fun at Lady Bracknell here, but he is identifying a class anxiety that runs through the play. Those who wish to escape from its implications may find refuge in his humour, divorcing it from the circumstances that have generated it; but to do so would be foolishly to ignore the basis of the drama, just as Lady Bracknell herself does '[n]ot approve of anything that tampers with natural ignorance' (*I*, p.368). Worry about one's position drives the action and consumes the characters. 'What between the duties expected of one during one's lifetime, and the duties exacted from one after one's death', complains Lady Bracknell, 'land has ceased to be either a profit or a pleasure. It gives one position, and prevents one from keeping it up' (*I*, p.368). This is why she is satisfied that Jack's income is mainly from investments. He does have a country house with about 15,000 acres, 'but I don't depend on that for my real income. In fact, as far as I can make out, the poachers are the only people making anything out of it' (*I*, p.368). The decreasing profitability of land was a fact of the time and the apprehension that the 'lower' classes were usurping one's rights was commonly held. Speaking to Cecily in defence of his name (which she still believes is Ernest), Algernon comments: 'it is rather an aristocratic name. Half of the chaps who get into the Bankruptcy Court are called Algernon' (*III*, p.396). It may be a joke, but it speaks of the fading fortunes of the upper class. Wilde would follow them into the court. Algernon's declaration that '[n]o gentleman ever has any money' (*II*, p.385) has a double-edged truth to it: gentlemen were losing their money and many of those who had money were losing their gentlemanliness. Later, Gribsby, the solicitor who serves the writ from the Savoy on Algernon (who is posing as Ernest), talks of the comforts of jail: it is 'fashionable and well-aired; and there are ample opportunities of taking exercise at certain stated hours of the day' (*II*, p.386). The following dialogue then occurs:

> ALGERNON: Exercise! Good God! No gentleman ever takes exercise. You don't seem to understand what a gentleman is.
>
> GRIBSBY: I have met so many of them, sir, that I am afraid I don't. There are the most curious varieties of them. The result of cultivation, no doubt. (*II*, pp.386–387)

In such seemingly light-hearted exchanges we discern the connectedness of Wilde's characters to the society they would prefer existed only with a capital 'S', and the connectedness of his play to the time that Wilde would prefer his art to transcend.

In *Lady Windermere's Fan* wealth (or its lack) and status are likewise to the fore. Early in the first act, when Lady Windermere voices her annoyance with Lord Darlington for having paid her elaborate compliments the previous evening, he smilingly excuses himself thus: 'Ah, nowadays we are all of us so hard up, that the only pleasant things to pay *are* compliments. They're the only things we *can* pay.'[51] They may not *all* be hard up – Lord Windermere's wife discovers that her husband has been making payments totalling at least 1,700 pounds to Mrs Erlynne – but enough of them are for it to be a concern.

In both plays financial confusion is mirrored by social and personal uncertainty. In *The Importance of Being Earnest* the plot twist is provided by the revelation (to the characters and the audience) that by birth

Jack is Algernon's brother and Lady Bracknell's nephew and his name really is Ernest. In *Lady Windermere's Fan* the secret of the play (known only to Lord Windermere and Mrs Erlynne and quickly deduced by the audience) is that the notorious Mrs Erlynne is mother to Lady Windermere, who believes her mother to have died when she, Lady Windermere, was a child. Wilde was not alone in dealing with orphans and discoveries of birth in his writings, but his treatment of them allows him to focus on the question of worth within and outside society. Dickens (whom Wilde spoke of less than positively) also did as much, but Wilde's unconventional views on morality and individualism mean that in an unsentimental, almost dispassionate way, he can examine the superficiality of character and society: that is to say, the judging of someone's character by their blood relations and material value. Much of the humour arises when Wilde shows just how ridiculous such assessments are. Yet it is an observant, uncommitted humour because it has nothing else to offer in their place. Moral worth counts for little to Wilde, because to him morality is a matter of style.

'[A]ll men are monsters' (*I*, p.427), exclaims the Duchess of Berwick early in the play. She is referring to their unfaithfulness. But Wilde seems more concerned with society's beastliness. In charting Mrs Erlynne's fall and limited rise he examines the effects of materialism and convention on estimations of personal worth apart from these things. He explores the corrupting influence of social and economic factors on individual growth. Since these are debilitating, they also inhibit social development as society is composed of individuals competing for recognition. Wilde's orphaned characters (orphaned in fact or by belief) afford multiple views of who they were, who they might have been, what they have become, and what in future might happen to them. Wilde shows that characters are socially determined.

Perhaps the play that most communicates class anxiety is *A Woman of No Importance* (written during August and September 1892, first produced in April 1893, and published in October 1894). Gender issues are also prominent, evidenced in its very title. The swing of power away from the aristocracy to the middle classes is addressed early in the first Act when Lady Caroline Pontefract, who gets the name of the M. P. Mr Kelvil not quite right, remarks: 'He must be quite respectable. One has never heard his name before in the whole course of one's life, which speaks volumes for a man, nowadays.'[52] The change in circumstances is underlined shortly afterwards when she comments to Hester Worsley that: 'In my young days ... one never met anyone in society who worked for their living. It was not considered the thing.' Her addressee, an American, replies simply: 'In America those are the people we respect most' (*I*, p.466). Hester is described by Lady Hunstanton as 'an orphan. Her father was a very wealthy millionaire or philanthropist, or both, I believe, who entertained my son quite hospitably, when he visited Boston. I don't know how he made his money, originally' (*I*, p.470). By contrast, Lord Alfred Rufford has, like his peers, no money.

It was only three years after the writing of this play that Wilde was himself declared bankrupt. (The naming of Lord Alfred might be significant: the play was written within eighteen months of Wilde's meeting Lord Alfred Douglas, who drained Wilde's finances; but I am less interested in such biographical speculation than in the type of person and predicament this character represents.)

The play questions the meaning of importance. It moves towards an inversion of its title. Thus, at the end of Act One, when Lord Illingworth sees Mrs Arbuthnot's handwriting and is reminded of her – though he does not yet know it is her hand – he dismisses her as '[a] woman of no importance' (*I*, p.477). At the end of the play, after Lord Illingworth has unwillingly turned his son against him and been made to realise that his money cannot buy filial affection, he is dismissed by Mrs Arbuthnot as '[a] man of no importance' (*IV*, p.514).[53]

Although Wilde rightly rejoices in the diminution of Illingworth, his sympathies do not seem to lie altogether with Mrs Arbuthnot, who appears stubborn and over-protective of her grown-up son. Neither parent enjoys complete authorial or audience support. But if, in his survey of upper-class marriage, Wilde cannot provide an answer, he can at least ask pertinent questions. In *A Woman of No Importance* these centre on the effects of money upon marriage. Lady Caroline insists that men should be kept in their 'proper place', which is looking after their wives. If they are not married, they should be compelled to by law. If they are in love with someone else who may be tied to another, they should 'be married off in a week to some plain respectable girl, in order to teach them not to meddle with other people's property'. To this, Mrs Allonby replies:

> I don't think that we should ever be spoken of as other people's property. All men are married women's property. That is the only true definition of what married women's property really is. But we don't belong to anyone. (*II*, p.478)

This glance at the debates about married women's property shows that even after the 1882 Married Women's Property Act 'removed most of the common law disabilities which denied a married woman the right to own property and earnings',[54] unease still existed.

Marriages in Wilde's plays are often tarnished by money. Many matches were made for financial gain and have been dulled by the pursuit or possession of wealth. This is nicely illustrated in the following from *A Woman of No Importance* when Mrs Allonby tells Lady Hunstanton: 'my husband is a sort of promissory note; I'm tired of meeting him' (*II*, p.479). Wilde understands – and shows his audience – that all human relations are defined by, and conducted through, economic relations. As Terence Brown has noted in a brief but suggestive introduction to the plays, 'Wilde does not flinch in the matter of money'.[55] Money is as central to the plays as it is to the characters' lives.

A changeful life

Wilde's grandson, Merlin Holland, a frequent commentator on his grandfather, has written of the difficulty in pinning Wilde down. He refers to the latter's fascinating and confusing duality:

> the Anglo-Irishman with Nationalist sympathies; the Protestant with life-long Catholic leanings; the married homosexual; the musician of words and painter of language who confessed to André Gide that writing bored him; the artist astride not two but three cultures, an Anglo-Francophile and a Celt at heart.[56]

Holland notes that on top of all this is 'the question of which facets of the Wildean dichotomy were real and involuntary and which were artificial and contrived for effect'.[57] Yet in addition, Holland observes, there is the unreliability of Wilde's biographies, Ellmann's monumental volume included. Their inaccuracies and lacunae are not helped by Wilde's own deceits. Holland quotes from a letter in which Wilde exposes his own fib about his circumstances, told in order to extract money from Ross, and he compares different statements by Wilde offering contradictory accounts of time spent with (or without) Frank Harris in Napoule. (Again, it seems the lie is to Ross and is designed to extract money.) Holland invites biographers to consider carefully '[t]his manipulation of the truth for financial advantage'.[58] Because of our uncertainties about Wilde, many of them fostered by his own pronouncements and behaviour, and because of the fragmentary views we get of him, so that contradiction and confusion seem to abound, Holland remarks that Wilde's duality is now 'more of a plurality'.[59] The multifarious beastly labels that were attached to him through the progress and transformation of his life reflect this. Their variability and the fluctuations in his fortunes (both metaphorically and materially) are further evidence that Wilde 'saw that the "self" ... was socially constructed'.[60] And *this* means that the self was buffeted by the winds of economic and social change. So, therefore, the terms used to describe it had regularly to be revised. In Wilde we see the complicated effort to retain the shape of the self against the prevailing forces. He remarks of Christ that: 'He felt life was changeful, fluid, active, and that to allow it to be stereotyped into any form was death.'[61] That is how Wilde tries to accommodate the changes in his life. It suits the originality of his art and person and it is reflected in the variety of animal imagery applied to and by him.

Notes

1 Henry James, quoted in Neil Sammells, *Wilde Style: The Plays and Prose of Oscar Wilde* (London: Pearson Education Limited, 2000), p.55. Sammells repeats the quotation from H. Montgomery Hyde, *Oscar Wilde* [1976].
2 For a detailed account of the trials, see H. Montgomery Hyde, *The Trials of Oscar Wilde* [1948, 1962] (New York, NY: Dover, 1973).
3 Richard Ellmann, *Oscar Wilde* (London: Penguin Books, 1988), p.412. Further page references will be given parenthetically preceded by *E*.
4 *Weekly Sun*, 16 June 1895, quoted in Ed Cohen, *Talk on the Wilde Side: Toward a Genealogy of a Discourse on Male Sexualities* (New York, NY: Routledge, 1993), p.17.
5 *Evening Standard*, 4 April 1895. Quoted in Cohen, *Talk on the Wilde Side*, p.166.
6 Cohen, *Talk on the Wilde Side*, pp.166–167.
7 Joseph Bristow, *Effeminate England: Homoerotic Writing after 1885* (Buckingham: Open University Press, 1995), p.37.
8 Quoted from *Pearson's Weekly*, 27 May 1893, in Holbrook Jackson, *The Eighteen Nineties* [1913] (Harmondsworth: Penguin, 1939), p.70.
9 This unattributed quotation is to be found in Jackson, *The Eighteen Nineties*, p.67.
10 Arthur Symons, 'Sex and Aversion', in Karl Beckson, ed., *The Memoirs of Arthur Symons: Life and Art in the 1890s* (University Park, PA: Pennsylvania State University Press, 1977), pp.146–147. Quoted in Bristow, *Effeminate England*, p.17.
11 Bristow, *Effeminate England*, p.2. Wilde's sentence, as Bristow reminds us, was two years in solitary confinement with hard labour.
12 Interestingly, the same image was used to describe Aubrey Beardsley. Jackson quotes H. C. Marillier: '"Poor Beardsley! His death has removed a quaint and amiable personality from among us; a butterfly who played at being serious, and yet a busy worker who played at being a butterfly."' Jackson, *The Eighteen Nineties*, p.88. That two apparently effeminate writers of the period should be so labelled is, I think, more than coincidence. The *OED* includes among its definitions of the word '[a] vain, gaudily attired person ... a light-headed, inconstant person' and 'vain, inconstant, frivolous'.

13 Oscar Wilde to Leonard Smithers, 11 December 1897. In Merlin Holland and Rupert Hart-Davis, eds, *The Complete Letters of Oscar Wilde* (London: Fourth Estate, 2000), p.1006. A version of this from an earlier edition of Wilde's letters is quoted by Bristow, *Effeminate England*, p.18. Holland and Hart-Davis footnote the Latin thus: '*Quantum mutatus ab illo* (How changed from what he once was). Virgil, *Aeneid*, II, 274.' Wilde applies the Latin to himself to convey his own sense of transformation.

14 Bristow, *Effeminate England*, p.18.

15 Jackson, *The Eighteen Nineties*, p.71. Jackson reports Sherard's description of Wilde as 'bloated' (p.71).

16 Bristow, *Effeminate England*, p.20.

17 Bristow, *Effeminate England*, p.20.

18 Bristow, *Effeminate England*, p.21.

19 Oscar Wilde, 'A Model Millionaire. A Note of Admiration', in *Lord Arthur Savile's Crime and Other Stories* [1891] (London: Penguin, 1994), p.77. Further page references will be given parenthetically with the abbreviation '*MM*'.

20 Oscar Wilde, 'The Happy Prince', in *Lord Arthur Savile's Crime and Other Stories* [1891] (London: Penguin, 1994), p.139. The tale was first published in *The Happy Prince and Other Tales* in 1888. Further page references will be given parenthetically with the abbreviation '*HP*'.

21 John Stokes, *Oscar Wilde* (Harlow: Longman for the British Council, 1978), p.22.

22 Stokes, *Oscar Wilde*, pp.21–22.

23 Stokes, *Oscar Wilde*, p.22.

24 Stokes, *Oscar Wilde*, p.22.

25 Oscar Wilde, 'The Soul of Man', in Oscar Wilde, *The Soul of Man and Prison Writings*, edited and with an introduction by Isobel Murray (Oxford: Oxford University Press, 1990), p.29. Further page references will be given parenthetically as '*SM*'. For the application of 'monster' to the French Revolution, see Chris Baldick, *In Frankenstein's Shadow: Myth, Monstrosity, and Nineteenth-Century Writing* (Oxford: Clarendon Press, 1987), Chapter One.

26 Oscar Wilde, 'The Ballad of Reading Gaol' (1898), in Oscar Wilde, *The Soul of Man and Prison Writings*, edited and with an introduction by Isobel Murray (Oxford: Oxford University Press, 1990), p.182, lines 433–436. I discuss this poem further in '"A Sonnet Out of Skilly": Oscar Wilde's "The Ballad of Reading Gaol"', *Critical Survey* 11, 3 (1999), 40–47.

27 Wilde, 'The Ballad of Reading Gaol', p.185, line 511. The information on Wooldridge is taken from Murray's endnote in Wilde, *The Soul of Man and Prison Writings*, edited and with an introduction by Isobel Murray, p.220. The poem's inscription begins 'In Memoriam/C.T.W.' (p.169).

28 Wilde, 'The Ballad of Reading Gaol', p.174, lines 169–174.

29 Stokes, *Oscar Wilde*, p.46.

30 Wilde, 'The Ballad of Reading Gaol', p.186, lines 547–552.

31 Wilde, 'The Ballad of Reading Gaol', p.187, lines 583–584.

32 Wilde, 'The Ballad of Reading Gaol', p.186, line 559.

33 'Wilde's Second Post-Prison Letter to the *Daily Chronicle*', in *The Soul of Man and Prison Writings*, edited by Isobel Murray, p.191. The letter was published on 24 March 1898.

34 'Wilde's First Post-Prison Letter to the *Daily Chronicle*', in *The Soul of Man and*

Prison Writings, edited by Isobel Murray, p.166. The letter was published on 28 May 1897.
35 Wilde, 'First Post-Prison Letter', p.167.
36 The first post-prison letter was written in defence of a warder who had been 'dismissed by the Prison Commissioners for having given some sweet biscuits to a little hungry child' (p.159). The scope of the letter widens into a protest against the inhumane treatment of children in prison. Their 'terror', writes Wilde, 'was quite limitless' (p.160). They are locked in their solitary, dimly lit cells for twenty-three hours per day, and Wilde recalls 'a child's face … like a white wedge of sheer terror' that had 'in his eyes the terror of a hunted animal' (p.161). Wilde's attack is fiercely against the society that inflicts such cruelty, not on what many of his contemporaries would presume to be the child's own animality.
37 Wilde, 'Second Post-Prison Letter', pp.193–194.
38 Wilde, 'The Ballad of Reading Gaol', p.185, line 534.
39 Wilde, 'First Post-Prison Letter', p.160.
40 Ellmann infers that James saw in Wilde a threat, because 'James's homosexuality was latent, Wilde's was patent', and Wilde's 'flouting and flaunting' made it difficult for society to tolerate it by turning a blind eye to it (p.171).
41 Reproduced in Ellmann, *Oscar Wilde*, between pp.226 and 227.
42 Quoted in Ellmann, *Oscar Wilde*, p.461, unnumbered footnote.
43 Karl Marx, *Capital*, quoted in Regenia Gagnier, 'Wilde and the Victorians', in Peter Raby, ed., *The Cambridge Companion to Oscar Wilde* (Cambridge: Cambridge University Press, 1997), p.21.
44 These symptoms were noted by most of Wilde's visitors, but are also concentrated in Ellmann's summary of Robert Ross's impressions of Wilde after a year of his imprisonment. Ellmann, *Oscar Wilde*, pp.468–469.
45 Oscar Wilde, 'De Profundis', in *The Soul of Man and other Prison Writings*, edited by Isobel Murray (Oxford: Oxford University Press, 1990), p.72. Further page references will be given parenthetically.
46 Details of some of this expenditure are given in the letter.
47 On Wilde and martyrdom, see, for example, Karl Beckson and Bobby Fong, 'Wilde as Poet', in Peter Raby, ed., *The Cambridge Companion to Oscar Wilde*, p.62; and John Stokes, 'Wilde the Journalist', in Raby, ed., *The Cambridge Companion to Oscar Wilde*, p.76.
48 Oscar Wilde, 'The Decay of Lying', in *Intentions* [1891] (London: Methuen & Co. Ltd., 1925), p.27. The essay first appeared in *The Nineteenth Century*, January 1889, and was revised for its publication in book form in *Intentions*.
49 Oscar Wilde, 'The Decay of Lying', p.8.
50 Oscar Wilde, *The Importance of Being Earnest*, in *Complete Works of Oscar Wilde* (Glasgow: HarperCollins Publishers, 1994), Act One, p.360. Further page references to the play will be given parenthetically, preceded by the Act number, and are to this edition. The edition gives the play in its full four Acts, including the second, which is often omitted from performances and from other texts after having been cut at the behest of Wilde's actor manager (p.352). The play was written in August and September of 1894, produced in January 1895, and published in January 1899.
51 Oscar Wilde, *Lady Windermere's Fan*, in *Complete Works of Oscar Wilde*, Act One, p.421. Further page references to the play will be given parenthetically, preceded by

the Act number, and are to this edition. The play was first produced in February 1892 and published in November the following year.

52 Oscar Wilde, *A Woman of No Importance* (Glasgow: HarperCollins Publishers, 1994), p.465. Further page references to the play will be given parenthetically, preceded by the Act number, and are to this edition.

53 The plot has a chance meeting between Lord Illingworth and Mrs Arbuthnot – the mother of their son, Gerald. Illingworth had made her pregnant, but had not kept his promise to marry her. She had left, refusing financial help. Again by chance, Illingworth has offered Gerald a post as his private secretary. Gerald wants to accept because it will boost both his income and social status, as well as broaden his horizons. It will involve geographical as well as social travel. Encouraged by Illingworth, once the latter has discovered – but not revealed to Gerald – the young man's true identity, Gerald grows impatient with his mother for her opposition, which looks like (and in part is) a maternal clinging. However, when Illingworth tries to seduce Hester, whom Gerald loves, Gerald loses all respect for him. At this point, in the near violence of the moment (Gerald has threatened Illingworth), his mother reveals the secret of his paternity. Once he has been told the story of Illingworth's deception of Mrs Arbuthnot, Gerald is more opposed to him.

54 J. F. C. Harrison, *Late Victorian Britain 1875–1901* (n.p.: Fontana Press, 1990), p.170.

55 Terence Brown, 'Introduction to the Plays', in *Complete Works of Oscar Wilde*, p.351.

56 Merlin Holland, 'Biography and the Art of Lying', in Peter Raby, ed., *The Cambridge Companion to Oscar Wilde*, p.3

57 Holland, 'Biography and the Art of Lying', p.3.

58 Holland, 'Biography and the Art of Lying', p.9.

59 Holland, 'Biography and the Art of Lying', p.16.

60 Regenia Gagnier, 'Wilde and the Victorians', in Peter Raby, ed., *The Cambridge Companion to Oscar Wilde*, p.20. Gagnier elaborates: 'It was constructed through language ... It was constructed through social institutions ... And it was constructed irrationally, unconsciously ...' I would place its economic construction (which is a part of Gagnier's analysis) above these.

61 Wilde, 'De Profundis', p.121.

Conclusion

The preceding chapters have argued that the shape assumed by beasts in the literature of the late 1880s and 1890s is moulded by the changing identity of Britain at that time. The 1880s were a 'period of extraordinary transition'.[1] The travels and transformations found in contemporary writing provide a response to those critical years, one that also resonates in more recent surveys and reviews of the period. This is illustrated in the following brief quotation (one of many such), which sums up what much of the foregoing discussion has shown: 'England in the 1880s was in transition, shedding the skin of Victorianism and moving towards a more modern age.'[2] The combination of social change, animal imagery, and travel metaphors concisely expressed here encapsulates the main themes of this book.

Before taking stock, let us glance at the forms taken by the early progeny of the beasts we have observed so far. In the main, the next generation, the descendants that inhabited the first third of the twentieth century, quiver from the fear of sex and slaver over the threat of national dissolution. John Lucas writes of the 1920s that: 'A deep anxiety underlies or is to be found within much writing by men during this period, and one of the ways it shows is in the depiction of women gone feral.'[3] At the very start of that decade, Edward Heron-Allen's short story 'The Cheetah-Girl' was expunged from the collection *The Purple Sapphire and Other Posthumous Papers* (1921) that it was meant to close. Under the story's title a parenthetical note explains: '[The Publishers regret that they are unable to print this M.S.].'[4]

In the title poem of Charlotte Mew's *The Farmer's Bride* (1916), 'the young wife flees from her husband's sexual demands and is described in a way that identifies her ... with a hunted animal: a leveret in her shyness, her fears, and her "soft, young down"'.[5] Lucas notes that the poem 'seems to set in ... train a number of works in which women become feral creatures'.[6] We might list among these David Garnett's novella *Lady into Fox* (1922), which, like his *A Man in the Zoo* (1924), unsettles with its representation of animals. The protagonist of the former, Mr Tebrick, attempts to reconcile himself to his wife Sylvia's metamorphosis into a vixen. The narrator encourages a lack of understanding:

> A grown lady is changed straightaway into a fox. There is no explaining that away by any natural philosophy. The materialism of our age will not help us here. It is indeed *a miracle*; something from outside our world altogether.[7]

It may be written tongue-in-cheek, but the narrator desires us to accept the thing just as it is; the event happens and cannot be rationalised. In keeping with many twentieth-century animal narratives, *Lady into Fox* encourages both sympathy and empathy. Tebrick loves his wife, regardless of her altered state, telling her: 'Though you are a fox I would rather live with you than any woman.' He pledges fidelity, 'respect and reverence'. He does so, 'not because of any hope that God in His mercy will see fit to restore your shape, but solely because I love you. However you may be changed, my love is not' (p.14). But Mr Tebrick grows impatient with his foxy wife, whose increasing slide into animal ways he finds repulsive.[8] When he begins to worry that she is losing what remains of her human characteristics he tests her by leaving her alone for five minutes with a present of flowers and a black-and-white rabbit. Before he steps outside the room to fetch a vase she shows no interest in the creature. When he returns he finds '[b]lood on the carpet, blood on the armchairs and antimacassars, even a little blood spurtled on to the wall, and what was worse, Mrs. Tebrick tearing and growling over a piece of the skin and the legs, for she had eaten up all the rest of it' (p.29). Shock and humour collide here, produced by Garnett's giving the fox its previous human appellation and marital title while it consumes the rabbit, staining the furniture red. Garnett's story introduces a second transformation as Tebrick's attitude towards his vulpine spouse changes. His vow of fidelity gives way to inconstancy, at least of feeling. Garnett thus shows that things – people – are not fixed. Furthermore, because the narrative itself presents Tebrick's reversal of view without commenting on the contradiction, it reveals a gap between intention and conduct; between declaration and behaviour. Promises are rendered unreliable; emotions and relationships are unsettled. It also creates distance between what is shown and what is said: Tebrick's growing distaste contravenes his declarations of love, but the discrepancy is not acknowledged. Mr Tebrick's own change advances with his retreat into misanthropy. He becomes a recluse, who 'had come to hate his fellow men and was embittered against all human decencies and decorum' (p.62). This state is reached after his fox-wife has turned against him and fled into the wild. She had earlier bit his hand when he prevented her escaping through a tunnel she was digging, and her eyes 'held his, with their split pupils looking at him with savage desperation and rage' (p.56). The language of escape and entrapment is associated with marriage: the story posits the vixen's efforts to flee as an attempt to achieve freedom. Mr Tebrick asks his wife: 'Are you trying to escape from me? I am your husband, and if I keep you confined it is to protect you, not to let you run into danger' (p.48). His words are those of the patriarch who insists he knows what is best for his wife. Garnett employs his animal metaphor at this point to critique contemporary marriage and gender relationships.

Neil Jordan, who directed Angela Carter's *Company of Wolves* (1984) and co-wrote the screenplay with her, states of Garnett's *Lady into Fox* and *A Man in the Zoo* that:

> The presence of animals in both intimates a parable, a meaning, a lesson, but the power of both stories lies actually in their resistance to interpretation, in the inscrutable balance Garnett has achieved between a subject that is primitive, outlandish, and a style that is almost prim in its reserve, its rectitude.[9]

Jordan's first remark oversimplifies animal tales, which are often much more complex and ambiguous than parables. On the other hand, his suggestion that their strength resides in their challenge to interpretation reminds us of both the indeterminacy of meaning created by the transformations we have witnessed to date and the uncertainty that sits at the heart of much modernist art. Jordan's comment on the discrepancy between subject and style can be applied to the stories of Saki (H. H. Munro) in which the ill-fit is for effect and exposes an unease about the suitability of appearance to substance; of outward form to inner nature. The rift between expression and topic is discomfiting and ensures that the text cannot be read unthinkingly: illusions of natural fit are shattered.

Saki's dry wit has the bestial intrude into the English drawing room in a number of his short tales. The contrast between his elegantly mannered prose and savage humour complements his coupling of the domestic and the wild. In 'The She-Wolf' (1912, 1914), hostess Mary Hampton tells her guest Leonard Bilsiter, who has travelled across Eastern Europe, 'I wish you would turn me into a wolf, Mr. Bilsiter.'[10] The story rests on the illusion of a transformation. Saki mocks the protagonist's pretensions to supernatural abilities. Bilsiter believes he has acquired mystical powers on his journey and as a result of his powerful imagination, but his fellow guest Clovis Sangrail secretly arranges for another guest to bring to the property a wolf that he owns. This wolf they introduce as though Bilsiter really has changed his hostess into a she-wolf, much to Bilsiter's embarrassment and consternation. The tale does not relate a real transformation, but it parodies those stories in which transmutations are said to occur, and it makes fun of readers who accept the illusion. Clovis casually assumes superior gifts, claiming:

> I happen to have lived for a couple of years in North-eastern Russia, and I have more than a tourist's acquaintance with the magic craft of that region. One does not care to speak about these strange powers, but once in a way, when one hears a lot of nonsense being talked about them, one is tempted to show what Siberian magic can accomplish in the hands of some one who really understands it. I yielded to that temptation. May I have some brandy? The effort has left me rather faint. (p.128)

It is in part the incongruity of Sangrail's urbane calmness and the fantastical tale he tells that provokes Bilsiter into thinking that if he 'could at that moment have transformed Clovis into a cockroach and then have stepped on him he would gladly have performed both operations' (p.129). It is noticeable that here, as in Garnett's work and other examples of shape-shifting narratives from the 1920s, humour is prominent. The juxtaposition of the quotidian and the fantastic that in the fin de siècle Gothic generated fear and horror now gives rise to a sardonic smile.

The anomalous is at the heart of Saki's writing. Introducing a collection of Saki's tales, Tom Sharpe writes of how, in them,

> [c]ivilization has been overthrown and replaced by a strange supernature, and all this worship of instinct comes at us more forcefully because it emerges from the setting of house party and afternoon tea, and all the hallowed conventions of Edwardian society.[11]

Sharpe's description inadvertently suggests a line connecting Saki to Machen and MacDonald: 'Step out through the French windows and you are in the realm of Pan and liable, unless you pay homage, to pay with your life for your arrogant belief in material progress and the virtues of middle-class respectability.'[12] There are obvious continuities with the late nineteenth-century works discussed in the previous pages, but, as ever, the new forms mark an adaptation to their own environment. The First World War increased the longing for escape as much as it hammered home the barbarity of a newly industrialised killing machine. The absurd combination of savagery and domestic interiors in Garnett's and Saki's darkly humorous tales owes something to this. It is evident, too, along with the build-up to the Second World War, in Karel Čapek's satirical allegory, *War with the Newts* (1937), which – using, like *Dracula* and *The Beetle*, multiple voices and documents – recounts the discovery, exploitation, adaptation, and militarisation of the eponymous Newts. Human greed, politics, nationalism, and international rivalry produce another slave trade and violence on a world-wide scale. Indeed, there is a subdivision of beastliness here as the German emphasis on the racial superiority of the Baltic Newt has the country's press describing with contempt 'the degenerate Mediterranean Newts, stunted both physically and morally; the savage tropical Newts; and altogether the low, barbarian, and bestial Salamanders of other nations'.[13]

In the twentieth century, beastliness arising from travel is often linked with a threat to authority. That authority is generally white and male. The challenges to it are frequently posed by colonial subjects moving towards independence, nations with alternative political systems, opposing political and class interests, and women striving for liberation. Those pressures are present in the later nineteenth century, too, but they intensify in the twentieth. Expressions of a governing body as a weakened animal or under attack from wild creatures are rife. At the beginning of his travel book *Filibusters in Barbary*, which sees the author travelling to Morocco, Wyndham Lewis complains that

> [t]he sedentary habits of six years of work had begun, I confess, to weary me. Then the atmosphere of our dying European society is to me profoundly depressing. Some relief is necessary from the daily spectacle of those expiring Lions and Eagles, who obviously will never recover from the death-blows they dealt each other (foolish beasts and birds) from 1914–1918 …
>
> Perhaps nothing short of the greatest desert in the world, or its proximity, would answer the case.[14]

Lewis seeks the sun, both literally and figuratively. He turns away from the cold and wet:

> England had its watercart on at full blast as I left; there had been no sun for ten months … England, my England! I gasped, my face streaming with rain – Shall I return; or, like so many of your sons, become from henceforth an exile? I wished frankly to escape for ever from this expiring Octopus, that held me to it by my mother-tongue (unless America can be said to share, with England, that advantage over me).[15]

Lewis was one of those modernists who were troubled by the encroachment of tourism on travel. The rise of mass tourism from the mid-nineteenth century provokes its own bestiary. Paul Fussell notes 'how traditional in anti-tourist fulminations animal images are ... And if not animals, insects'.[16] By way of example, Fussell quotes from Charles Lever, Francis Kilvert, and Osbert and Edith Sitwell, but many more could be added to the list. Scorning the herd or the swarm is to individualise and humanise oneself.[17]

The impulse to travel and to do so in ways distinct from group tourism was also a reaction against the 1914–1918 war. In the decade after that conflict, many artists presented a vision of a world in which human behaviour and feelings were mechanised. D. H. Lawrence's characters are insentient victims of, or seek an antidote to, this machine state. In Lawrence's writing and that of several of his contemporaries, sex is a focus for this robotic condition, regarded either with disgust or as a revitalising remedy. John Lucas reminds us that in T. S. Eliot's poem *The Waste Land*, Tiresias 'emerges as the prurient, disgusted voyeur of the animal-like sexual couplings which such critics as F.R. Leavis and Cleanth Brooks took to characterise relationships in the modern world: mechanical, sterile, joyless'.[18] The decadence that was perceived – even sought and promoted – in these years heightened the atmosphere of animalistic pleasure. Lucas writes of the 1920s: 'Sex, drugs, dance music. Signs of the times, elements in the vortex of beastliness.'[19] That which had previously been shunned or feared now enticed and was embraced with a frisson of danger. In art (visual and aural), the appetite for it is manifested in the appropriation and adaptation of indigenous culture. In music, what Lucas calls 'the fearful fascination of an earlier generation of European writers and artists with [the] heart of darkness' becomes 'modulated into or ... focused on what was commonly called "jungle music" – in a word, jazz'.[20] Drugs themselves became the means of achieving an altered state. When Kathleen Hale unwittingly takes hashish at a party in 1922 she experiences 'horrendous nightmares about colossal and malign elephants', and, on awaking the next morning, '[s]till under the influence of hashish, I was convinced that I had become an object of utter ridicule with a monstrous body and eyes that had totally disappeared behind puffed eyelids'.[21]

The year after the end of the First World War saw the publication of W. B. Yeats's 'The Second Coming', a poem that itself took on many forms as the poet revised it several times. Anticipating the Second Coming, the speaker remarks:

> The Second Coming! Hardly are those words out
> When a vast image out of *Spiritus Mundi*
> Troubles my sight: somewhere in sands of the desert

A shape with lion body and the head of a man,
A gaze blank and pitiless as the sun,
Is moving its slow thighs, while all about it
Reel shadows of the indignant desert birds.

As darkness descends, the speaker now knows '[t]hat twenty centuries of stony sleep/Were vexed to nightmare by a rocking cradle'. The original version closes with the threatening question: 'And what rough beast, its hour come round at last,/Slouches towards Bethlehem to be born?'[22] Declan Kiberd proffers those last lines as examples of what he finds to be characteristic of 'many of Yeats's most memorable [ones]': that they 'are striking without being lucid'. The rough beast, Kiberd suggests, may be 'a divine agent of inspiration, heralding not only a new era but also new subjects for poetry'.[23] That may be, but it is an unsettling, even a sinister, image. Yeats's rough beast is of an indeterminate hue, symptomatic of modernism's amorphous shapes. Noting Yeats's preoccupation with Socialism and his apprehension of its spread in Russia, Germany, and Italy both during and after the war, Lucas identifies the slouching beast with the working classes, the 'plebs'. In Lucas's reading, 'Yeats' fear is that history now shapes and is shaped by "the roof-levelling wind" of democratic energies which will actively threaten and destroy a culture, a civilisation, where "all's accustomed, ceremoniousness".'[24] We might record here that Churchill wrote to Mussolini, supporting his struggle 'against the bestial appetites and passions of Leninism'.[25]

Naturalistic descriptions of workers and the masses continue into the twentieth from the nineteenth century. In Ellen Wilkinson's 1929 novel *Clash*, miners are depicted as the victims of a voracious industrial monster:

> The coal-pit was the only thing in each village that mattered, the only part of life on which capital and care and brains were expended. Human beings were usually fed into its mouth at eight-hourly intervals, and just as regularly coughed up again. Now the wheels of the winding cage were silent, but the domination of the pit remained. On the refuse-heaps men, women and children grubbed, like maggots trying to find precious bits of coal to sell for bread.[26]

In the opening section of *The Road to Wigan Pier* (1937), George Orwell writes of people like 'blackbeetles'.[27] But Orwell sees through the outer coat. He urges: 'if one remembers that a tramp is only an Englishman out of work, forced by law to live as a vagabond, then the tramp-monster vanishes'.[28] Orwell's vision restores humanity to those who have been brutalised. Bernard Schweizer asserts that: 'For George Orwell, both the act and the rhetorical figure of travelling were linked with the idea of social and political transformation.' Travel was 'also tied up with a sense of responsibility, of promoting a silenced perspective'.[29] If one accepts Schweizer's case, Orwell reverses the processes that have been described in much of the present work; rather than Othering in his travels, Orwell strips away difference. But in Orwell's travel writing,

> guilt is the sign of an incomplete social transformation … In facing the poor and the colonized, Orwell is constantly torn between his liberationist, egalitarian ideals and his bourgeois background. And each time the repressed middle-class consciousness rears its head, the result is an uncanny impression.[30]

One might contend that in the self-consciously comic construction of domestic beastliness in Saki and Garnett, in the knowingly allegorical warning of the effects of slavery and exploitation in *War with the Newts*, and in the proletarian sympathies – however qualified or compromised – of Orwell, the beasts of the half century after the fin de siècle are less an object of fear or correction and more an artifice. If we have moved on, it may be at the cost of attention to the real causes of deformation, though to speak in terms of progress or regression is unwise. The pattern is uneven. The narrator of African American James Weldon Johnson's 1912 novel *Autobiography of an Ex-Coloured Man* may hurl back the animal label often used against his people by writing of whites who commit a lynching – 'Have you ever witnessed the transformation of human beings into savage beasts?'[31] – but a century later a prominent and distinguished British commentator could write of young people who took part in rioting that they were wild beasts, with instincts only to sleep, eat, drink, have sex, and steal or destroy others' property.[32]

The processes discussed in this book are not unique to the last years of the nineteenth century, but the examples presented here display in concentrated form the operation of material contexts on cultural metaphors. The number of survivals from the last fifteen years of the nineteenth century is remarkable and testament to the profundity of the symbolic representation of social and economic forces and fears at the time, but the mutation of the originals reflects subsequent concerns, too. The creatures paraded between these covers serve to show that, in literature as in life, animals adapt to their environment. In literary texts, this means adaptation to form and genre, which respond in turn to their own context, and also to the society in which those works are produced. In the last fifteen years or so of the nineteenth century we witness the extraordinary coincidence of factors – economic, social, intellectual, and technological – that bore on the shapes of humans, the world they inhabited, and how they travelled. On the cusp of the modern, they look both ahead and back. The economic catalysts so evident to nineteenth-century readers are largely erased from retellings, but remain preserved in the originals ready for excavation.

It is tempting to conclude by identifying a movement towards greater empathy with animals. Taking his lead from Kate Soper, Steve Baker discusses

> the diverse ways in which post-modern art has dealt with the animal across a spectrum ranging from the *animal-endorsing* to the *animal-sceptical*. These terms ... point to the complexity of what it is that is called 'animal' here. Animal-endorsing art will tend to endorse animal life itself (and may therefore align itself with the work of conservationists, or perhaps of animal advocacy), rather than endorsing cultural constructions of the animal. Animal-sceptical art, on the contrary, is likely to be sceptical not of animals themselves (as if the very existence of non-human life was in question), but rather of culture's means of constructing and classifying the animal in order to make it meaningful to the human.[33]

Works such as Franz Kafka's *The Metamorphosis* (1915) take a more sympathetic view of the perspective and plight of the animal. In Kafka's tale finance is, as in so many of the works discussed here, central to the story. The family of the protagonist, Gregor Samsa, struggle to feed themselves when Gregor is unable to work as a result of his transformation. They then start saving money as a result of his cheaper living. Syed Islam cites Kafka as an example of what he calls a 'nomadic' as opposed to a 'sedentary' traveller: that is, Kafka is able to have his view altered by his engagement with the Other.[34] In such readings Otherness is not demonised, but is understood.

In academia, the growth in ecocriticism, often in conjunction with postcolonialism, may be taken to signal a greater recognition of, and sympathy with, the situation of the animal. Here, humans are the danger to the natural order, not themselves at threat from nature. Certainly, one may also deduce from works such as Baker's that modern and postmodern art interrogate the meanings we ascribe to the animal and the human; that art now is concerned with breaking down these categories in ways that develop our understanding, rather than identifying commingling as a threat. But this movement is a tendency, not the whole or even a general picture. Questioning and sympathy may exist and they may constitute a significant departure from art that is characteristic of the period we have been looking at, but many examples of the kind associated with late nineteenth-century representations continue to be produced.

Those similar cases notwithstanding, one would probably infer from cultural criticism that the later twentieth and twenty-first centuries have witnessed more positive, less fearful views of the animal and self-critical explorations of the relationship between the animal and the human. Cary Wolfe refers to the 'radical revaluation of the status of nonhuman animals that has taken place in society at large' and to work in areas such as cognitive ethology and field ecology that has 'more or less permanently eroded the tidy divisions between human and nonhuman ... [which] in turn, has led to a broad reopening of the question of the ethical status of animals in relation to the human'.[35] Wolfe points to the irony, however, that an essentially humanist philosophy erases the very difference of the animal that those concerned with animal rights 'sought to respect in the first place'.[36] Donna Haraway writes of her belief that

> ethical relating, within or between species, is knit from the silk-strong thread of ongoing alertness to otherness-in-relation. We are not one, and being depends on getting on together.[37]

Moving beyond a positive attitude towards the Other, Haraway calls for recognition of 'significant otherness as something other than a reflection of one's own intentions'.[38] Derrida has problematised 'the purity and indivisibility of a line between reaction and response, and especially the possibility of tracing such a line, between the human *in general* and the animal *in general*'.[39] Deleuze and Guattari have written on 'becoming animal', in which '[b]ecoming produces nothing other than itself ... What is real is the becoming itself, the block of becoming, not the supposedly fixed terms through which that which becomes passes.'[40]

Seemingly more enlightened views, such as Haraway's and those of others who attempt to honour the difference of the animal, do not mean that horror is no longer generated from tales of transformation, as the original and sequel of the film *The Human Centipede* (2010; 2011) prove. Repeats and reworkings of familiar characters and creatures – Dracula and vampires, werewolves, Hyde – continue to appear. What does seem to happen though is that the dissolution of the boundary between the human and the beast becomes something increasingly to be desired or to be explored dispassionately rather than feared. Besides the popularity of 'green' issues and ecocriticism, there is the fact, observed by Baker, that

> Many postmodern or poststructuralist artists and writers seem, at one level or another, to adopt or to identify with the animal as a metaphor for, or as an image of, their own creativity. Whether it connotes a sense of alienation from the human or a sense of bodily freedom and unboundedness, this

willing taking-on of animal form casts the fixity of identity as an inhibition of creativity.[41]

What we can be sure of is that animals, journeys, and literary genres all inherit characteristics of their progenitors; and they combine original features with responses to their present circumstances. They change shape, but remain recognisable. Of course they are not simply 'out there'. Their meaning derives from the onlooker. No less than narrators do we define, classify, and judge. And this is often in the service of power: 'Society and the State need animal characteristics to use for classifying people', Deleuze and Guattari point out.[42] Against this urge towards classification, the movement of genres (of animals and literature) can introduce fluidity. Metaphors, like actual travel, cross space and time and forge connections. They always speak of at least two conditions and inherent in them therefore is the potential to destabilise the very urge to fix that has impelled them. They can operate interrogatively or affirmatively, radically or conservatively.

Luckhurst claims that

> for many critics, the phantasmagoric imagination of the Gothic actually begins to provide many of the metaphors for how we conceive of our modern subjectivity, mysterious to itself, labyrinthine, haunted by half-glimpsed spectres of memory and desire, never quite successfully burying its dead, fearful that all the skeletons in the closet will one day return.

Here he is hinting at the process by which we revivify texts and genres that might otherwise become or stay moribund.[43] Genres are in any case in flux, as are individual works within them. As John Frow observes, 'all texts are strongly shaped by their relation to one or more genres, which in turn they may modify'.[44] Genres are not fixed but dynamic. In Frow's words:

> because the range of possible uses is always open-ended, genre classifications are necessarily unstable and unpredictable. And this is so above all because texts do not simply have uses which are mapped out in advance by the genre: they are themselves *uses of genre*, performances of or allusions to the norms and conventions which form them and which they may, in turn, transform.[45]

Like their subjects, then, the texts studied in this volume are themselves examples of unstable forms, with Stoker transforming the Gothic that he has inherited, MacDonald doing the same with fairy tales and the fantastic, Wells shaping the scientific romance, and so on. Journeys, beasts, and literary genres are all in motion. Their congruence in the last fifteen years of the nineteenth century at a time of extraordinary social movement, political tension, and economic crisis has endowed us with a uniquely rich corpus that has survived its original setting, but that has been divested, in revivals, of its financial roots. In her *In Darkest London*, Margaret Harkness writes: 'This is metaphorical language, but some things can only be expressed in metaphors.'[46] These beastly journeys, whose figures of speech reflect their origins and that have survived, if modified, in our own time, help demonstrate why.

Notes

1. R. A. Biderman, 'Introduction', in Israel Zangwill, *Children of the Ghetto: A Study of a Peculiar People* [1895] (Cambridge: Black Apollo Press, 2004), p.9.
2. Paul Begg, *Jack the Ripper: The Definitive History* (London: Longman, 2003), p.3.
3. John Lucas, *The Radical Twenties* (Nottingham: Five Leaves Press, 1997), p.71.
4. Christopher Blayre, *The Purple Sapphire and Other Posthumous Papers* (London: Philip Allan and Co., 1921), p.211. Blayre was the pseudonym of polymath Edward Heron-Allen. I am grateful to Christopher Barker for informing me of the existence of 'The Cheetah-Girl' and to Ray Russell for supplying me with a copy of the text. The story was apparently dropped for fear that its treatment of sexual themes, including bestiality and lesbianism, would render the publishers liable to prosecution. Heron-Allen circulated it in a private edition of twenty copies and it was printed in *The Collected Strange Papers of Christopher Blayre* (Leyburn: Tartarus Press, 1998) and separately as *The Cheetah-Girl (Being the MS. Not Published with the Collection Under the Title of The Purple Sapphire) – Deposited By the Professor of Physiology in the University of Cosmopoli* (East Sussex: Tartarus Press, 1998).
5. Lucas, *The Radical Twenties*, p.72.
6. Lucas, *The Radical Twenties*, p.73.
7. David Garnett, *Lady into Fox* and *A Man in the Zoo* [1928] (London: The Hogarth Press, 1985), p.2. Further page references will be to this edition and given parenthetically.
8. The *OED*'s first citation of foxy as meaning of a woman 'attractive, desirable, pretty; sexy' is from the United States in 1913.
9. Neil Jordan, 'Introduction', in David Garnett, *Lady into Fox* and *A Man in the Zoo* [1928] (London: The Hogarth Press, 1985), n.p.
10. H. H. Munro, 'The She-Wolf', in *The Best of Saki*, introduced by Tom Sharpe (London: Picador, 1976), p.123. Further page references will be given parenthetically.
11. Tom Sharpe, 'Introduction', in *The Best of Saki*, p.8
12. Tom Sharpe, 'Introduction', in *The Best of Saki*, p.8.
13. Karel Čapek, *War with the Newts*, translated by M. and R. Weatherall (London: George Allen and Unwin Ltd., 1937), p.276.
14. Wyndham Lewis, *Filibusters in Barbary* (London: Grayson and Grayson, 1932), pp.vii–viii.
15. Lewis, *Filibusters*, p.3.
16. Paul Fussell, *Abroad: British Literary Traveling between the Wars* (New York, NY: Oxford University Press, 1980), p.40.

17 See also Jean-Yves Le Disez, 'Animals as Figures of Otherness in Travel Narratives of Brittany, 1840–1895', in Glenn Hooper and Tim Youngs, eds, *Perspectives on Travel Writing* (Aldershot: Ashgate, 2004), pp.71–84.
18 Lucas, *The Radical Twenties*, p.122.
19 Lucas, *The Radical Twenties*, p.117.
20 Lucas, *The Radical Twenties*, p.126.
21 Kathleen Hale, *A Slender Reputation: An Autobiography* (London: Frederick Warne, 1994), p.127. Quoted in Lucas, *The Radical Twenties*, p.111.
22 W. B. Yeats, 'The Second Coming', in W. B. Yeats, *Selected Poetry*, edited by A. Norman Jeffares (London: Pan, 1974), p.100.
23 Declan Kiberd, *Inventing Ireland: The Literature of the Modern Nation* [1995] (London: Vintage, 1996), p.312.
24 Lucas, *The Radical Twenties*, p.138. Lucas explains that the phrase he has quoted comes from 'A Prayer for My Daughter', which follows 'The Second Coming' in the volume *Michael Robartes and the Dancer*.
25 Quoted in Lucas, *The Radical Twenties*, p.173, n.62. Lucas is in turn quoting from Douglas Goldring, *The Nineteen Twenties: A General Survey and Some Personal Memories* (London: Nicholson & Watson, 1945).
26 Quoted in Lucas, *The Radical Twenties*, p.241.
27 Quoted in Bernard Schweizer, *Radicals on the Road: The Politics of English Travel Writing in the 1930s* (Charlottesville, VA: University Press of Virginia, 2001), p.161.
28 Orwell, quoted in Schweizer, *Radicals on the Road*, p.24.
29 Schweizer, *Radicals on the Road*, p.17.
30 Schweizer, *Radicals on the Road*, p.173.
31 James Weldon Johnson, *The Autobiography of an Ex-Coloured Man* [1912] (New York, NY: Hill and Wang, 1960), p.186.
32 Max Hastings, 'Years of Liberal Dogma Have Spawned a Generation of Amoral, Uneducated, Welfare Dependent, Brutalised Youngsters', *Daily Mail*, 12 August 2011.
33 Steve Baker, *The Postmodern Animal* (London: Reaktion Books, 2000), p.9. The Soper reference is to Kate Soper, *What is Nature? Culture, Politics and the Non-Human* (Oxford: Wiley-Blackwell, 1995).
34 Syed Manzurul Islam, *The Ethics of Travel: From Marco Polo to Kafka* (Manchester: Manchester University Press, 1996).
35 Cary Wolfe, 'Introduction', in Cary Wolfe, ed., *Zoontologies: The Question of the Animal* (Minneapolis, MN: University of Minnesota Press, 2003), p.xi.
36 Wolfe, 'Introduction', p.xii.
37 Donna Haraway, *The Companion Species Manifesto: Dogs, People, and Significant Otherness* (Chicago, IL: Prickly Paradigm Press, 2003), p.50.
38 Haraway, *The Companion Species Manifesto*, p.28. Of course, however desirable and well-intentioned this stance, it also serves to affirm one's own ethical principles and to differentiate oneself from those who do not hold them, thus functioning as a means of self-definition as much as an observance of the distinctness of other species.
39 Jacques Derrida, 'And Say the Animal Responded?', translated by David Wills, in Cary Wolfe, ed., *Zoontologies*, p.128.
40 Gilles Deleuze and Félix Guattari, '1730: Becoming Intense, Becoming-Animal, Becoming-Imperceptible ... [sic]', in *A Thousand Plateaus: Capitalism and*

Schizophrenia, translated and with a foreword by Brian Massumi (London: Athlone Press, 1988), p.238.
41 Baker, *The Postmodern Animal*, p.18.
42 Deleuze and Guattari, '1730: Becoming Intense, Becoming-Animal', p.239.
43 Roger Luckhurst, 'Introduction', in Bram Stoker, *Dracula* (Oxford: Oxford University Press, 2011) p.xiii.
44 John Frow, *Genre* (London: Routledge, 2006), p.1.
45 Frow, *Genre*, p.25.
46 Margaret Harkness, *In Darkest London* [1889 as *Captain Lobe: A Story of the Salvation Army*] (Cambridge: Black Apollo Press, 2003), p.164.

Bibliography

Primary

Anonymous. *Teleny or The Reverse of the Medal* [1883]. Ware: Wordsworth Editions Limited, 1995.

Besant, Walter. *All Sorts and Conditions of Men* [1882]. Oxford: Oxford University Press, 1997.

Čapek, Karel. *War with the Newts*. Translated by M. and R. Weatherall. London: George Allen and Unwin Ltd., 1937.

Darwin, Charles. *The Origin of Species by Means of Natural Selection*, last (sixth) edition [1872]. London: Watts & Co., n.d.

Davidson, John. 'A Northern Suburb' [1897]. Reprinted in R. K. R. Thornton, ed., *Poetry of the 'Nineties*. Harmondsworth: Penguin, 1970, pp.63-64.

Dreiser, Theodore. *Sister Carrie* [1900]. Harmondsworth: Penguin, 1981.

Garnett, David. *Lady into Fox* and *A Man in the Zoo* [1928]. London: The Hogarth Press, 1985.

Gissing, George. *The Nether World* [1889]. Edited with an introduction by Stephen Gill. Oxford: Oxford University Press, 1992.

Harkness, Margaret. *In Darkest London* [1889 as *Captain Lobe: A Story of the Salvation Army*]. Cambridge: Black Apollo Press, 2003.

Holland, Merlin and Rupert Hart-Davis, eds. *The Complete Letters of Oscar Wilde*. London: Fourth Estate, 2000.

James, Henry. 'The Art of Fiction' [1884]. In Roger Gard, ed., *Henry James: The Critical Muse. Selected Literary Criticism*. London: Penguin, 1987, pp.186–208.

Johnson, James Weldon. *The Autobiography of an Ex-Coloured Man* [1912]. New York, NY: Hill and Wang, 1960.

Lang, Andrew. 'Mr. Stevenson's Works'. In *Essays in Little*. London: Henry and Co., 1891, pp.21–35.

Lewis, Wyndham. *Filibusters in Barbary*. London: Grayson and Grayson, 1932.

MacDonald, George. 'The Imagination: Its Functions and Its Culture' [1867]. In *A Dish of Orts* [1893]. Whitethorn, CA: Johannesen, 1996, pp.1–42.

MacDonald, George. *Lilith: A Romance* [1895]. Grand Rapids, MI: Wm. B. Eerdmans, 1981.

MacDonald, George. *The Princess and the Goblin* and *The Princess and Curdie*. Edited with an Introduction by Roderick McGillis. Oxford: Oxford University Press, 1990.

MacDonald, George. *The Complete Fairy Tales*. Edited with an Introduction and Notes by U.C. Knoepflmacher. London: Penguin Books, 1999.

Machen, Arthur. *The Great God Pan* [1894]. London: Creation Books, 1996.

Marsh, Richard. *The Beetle* [1897]. Stroud: Alan Sutton Publishing, 1994.

Morrison, Arthur. *Tales of Mean Streets* [1894]. London: Methuen and Co. Ltd., 1927.

Morrison, Arthur. *A Child of the Jago* [1896]. Edited by Peter Miles. London: Everyman, 1996.

Munro, H. H. *The Best of Saki*. Introduced by Tom Sharpe. London: Picador, 1976.

Nordau, Max. *Degeneration* [1892]. Translated from the second edition of the German [1895]. Introduction by George L. Mosse. Lincoln, NE: University of Nebraska Press, 1993.

Shaw, Bernard. *Plays Unpleasant: Widowers' Houses, The Philanderer, Mrs. Warren's Profession*. Harmondsworth: Penguin, 1946.

Stead, W. T. 'The Maiden Tribute of Modern Babylon' (The Report of the *Pall Mall Gazette* Secret Commission). *Pall Mall Gazette*, 6, 7, 8, 10 July 1885.

Stevenson, Robert Louis. 'The Strange Case of Dr. Jekyll and Mr. Hyde'. In *Dr. Jekyll and Mr. Hyde, The Merry Men and Other Tales*. London: J. M. Dent & Sons Ltd., 1925, pp.1-62.

Stoker, Bram. *Dracula*. Edited with Introduction and Notes by Roger Luckhurst. Oxford: Oxford World's Classics, 2011.

Wells, H. G. 'The Time Machine' [1895]. In *Selected Short Stories*. Harmondsworth: Penguin, 1958, pp.7–83.

Wells, H. G. *The Island of Doctor Moreau* [1896]. Harmondsworth: Penguin Books, 1946.

Wells, H. G. *The Wheels of Chance* [1896]. London: J. M. Dent & Sons Ltd., n.d.

Wells, H. G. *The War of the Worlds* [1898]. London: Pan Books Ltd., 1975.

Wells, H. G. *First and Last Things: A Confession of Faith and Rule of Life* [1908]. London: Watts & Co., 1929.

Wells, H. G. *Experiment in Autobiography: Discoveries and Conclusions of a Very Ordinary Person (Since 1866)*. New York, NY: The Macmillan Company, 1934.

Wilde, Oscar. *The Picture of Dorian Gray* [1891]. Oxford: Oxford University Press, 1981.

Wilde, Oscar. *Lord Arthur Savile's Crime and Other Stories* [1891]. London: Penguin, 1994.

Wilde, Oscar. *A Woman of No Importance* [1893]. Glasgow: HarperCollins Publishers, 1994.

Wilde, Oscar. *The Soul of Man and Prison Writings*. Edited with an Introduction by Isobel Murray. Oxford: Oxford University Press, 1990.

Wilde, Oscar. *Complete Works of Oscar Wilde*. Glasgow: HarperCollins Publishers, 1994.

Yeats, W. B. *Selected Poetry*. Edited by A. Norman Jeffares. London: Pan, 1974.

Zangwill, Israel. *Children of the Ghetto: A Study of a Peculiar People* [1895]. Cambridge: Black Apollo Press, 2004.

Secondary

Arata, Stephen D. 'The Occidental Tourist: *Dracula* and the Anxiety of Reverse Colonization'. *Victorian Studies* 33, 4 (Summer 1990), 621–645.
Asma, Stephen T. *On Monsters: An Unnatural History of our Worst Fears*. Oxford: Oxford University Press, 2009.
Baker, Steve. *The Postmodern Animal*. London: Reaktion Books, 2000.
Bakhtin, M. M. 'Forms of Time and of the Chronotope in the Novel'. In *The Dialogic Imagination: Four Essays by M. M. Bakhtin*, edited by Michael Holquist. Translated by Caryl Emerson and Michael Holquist. Austin, TX: University of Texas Press, 1981, pp.84–258.
Baldick, Chris. *In Frankenstein's Shadow: Myth, Monstrosity, and Nineteenth-century Writing*. Oxford: Clarendon Press, 1987.
Batchelor, John. *H. G. Wells*. Cambridge: Cambridge University Press, 1985.
Beaulieu, Alain. 'The Status of Animality in Deleuze's Thought'. *Journal for Critical Animal Studies* IX, 1/2 (2011), 69–88.
Beckson, Karl. *London in the 1890s: A Cultural History*. New York, NY: W.W. Norton, 1992.
Beer, Gillian. *Darwin's Plots: Evolutionary Narrative in Darwin, George Eliot and Nineteenth-Century Fiction* [1983]. London: Ark, 1985.
Begg, Paul. *Jack the Ripper: The Definitive History*. London: Longman, 2003.
Belsey, Catherine. *Critical Practice*. London: Methuen, 1980.
Bergonzi, Bernard. *The Early H. G. Wells: A Study of the Scientific Romances*. Manchester: Manchester University Press, 1961.
Biderman R.A. 'Introduction'. In Israel Zangwill, *Children of the Ghetto: A Study of a Peculiar People* [1895]. Cambridge: Black Apollo Press, 2004, pp.7–12.
Botting, Fred. *Gothic*. London: Routledge, 1996.
Bowler, Peter J. *The Eclipse of Darwinism: Anti-Darwinian Evolution Theories in the Decades around 1900*. Baltimore, MD: Johns Hopkins University Press, 1983.
Brantlinger, Patrick and Richard Boyle. 'The Education of Edward Hyde: Stevenson's "Gothic Gnome" and the Mass Readership of Late-Victorian England'. In William Veeder and Gordon Hirsch, eds, *Dr. Jekyll and Mr. Hyde after One Hundred Years*. Chicago, IL: Chicago University Press, 1988, pp.265–282.
Briggs, Asa. *Victorian Cities* [1963]. London: Penguin, 1968.
Bristow, Joseph. *Effeminate England: Homoerotic Writing after 1885*. Buckingham: Open University Press, 1995.
Budge, E. A. Wallis. *Egyptian Magic* [1901]. New York, NY: Dover Publications Inc., 1971.
Byron, Glennis, ed. *Dracula: New Casebooks*. Basingstoke: Macmillan, 1999.
Cannadine, David. *The Decline and Fall of the British Aristocracy*. London: Macmillan, 1996.
Cohen, Ed. *Talk on the Wilde Side: Toward a Genealogy of a Discourse on Male Sexualities*. New York, NY: Routledge, 1993.

Curtis, L. Perry, Jr. *Apes and Angels: The Irishman in Victorian Caricature*. Newton Abbot: David & Charles, 1971.
Dekkers, Midas. *Dearest Pet: On Bestiality*. Translated by Paul Vincent. London: Verso, 1994.
Deleuze, Gilles and Félix Guattari. '1730: Becoming Intense, Becoming-Animal, Becoming-Imperceptible … '. In *A Thousand Plateaus: Capitalism and Schizophrenia*. Translated and foreword by Brian Massumi. London: Athlone Press, 1988, pp.232–309.
Dentith, Simon. *Society and Cultural Forms in Nineteenth-Century England*. Basingstoke: Palgrave Macmillan, 1998.
Derrida, Jacques. 'And Say the Animal Responded?' Translated by David Wills. In Cary Wolfe, ed., *Zoontologies: The Question of the Animal*. Minneapolis, MN: University of Minnesota Press, 2003, pp.121–146.
Dickson, Lovat. *H. G. Wells: His Turbulent Life and Times*. London: Readers Union, Macmillan, 1971.
Dryden, Linda. *The Modern Gothic and Literary Doubles: Stevenson, Wilde and Wells*. Basingstoke: Palgrave Macmillan, 2003.
Eckley, Grace. *Maiden Tribute: A Life of W. T. Stead*. Philadelphia, PA: Xlibris, 2007.
Elias, Norbert. *Time: An Essay*. Translated by Edmund Jephcott. Oxford: Blackwell, 1993.
Ellmann, Richard. *Oscar Wilde* [1987]. London: Penguin, 1988.
Filmer, Kath. 'Introduction'. In Kath Filmer, ed., *The Victorian Fantasists: Essays on Culture, Society and Belief in the Mythopoeic Fiction of the Victorian Age*. Houndmills: Macmillan, 1991, pp.1–12.
Filmer, Kath. 'La Belle Dame Sans Merci: Cultural Criticism and Mythopoeic Vision in *Lilith*'. In Kath Filmer, ed., *The Victorian Fantasists: Essays on Culture, Society and Belief in the Mythopoeic Fiction of the Victorian Age*. Houndmills: Macmillan, 1991, pp.90–103.
Fishman, William J. *East End 1888: A Year in a London Borough among the Labouring Poor* [2005]. Nottingham: Five Leaves Publications, 2009.
Freud, Sigmund. 'From the History of an Infantile Neurosis' ('The "Wolf Man"')' [1914; 1918]. In Angela Richards, ed., *Case Histories II*. The Penguin Freud Library vol. 9. London: Penguin, 1991, pp.233–366.
Frow, John. *Genre*. London: Routledge, 2006.
Gagnier, Regenia. 'Wilde and the Victorians'. In Peter Raby, ed., *The Cambridge Companion to Oscar Wilde*. Cambridge: Cambridge University Press, 1997, pp.18–33.
Gelder, Ken. *Reading the Vampire*. London: Routledge, 1994.
Glendening, John. *The Evolutionary Imagination in Late-Victorian Novels: An Entangled Bank*. Aldershot: Ashgate, 2007.
Glover, David. *Vampires, Mummies, and Liberals: Bram Stoker and the Politics of Popular Fiction*. Durham, NC: Duke University Press, 1996.
Goode, John. *George Gissing: Ideology and Fiction*. London: Vision, 1978.
Gould, Stephen Jay. *Time's Arrow, Time's Cycle: Myth and Metaphor in the Discovery of Geological Time* [1987]. London: Penguin, 1991.

Griffith, David L. 'George MacDonald's *Lilith* A: A Transcription'. MA Thesis, Virginia Polytechnic Institute and State University, 2001.

Haraway, Donna. *The Companion Species Manifesto: Dogs, People, and Significant Otherness*. Chicago, IL: Prickly Paradigm Press, 2003.

Harris, Jose. *Private Lives, Public Spirit: Britain 1870–1914* [1993]. London: Penguin Books, 1994.

Harrison, J. F. C. *Late Victorian Britain 1870–1901*. London: Fontana Press, 1990.

Harvey, David. *The Urban Experience*. Oxford: Basil Blackwell, 1989.

Hein, Rolland. *George MacDonald: Victorian Mythmaker* [1993]. Whitethorn, CA: Johannesen, 1999.

Helsinger, Elizabeth K., Robin Lauterbach Sheets and William Veeder. *The Woman Question: Society and Literature in Britain and America, 1837–1883* (3 vols), vol. 2: *The Woman Question: Social Issues, 1837–1883*. Manchester: Manchester University Press, 1983.

Hendershot, Cyndy. *The Animal Within: Masculinity and the Gothic*. Ann Arbor, MI: University of Michigan Press, 1998.

Herbert, Christopher. *Culture and Anomie: Ethnographic Imagination in the Nineteenth Century*. Chicago, IL: University of Chicago Press, 1991.

Himmelfarb, Gertrude. *Poverty and Compassion: The Moral Imagination of the Late Victorians*. New York, NY: Vintage Books, 1992.

Holland, Merlin. 'Biography and the Art of Lying'. In Peter Raby, ed., *The Cambridge Companion to Oscar Wilde*. Cambridge: Cambridge University Press, 1997, pp.3–17.

Howell, Michael and Peter Ford. *The True History of the Elephant Man*. Harmondsworth: Penguin, 1980.

Humpherys, Anne. 'Knowing the Victorian City: Writing and Representation'. *Victorian Literature and Culture* 30, 2 (September 2002), 601–612.

Huntington, John. *H. G. Wells and Science Fiction*. New York, NY: Columbia University Press, 1982.

Hurley, Kelly. '"The Inner Chambers of All Nameless Sin": *The Beetle*, Gothic Female Sexuality, and Oriental Barbarism'. In Lloyd Davis, ed., *Virginal Sexuality and Textuality in Victorian Literature*. Albany, NY: State University of New York Press, 1993, pp.193-213.

Hyde, H. Montgomery. *The Trials of Oscar Wilde* [1948; 1962]. New York, NY: Dover, 1973.

Islam, Syed Manzurul. *The Ethics of Travel: From Marco Polo to Kafka*. Manchester: Manchester University Press, 1996.

Jackson, Rosemary. *Fantasy: The Literature of Subversion*. London: Routledge, 1981.

James, Simon J. *Unsettled Accounts: Money and Narrative in the Novels of George Gissing*. London: Anthem, 2003.

Jones, Gareth Stedman. *Outcast London: A Study in the Relationship between Classes in Victorian Society* [1971]. Harmondsworth: Penguin Books, 1976.

Jordan, Neil. 'Introduction'. In David Garnett, *Lady into Fox* and *A Man in the Zoo* [1928]. London: The Hogarth Press, 1985, n.p.

Keating, Peter, ed. *Into Unknown England 1866–1913: Selections from the Social Explorers*. Manchester: Manchester University Press, 1976.

Keating, Peter. *The Haunted Study: A Social History of the English Novel 1875–1914* [1989]. London: Fontana Press, 1991.

Kirk, Neville. *Change, Continuity and Class: Labour in British Society, 1850–1920*. Manchester: Manchester University Press, 1998.

Knoepflmacher, U. C. 'Introduction'. In George MacDonald, *The Complete Fairy Tales*. Edited with an Introduction and Notes by U. C. Knoepflmacher. London: Penguin Books, 1999, pp.vii–xx.

Le Disez, Jean-Yves. 'Animals as Figures of Otherness in Travel Narratives of Brittany, 1840–1895'. In Glenn Hooper and Tim Youngs, eds, *Perspectives on Travel Writing*. Aldershot: Ashgate, 2004, pp.71–84.

Ledger, Sally. *The New Woman: Fiction and Feminism at the Fin de Siècle*. Manchester: Manchester University Press, 1997.

Lee, Michael Parrish. 'Reading Meat in H. G. Wells'. *Studies in the Novel* 42, 3 (Fall 2010), 249–268.

Lehan, Richard. *The City in Literature: An Intellectual and Cultural History*. Berkeley, CA: University of California Press, 1998.

Lem, Stanislaw. 'H. G. Wells's *The War of the Worlds*'. In Rhys Garnett and R. J. Ellis, eds, *Science Fiction Roots and Branches: Contemporary Critical Approaches*. Basingstoke: Palgrave Macmillan, 1990, pp.18–29.

Lester, John A., Jr. *Journey through Despair 1880–1914: Transformations in British Literary Culture*. Princeton, NJ: Princeton University Press, 1968.

Lewis, C. S. 'Introduction'. In George MacDonald, *Lilith: A Romance* [1895]. Grand Rapids, MI: Wm. B. Eerdmans, 1981, pp.v–xii.

Lucas, John. *The Radical Twenties*. Nottingham: Five Leaves Press, 1997.

Luckhurst, Roger. 'Introduction'. In *Late Victorian Gothic Tales*. Oxford: Oxford University Press, 2005, pp.ix–xxxi.

Luckhurst, Roger. 'Introduction'. In Robert Louis Stevenson, *Strange Case of Dr Jekyll and Mr Hyde and Other Tales*. Oxford: Oxford University Press, 2006, pp.vii–xxxii.

Luckhurst, Roger. 'Introduction'. In Bram Stoker, *Dracula*. Oxford: Oxford University Press, 2011, pp.vii–xxxii.

Lukács, Georg. 'Narrate or Describe?' In *Writer and Critic and Other Essays*. London: Merlin Press, 1978, pp.110–148.

Lukács, Georg. 'Realism in the Balance'. In *Aesthetics and Politics: Ernst Bloch, Georg Lukács, Bertolt Brecht, Walter Benjamin, Theodor Adorno*. London: Verso, 1980, pp.28–59.

Lynd, Helen Merrell. *England in the Eighteen-Eighties: Toward a Social Basis for Freedom*. London: Oxford University Press, 1945.

McGillis, Roderick. 'Introduction'. In George MacDonald, *The Princess and the Goblin* and *The Princess and Curdie*. Edited with an Introduction by Roderick McGillis. Oxford: Oxford University Press, 1990, pp.vii–xxiii.

Manlove, C. N. *Modern Fantasy: Five Studies*. Cambridge: Cambridge University Press, 1975.

Margree, Victoria. '"Both in Men's Clothing": Gender, Sovereignty and Insecurity in Richard Marsh's *The Beetle*'. *Critical Survey* 19, 2 (2007), 63–81.

Marx, Karl. *Capital: A Critique of Political Economy* [1867], vol. 1. Introduced by Ernest Mandel. Translated by Ben Fowkes. London: Penguin Books in association with New Left Review, 1990.

Massey, Irving. *The Gaping Pig: Literature and Metamorphosis*. Berkeley, CA: University of California Press, 1976.

Mendlesohn, Farah. *Rhetorics of Fantasy*. Middletown, CT: Wesleyan University Press, 2008.

Miles, Peter. 'Introduction'. In Arthur Morrison, *A Child of the Jago* [1896]. Edited by Peter Miles. London: Everyman, 1996, pp.xxxv–lv.

Moretti, Franco. 'Dialectic of Fear'. In *Signs Taken for Wonders: Essays in the Sociology of Literary Form*. London: Verso, 1988, pp.83–108.

Mosse, George L. 'Introduction'. In Max Nordau, *Degeneration* [1892]. Translated from the second edition of the German [1895]. Lincoln, NE: University of Nebraska Press, 1993, pp.xiii–xxxvi.

Neetens, Wim. *Writing and Democracy: Literature, Politics and Culture in Transition*. London: Harvester Wheatsheaf, 1991.

Norris, Margot. *Beasts of the Modern Imagination: Darwin, Nietzsche, Kafka, Ernst, and Lawrence*. Baltimore, MD: The Johns Hopkins University Press, 1985.

Parry, Jonathan and Maurice Bloch. 'Introduction: Money and the Morality of Exchange'. In J. Parry and M. Bloch, eds, *Money and the Morality of Exchange*. Cambridge: Cambridge University Press, 1989, pp.1–32.

Petzold, Dieter. 'Beasts and Monsters in MacDonald's Fantasy Stories'. *North Wind* 14 (1995), 4–21.

Phillips, Adam. *Darwin's Worms*. London: Faber and Faber Limited, 1999.

Prickett, Stephen. 'The Two Worlds of George MacDonald'. *North Wind* 2 (1983), 14–23.

Punter, David. *The Literature of Terror: A History of Gothic Fictions from 1765 to the Present Day*, vol. 2. *The Modern Gothic*. London: Longman, 1996.

Purkiss, Diane. *Troublesome Things: A History of Fairies and Fairy Stories*. London: Penguin Books, 2001.

Raeper, William. *George MacDonald*. Tring: Lion, 1987.

Richter, Virginia. *Literature after Darwin: Human Beasts in Western Fiction, 1859–1939*. Basingstoke: Palgrave Macmillan, 2011.

Ritvo, Harriet. *The Animal Estate: The English and Other Creatures in the Victorian Age*. Cambridge, MA: Harvard University Press, 1987.

Rowland, Beryl. *Animals with Human Faces: A Guide to Animal Symbolism*. Knoxville, TN: University of Tennessee Press, 1973.

Sammells, Neil. *Wilde Style: The Plays and Prose of Oscar Wilde*. London: Pearson Education Limited, 2000.

Schults, Raymond L. *Crusader in Babylon: W.T. Stead and the Pall Mall Gazette*. Lincoln, NE: University of Nebraska Press, 1972.

Showalter, Elaine. *Sexual Anarchy: Gender and Culture at the Fin de Siècle*. New York, NY: Viking, 1990.

Silver, Carole G. *Strange and Secret Peoples: Fairies and Victorian Consciousness*. Oxford: Oxford University Press, 1999.

Sloan, John. *George Gissing: The Cultural Challenge*. Basingstoke: Macmillan, 1989.

Small, Helen. 'Introduction'. In Walter Besant, *All Sorts and Conditions of Men* [1882]. Oxford: Oxford University Press, 1997, pp.x–xxv.

Spencer, Herbert. 'Progress: Its Law and Cause'. In *Essays on Education and Kindred Subjects*. London: J. M. Dent & Sons, 1911, pp.153-197.

Stocking, George W., Jr. *Victorian Anthropology*. New York, NY: The Free Press, 1987.

Stokes, John. *Oscar Wilde*. Harlow: Longman for the British Council, 1978.

Stokes, John. *In the Nineties*. London: Harvester Wheatsheaf, 1989.

Stokes, John. *Fin de Siècle/Fin du Globe: Fears and Fantasies of the Late Nineteenth Century*. Basingstoke: Macmillan, 1992.

Sturgis, Matthew. *Passionate Attitudes: The English Decadence of the 1890s*. London: Macmillan, 1995.

Suvin, Darko. 'Wells as the Turning Point of the SF Tradition'. In Bernard Waites, Tony Bennett and Graham Martin, eds, *Popular Culture: Past and Present*. London: Croom Helm, 1982, pp.122–132.

Swafford, Kevin R. 'Translating the Slums: The Coding of Criminality and the Grotesque in Arthur Morrison's "A Child of the Jago"'. *The Journal of the Midwest Modern Language Association* 35, 2: *Translating in and across Cultures* (Autumn 2002), 50–64.

Veeder, William. 'Collated Fractions of the Manuscript Drafts of *Strange Case of Dr Jekyll and Mr Hyde*'. In William Veeder and Gordon Hirsch, eds, *Dr. Jekyll and Mr. Hyde after One Hundred Years*. Chicago, IL: Chicago University Press, 1988, pp.14–56.

Vint, Sherryl. *Animal Alterity: Science Fiction and the Question of the Animal*. Liverpool: Liverpool University Press, 2010.

Vuohelainen, Minna. 'Richard Marsh's *The Beetle* (1897): A Late-Victorian Popular Novel'. *Working with English: Medieval and Modern Language, Literature and Drama* 2, 1: Literary Fads and Fashions (2006), 89–100.

Wakeford, Iain. 'Wells, Woking and *The War of the Worlds*'. *The Wellsian* 14 (Summer 1991), 18–29.

Walkowitz, Judith R. *City of Dreadful Delight: Narratives of Sexual Danger in Late-Victorian London* [1992]. London: Virago, 1994.

Wallace, Jeff. 'Introduction: Difficulty and Defamiliarisation – Language and Process in *The Origin of Species*'. In David Amigoni and Jeff Wallace, eds, *Charles Darwin's The Origin of Species: New Interdisciplinary Series*. Manchester: Manchester University Press, 1995, pp.1–46.

Warner, Marina. *No Go the Bogeyman: Scaring, Lulling and Making Mock*. London: Chatto & Windus, 1998.

Warner, Marina. *Fantastic Metamorphoses, Other Worlds: Ways of Telling the Self*. Oxford: Oxford University Press, 2002.

Warwick, Alexandra. 'Vampires and the Empire: Fears and Fictions of the 1890s'. In Sally Ledger and Scott McCracken, eds, *Cultural Politics at the Fin de Siècle*. Cambridge: Cambridge University Press, 1995, pp.202–220.

Williams, Raymond. 'Forms of English Fiction in 1848'. In *Writing in Society*. London: Verso, n.d., pp.150–165.

Williams, Raymond. *The English Novel from Dickens to Lawrence* [1971]. London: The Hogarth Press, 1984.

Wolfe, Cary. 'Introduction'. In Cary Wolfe, ed., *Zoontologies: The Question of the Animal*. Minneapolis, MN: University of Minnesota Press, 2003, pp.ix–xxiii.

Wolfreys, Julian. 'Introduction'. In Richard Marsh, *The Beetle* [1897]. Edited by Julian Wolfreys. Peterborough, Ontario: Broadview Press, 2004, pp.9–34.

Youngs, Tim. *Travellers in Africa: British Travelogues, 1850–1900*. Manchester: Manchester University Press, 1994.

Youngs, Tim. 'Stevenson's Monkey-Business: *The Strange Case of Dr. Jekyll and Mr. Hyde*'. In Peter Liebregts and Wim Tigges, eds, *Beauty and the Beast: Christina Rossetti, Walter Pater, R.L. Stevenson and their Contemporaries*. Amsterdam and Georgia: Rodopi, 1996, pp.157–170.

Youngs, Tim. 'Wells's Fifth Dimension: *The Time Machine* at the Fin de Siècle'. In Tracey Hill and Alan Marshall, eds, *Decadence and Danger: Writing, History and the Fin de Siècle*. Bath: Sulis Press, 1997, pp.64–74.

Youngs, Tim. 'The Plasticity of Living Forms: Beasts and Narrative in *The Octopus* and *The Island of Doctor Moreau*'. *Symbiosis: A Journal of Anglo-American Literary Relations* 1, 1 (April 1997), 86–103.

Youngs, Tim. 'White Apes at the Fin de Siècle'. In Tim Youngs, ed., *Writing and Race*. London: Longman, 1997, pp.166–190.

Youngs, Tim. '"A Sonnet out of Skilly": Oscar Wilde's "The Ballad of Reading Gaol"'. *Critical Survey* 11, 3 (1999), 40–47.

Index

'.007' 13

agency, human 12, 19
Albert Victor, Prince 27
Alice's Adventures in Wonderland 149
allegory 142, 150, 201
All Sorts and Conditions of Men 2
animal imagery 2, 26, 30, 31, 39, 49, 50, 54, 59, 70, 74, 75, 79, 91, 165, 178, 179, 181, 193, 197, 198, 199, 202, 204
animality 2, 6, 20, 27, 30, 40, 50, 58, 61, 63, 68, 114, 122, 123, 124, 127, 130, 132, 154, 159, 165, 176, 180, 198, 202
animals 4, 18, 19, 20, 24, 31, 40, 57, 76, 78, 102, 109, 115, 116, 117, 120, 123, 124, 147, 157, 161, 169, 175, 177, 178, 197, 199, 202, 204, 205
Arata, Stephen 80
aristocracy and aristocratic rule 10, 14–16, 81, 82, 83, 103, 118, 151, 161, 166, 171, 189, 190
Armstrong, Eliza 64
Autobiography of an Ex-Coloured Man 204

Baker, Steve 205–207
Bakhtin, Mikhail 110; *see also* 'chronotope'
Baldick, Chris 16, 123
Ball, Benjamin 26
'The Ballad of Reading Gaol' 177–178, 183
Balzac, Honoré de 167
banking 45
Barrett, Wilson 181
Batchelor, John 135
beasts 1, 4, 5, 12, 18, 20, 24, 27, 30, 31, 39, 40, 42, 51, 55, 56, 57, 60, 61, 105, 126, 146, 154, 161, 162, 175, 180, 197, 201, 204, 207
Beer, Gillian 3, 18–26
The Beetle 7, 31, 70, 84–104, 131, 201
Begg, Paul 69–70
Belsey, Catherine 128, 130
Bennett, Arnold 30
Bergonzi, Bernard 118–119

Besant, Walter 2, 13, 59, 136; *see also All Sorts and Conditions of Men*
bestiality 1, 7, 12, 26, 31, 39, 48, 56, 61, 70, 74, 165, 167, 184, 208
Bloch, Maurice 11–12
Booth, William 7; *see also In Darkest England*
Botting, Fred 76–77, 81
Boulton, Ernest 27
Boyle, Richard 48
Brabazon, Lord 43
Brabourne, Lord 16
Brantlinger, Patrick 48
'breadline', use of term 40
Briggs, Asa 39
Bristow, Joseph 29, 166–168
Brooks, Cleanth 202
Broughton, Nancy 64
Brown, Terence 192
Browning, Oscar 182
Bunyan, John 158; *see also The Pilgrim's Progress*
Burke, Edmund 16
Burne-Jones, Edward 182

Cannadine, David 10, 14
cannibalism 60, 111, 118–120
Čapek, Karel 200–201; *see also War with the Newts*
Capital 12
capitalism 1, 6, 11–12, 29, 41, 53, 59, 70, 78, 90, 117, 123, 126
Captain Lobe 53–61, 208
Carlyle, Thomas 142
Carroll, Lewis 149; *see also Alice's Adventures in Wonderland*
Carson, Edward 165–166, 181
Carter, Angela 199; *see also The Company of Wolves*
'The Cheetah-Girl' 197
A Child of the Jago 40, 49–53, 62

Children of the Ghetto 117
Christianity 57, 96, 126, 141, 148, 151; *see also* Jesus Christ
'chronotope' 110, 112
Churchill, Winston 203
A City Girl 40
Clash 203
class distinctions 7, 17, 65–66, 134, 153, 166, 184, 188
Cleveland Street affair 27
Cohen, Ed 28, 165–166
colonialism 3, 15, 101–102, 103, 121–122, 201
The Company of Wolves (film) 199
Conan Doyle, Sir Arthur 136
Conrad, Joseph 78, 108, 120, 125, 128; *see also* Heart of Darkness
copyright protection 13
Corelli, Marie 136
Crane, Stephen 51; *see also Maggie*
Criminal Law Amendment Act (1885) 67, 165
Cromer, Lord 102
cycling 133, 134, 135–136

Daily Chronicle 183
Daily Telegraph 68
Darwin, Charles 6, 18–26, 111, 113, 114, 122–123, 155
Darwinism 5–7, 18–25, 43, 110, 120–121, 128, 147; *see also* Social Darwinism
Davidson, John 1, 4, 23
decadence 5, 26, 28–29, 43, 111, 114–115, 125, 202
'The Decay of Lying' 186
degeneracy and degeneration 7, 9, 26–27, 30–31, 42–44, 62, 75, 89, 111, 112, 115–116, 122, 125, 149, 165, 179, 184–185, 201
Degeneration 2, 26–27, 30–31, 165
Deleuze, Gilles 206–207
democracy and democratisation 14–16, 30, 47, 64–65, 83, 135, 153, 177, 181, 203
Dentith, Simon 5
De Profundis 183–186
Derrida, Jacques 206
diachrony 18
Dickens, Charles 7, 12, 39, 190; *see also Our Mutual Friend*
Dilke, Sir Charles 27
Disraeli, Benjamin 16
Douglas, Anna Maria 181
Douglas, Lord Percy 181
Dracula 4, 7, 43, 70, 74–85, 88–90, 104, 201, 206

Dreiser, Theodore 61, 124; *see also Sister Carrie*
Drumlanrig, Lord 27
Dryden, Linda 107, 126, 132

The Earth 23
ecocriticism 205, 206
effeminacy 29–30, 165, 167
Egypt, attitudes to 101–102, 104
Eight Hours Bill 86
'The Elephant Man' 4, 54; *see also* Merrick, Joseph
Elias, Norbert 109
Eliot, George 128; *see also Middlemarch*
Eliot, T. S. 202; *see also The Waste Land*
Ellmann, Richard 19–20, 180–183, 192
Engels, Friedrich 58
evolutionism 18–19, 21–23, 25, 113, 115, 121, 124, 127, 130, 147; *see also* Darwinism

fairy tales 16, 140–142, 148, 162, 173, 174, 207
fantasy literature 99–100, 107, 125, 132, 141, 149, 150, 155–156, 159–160
The Farmer's Bride 197
femininity 27, 29, 61
feminism 27; *see also* New Woman phenomenon
Fenian activism 42
Filibusters in Barbary 201
fin de siècle context 2, 5, 9, 13, 26, 28, 43, 44, 68, 107–110, 112, 131, 200, 204
First and Last Things 114
First World War 200, 202–203
Fishman, William 39–40
Frankenstein 16, 55, 84, 144
Freud, Sigmund 6, 27; *see also* Freudian
Freudian 6, 150
Frow, John 207
Fussell, Paul 201–212

Gagnier, Regenia 166, 183
Garnett, David 197–200, 204; *see also Lady into Fox*, *A Man in the Zoo*
Gaskell, Elizabeth 7, 12, 39; *see also Mary Barton*
gender 5, 9, 16, 28, 30, 55, 81, 88, 92, 95, 102, 110–111, 116, 133, 134, 147, 165, 166, 167, 190, 199
genres 6, 12–13, 107, 136, 155, 204, 207; *see also* fairy tales; fantast literature; Gothic literature; naturalism, literary;

realism, literary; science fiction; 'scientific romance'
Gide, André 192
Gissing, George 8, 12, 27, 30, 50, 61, 62–63, 136, 175; see also *The Nether World*
Glendening, John 131
Glover, David 75, 77, 80–81
Goode, John 63
Gordon, Charles George 42, 103
Gothic literature 6, 41, 43, 68, 76, 79–80, 82, 83, 84, 96, 104–105, 107, 132, 150, 155, 158, 200, 207
The Great God Pan 143–147
Guattari, Félix 206–207

Haggard, H. Rider 13, 116, 136; see also *She* and *King Solomon's Mines*
Hale, Kathleen 202
'The Happy Prince' 171–174
Haraway, Donna 206
Hardy, Thomas 8, 30; see also *Jude the Obscure*
Harkness, Margaret 40, 53, 56–61, 208; see also *Captain Lobe* and *A City Girl*
Harris, Frank 192
Harris, Jose 14
Harrison, J. F. C. 14
Harvey, David 41
Hawthorne, Nathaniel 150
Heart of Darkness 75, 78, 108, 119, 129–130
Hein, Rolland 142, 148, 150, 153
Heron-Allen, Edward 197; see also 'The Cheetah-Girl' and *The Purple Sapphire*
Hill, Octavia 148
The Hobbit 128
Holland, Merlin 192
homosexuality 27–29, 46, 88, 90–92, 95, 167–168, 180–182, 192
Hoopdriver's Holiday 136
The Human Centipede (films) 206
Humpherys, Anne 40–41
Hurley, Kelly 101–102

Ibsen, Henrik 27, 136
imperialism 125, 128
The Importance of Being Earnest 187–190
In Darkest Africa 7
In Darkest England 7
In Darkest London 53–61, 208; see also *Captain Lobe*
The Invisible Man 136
Irving, Henry 84

Isis, cult of 85, 97, 98–103
Islam, Syed Manzurul 205
The Island of Doctor Moreau 4, 7, 43, 78, 107, 119–124, 140, 144

Jack the Ripper 28, 60, 68–70, 144
Jackson, Holbrook 166–168
Jackson, Rosemary 107, 129, 132
Jackson, Thomas 40
James, Henry 13, 56, 132, 180; see also *Washington Square*
James, Simon 12
Jarrett, Rebecca 64
Jay, Arthur Osborne 51
Jekyll and Hyde see *The Strange Case of Dr Jekyll and Mr Hyde*
Jesus Christ 66, 126, 178, 185–186, 193
Jewish communities 54, 60, 80; see also Jewishness
Jewishness 88
Johnson, James Weldon 204; see also *Autobiography of an Ex-Coloured Man*
Jones, Gareth Stedman 42–43
Jordan, Neil 199; see also *The Company of Wolves*
Joyce, James 30
Jude the Obscure 8
Jung, Carl 155

Kafka, Franz 205; see also *The Metamorphosis*
Keating, Peter 1, 8–9, 12–13, 22, 30
Kennel Club 24
Kiberd, Declan 203
Kilvert, Francis 202
King Solomon's Mines 116
Kingsley, Charles 25, 148
Kipling, Rudyard 13, 136; see also '.007' and 'Wireless'
Kirk, Neville 14
Kitchener, Horatio Herbert 103
Knoepflmacher, U. C. 141–143, 148

Labouchere Amendment 46
Labour Party 17, 60
Lady into Fox 197–199
Lady Windermere's Fan 189–190
Lang, Andrew 49
Lautrec, Henri de Toulouse 167
Lawrence, D. H. 30, 202; see also *The Rainbow*
Leavis, F. R. 202
Ledger, Sally 28

INDEX

Lee, Michael Parrish 119–120
Lehan, Richard 99–100
Lem, Stanislaw 125
Lenin, Vladimir Ilyich 203
Lever, Charles 202
Lewis, C. S. 150
Lewis, Wyndham 201; *see also Filibusters in Barbary*
Lilith 141, 147–162
Lincoln, Abraham 177
Lincoln Penitentiary, Nebraska 180
literary agents 13
London: East and West parts of 8–9, 39, 68–69, 117; population growth in 3, 39
Lucas, John 197, 202–203
Luckhurst, Roger 84–85, 104–105, 207
Lukács, Georg 1, 131–132
Lynd, Helen Merrell 17

MacDonald, George 9, 13, 16, 31, 140–143, 147–162, 200, 207; *see also Lilith*; *Phantastes*; *The Princess and Curdie*; and *There and Back*
MacDonald, Louisa, 142
McGillis, Roderick 149
Machen, Arthur 142, 143, 200; *see also The Great God Pan*
Maggie 51
A Man in the Zoo 197–199
Margree, Victoria 86–87
Married Women's Property Acts (1870 and 1882) 28–30, 191–192
Marsh, Richard 7, 31, 70, 84–85, 94, 101–104, 131; *see also The Beetle*
Marx, Karl 10–12, 21, 110, 117, 183; *see also Capital*
Mary Barton 7
Massey, Irving 5
Maudsley, Henry 26
Mayhew, Henry 8, 176
meat-eating 111, 120
medievalism, cult of 140–141
Melville, Herman 120
Mendlesohn, Farah 141, 159–160
Merrick, Joseph 54–55; *see also* 'The Elephant Man'
Metamorphoses (Ovid) 3
metamorphosis, concepts of 1–5, 6–7, 9–11, 14, 23, 76, 77, 92, 143, 161, 198
The Metamorphosis (Kafka) 205
metaphor, use of 2, 6–7, 8, 9, 10–11, 14, 19–20, 23, 26–27, 30–31, 48, 54–55, 64, 70, 75, 81, 107, 132, 153, 162, 181, 184, 187, 197, 199, 204, 207–208
Mew, Charlotte 197; *see also The Farmer's Bride*
Middlemarch 128
Miles, Peter 52
Milton, John 162; *see also Paradise Lost*
'The Model Millionaire' 169–173
money: as an agent of social transformation 11–12, 29, 41; in literature 41, 140, 187–192
monogenesis 25
Morris, William 142
Morrison, Arthur 40, 49–53, 61; *see also A Child of the Jago*
Munro, H. H. 199; *see also* Saki
Mussolini, Benito 203

natural selection, theory of 18–22; *see also* Darwin, Charles; Darwinism; survival of the fittest
naturalism, literary 1, 3, 22, 23, 27, 39, 40, 41, 50, 52, 58, 63, 123, 124, 177, 203
Neetens, Wim 3, 13–16, 29
The Nether World 8, 61–63
New Woman phenomenon 27, 28–30, 81–82, 111, 133, 134
Nietzsche, Friedrich 4, 22
Nordau, Max 2, 5, 19, 26–27, 30–31, 165; *see also Degeneration*
Norman, Tom 54

Orientalism 80
Orwell, George 203–204; *see also The Road to Wigan Pier*
Ouida 136
Our Mutual Friend 12
Ovid 3; *see also The Metamorphosis*

Paine, Thomas 16
Paley, William 25
Paradise Lost 162
Park, Fredrick 27
Parnell, Charles Stewart 27, 181
Parry, Jonathan 11–12
Pater, Walter 185
Phantastes 142
Phillips, Adam 6
The Picture of Dorian Gray 43, 69, 78, 88, 166
The Pilgrim's Progress 158
Poe, Edgar Allan 150
Police Illustrated News 68
polygenesis 25

portal-quest narratives 141, 159–160
'The Portrait of Mr. W. H.' 173–174
postmodern art 205–206
poverty 42–3, 50, 52–53, 68, 144, 148, 153, 170–171, 173, 175–176
The Princess and Curdie 149
prostitution 28, 43, 59, 64–67, 180
psychoanalysis 6–8, 22, 83, 99, 120
Punch 16
Punter, David 43, 76, 78
The Purple Sapphire 197

Queensberry, Marquis of 27, 165, 181, 184

Raeper, William 140–141, 148–149, 154–155, 162
The Rainbow 128
realism, literary 1, 9, 12, 40, 41, 50, 52, 63, 104, 121, 125, 128–132, 186
Reform Acts (1884–85) 15–16, 42
revolutionary threats 42, 52–53, 69–70
Richter, Virginia 18
ripper murders 68–69, 144; *see also* Jack the Ripper
Ritvo, Harriet 24–25
The Road to Wigan Pier 203
Rosebery, Lord 27
Ross, Robert 180, 182–183, 192
Rossetti, Christina 136
Ruskin, John 148

Said, Edward 79
Saki 199–200, 204; *see also* 'The She-Wolf'
Salisbury, Lord 15–16
Schopenhauer, Arthur 22
Schreiner, Olive 136
Schweizer, Bernard 203–204
science fiction 6, 13, 107–108, 121, 125, 132, 141, 155
'scientific romance' 107, 121, 123, 125–127, 207
'The Second Coming' 202–203
Second World War 201
sexual relationships and sexual behaviour 27–30
sexuality: changes in 167; female 92; male 180; *see also* homosexuality
Shakespeare, William 136; *see also The Tempest*
Sharpe, Tom 200
Shaw, George Bernard 4, 52–53, 69–70, 175; *see also Widowers' Houses*

She 13
Shelley, Mary 84; *see also Frankenstein*
Sherard, Robert H. 168, 180
'The She-Wolf' 199–200
short stories 12–13, 135; of Oscar Wilde 169–175
Showalter, Elaine 9, 27
Sickert, Helena 180
Silver, Carole 162
Simmel, Georg 11
Sister Carrie 61, 124
Sitwell, Edith 202
Sitwell, Osbert 202
'slumming' 69
slumps 42
Small, Helen 2
Smith, Adam 11
Smith, Samuel 42
Smithers, Leonard 168
Social Darwinism 20, 114–117
socialism 16–17, 25, 58–59, 60, 69, 118, 168, 173, 175–178, 208
Society of Authors 13
'The Soul of Man under Socialism' 175–178, 186
Soper, Kate 205
speech codes 52
Spencer, Herbert 19, 112, 115
'The Sphinx' 180
Stanley, Henry M. 7, 78; *see also In Darkest Africa*
The Star 68, 69
Stead, W. T. 28, 64–68
Stevenson, Robert Louis 7, 41, 42, 45, 46, 47, 48–49, 68, 78, 113; *see also The Strange Case of Dr Jekyll and Mr Hyde*
Stoker, Bram 7, 31, 70, 74, 75, 74–85, 207; *see also Dracula*
Stokes, John 173–175, 178
The Strange Case of Dr Jekyll and Mr Hyde 7, 41–49, 56, 66, 68, 78, 84, 113, 129–130, 153
Sturgis, Matthew 5–6, 23
survival of the fittest 20, 24–25; *see also* Darwin, Charles; Darwinism; natural selection, theory of
Suvin, Darko 121, 123
Swafford, Kevin 52–53
Symons, Arthur 167

Teleny 95
The Tempest 103

Terry, Ellen 181
There and Back 154
Tillett, Ben 39–40
The Time Machine 4, 6–8, 21, 43–44, 62, 107–116, 119–121, 125, 135, 153, 156, 159
The Times 86
Tolkien, J. R. R. 128; *see also The Hobbit*
trade unionism 13, 17
travel 5, 6–9, 10, 26, 31, 56, 60–62, 79, 80–81, 85, 107, 108–110, 115–116, 126, 132, 141, 153, 156, 157, 159, 162, 197, 201–204, 207
Treves, Sir Frederick 54–55

unemployment 15, 22, 39–40, 42, 57–58, 70, 86, 89–90, 166, 175, 176

vegetarianism 111
Vint, Sherryl 31
Vizetelly, Henry 23
Vuohelainen, Minna 94

Wagner, Richard 26, 30
Walkowitz, Judith 68–69
Wallis Budge, E. A. 99
War with the Newts 200–201, 204
The War of the Worlds 4, 7, 80, 104, 107, 125–132, 135, 136
Warner, Marina 3–4, 10, 76
Warwick, Alexandra 81
Washington Post 180
Washington Square 56
The Waste Land 202
Watt, A. P. 13
Waugh, Benjamin 64
Webb, Beatrice 40
Weekly Sun 165
Wells, H. G. 4, 6–7, 8, 9, 12–13, 21, 30, 31, 78, 80, 87, 94, 107–136, 155, 175, 207; *see also First and Last Things*; *Hoopdriver's Holiday*; *The Invisible Man*; *The Island of Doctor Moreau*; *The Time Machine*; *The War of the Worlds*; *The Wheels of Chance*
Westminster Review 112
The Wheels of Chance 132–136
Whistler, James McNeill 180
Whitechapel 53–54, 55–57, 68–69
Whitman, Walt 26
Widowers' Houses 52–53
Wilde, Constance 181–182
Wilde, Jane Francesca 181
Wilde, Lily 181
Wilde, Oscar 9, 19–20, 27, 28–30, 31, 78, 81, 91, 142, 148, 165–93; biographies of 192; effect of imprisonment on 182–186; plays by 187–192; prison and post-prison writings of 177–179, 183, 186; short stories by 169–175; *see also* 'The Ballad of Reading Gaol'; 'The Decay of Lying'; *De Profundis*; 'The Happy Prince'; *The Importance of Being Earnest*; *Lady Windermere's Fan*; 'The Model Millionaire'; *The Picture of Dorian Gray*; 'The Portrait of Mr. W. H.'; 'The Soul of Man under Socialism'; 'The Sphinx'; *A Woman of No Importance*; 'The Young King'
Wilde, William 182
Wilkinson, Ellen 203; *see also Clash*
Williams, Raymond 7, 21–22, 39
'Wireless' 13
Wolfe, Cary 206
Wolfreys, Julian 104
A Woman of No Importance 190–192
women's rights 28–29
Wooldridge, Charles Thomas 177–178
Wordsworth, William 143, 185

Yeats, W. B. 202–203; *see also* 'The Second Coming'
'The Young King' 173–174

Zangwill, Israel 117; *see also Children of the Ghetto*
Zola, Emile 23, 31; *see also The Earth*